Martin Scorsese's Documentary Histories

Martin Scorsese's Documentary Histories

Migrations, Movies, Music

Mike Meneghetti

BLOOMSBURY ACADEMIC
NEW YORK · LONDON · OXFORD · NEW DELHI · SYDNEY

BLOOMSBURY ACADEMIC
Bloomsbury Publishing Inc
1385 Broadway, New York, NY 10018, USA
50 Bedford Square, London, WC1B 3DP, UK
29 Earlsfort Terrace, Dublin 2, Ireland

BLOOMSBURY, BLOOMSBURY ACADEMIC and the Diana logo are trademarks of
Bloomsbury Publishing Plc

First published in the United States of America 2021
This paperback edition published 2022

Copyright © Mike Meneghetti, 2021

For legal purposes the Acknowledgments on p. x constitute an
extension of this copyright page.

Cover design: Namkwan Cho
Cover image © Ronald Grant Archive / ArenaPAL

All rights reserved. No part of this publication may be reproduced or transmitted
in any form or by any means, electronic or mechanical, including photocopying,
recording, or any information storage or retrieval system, without prior
permission in writing from the publishers.

Bloomsbury Publishing Inc does not have any control over, or responsibility for, any
third-party websites referred to or in this book. All internet addresses given in this
book were correct at the time of going to press. The author and publisher regret
any inconvenience caused if addresses have changed or sites have ceased
to exist, but can accept no responsibility for any such changes.

Library of Congress Cataloging-in-Publication Data
Names: Meneghetti, Mike, author.
Title: Martin Scorsese's documentary histories: migrations, movies,
music / Mike Meneghetti.
Description: New York : Bloomsbury Academic, 2021. |
Includes bibliographical references and index.
Identifiers: LCCN 2020035900 | ISBN 9781501336874 (hardback)
| ISBN 9781501336881 (epub) | ISBN 9781501336898 (pdf)
Subjects: LCSH: Scorsese, Martin–Criticism and interpretation. |
Documentary films–United States–History and criticism.
Classification: LCC PN1998.3.S39 M46 2021 | DDC 791.4302/33092–dc23
LC record available at https://lccn.loc.gov/2020035900

ISBN: HB: 978-1-5013-3687-4
       PB: 978-1-5013-7595-8
       ePDF: 978-1-5013-3689-8
       ePUB: 978-1-5013-3688-1

Typeset by Integra Software Services Pvt. Ltd.

To find out more about our authors and books visit www.bloomsbury.com
and sign up for our newsletters.

For my family

Contents

List of Illustrations	viii
Acknowledgments	x
Introduction: Martin Scorsese's Documentary Histories	1
1 Historical Migrations: *Italianamerican* and *American Boy: A Profile of Steven Prince*	17
2 Foreclosed Journeys: *The Last Waltz* and *Shine a Light*	59
3 Archival Expeditions: *Feel Like Going Home* and *No Direction Home: Bob Dylan*	105
4 Personal Pilgrimages: *Il mio viaggio in Italia* and *A Letter to Elia*	153
Conclusion: Martin Scorsese's Documentary Profiles	197
Notes	209
References	245
Index	257

List of Illustrations

0.1	*Italianamerican* (Martin Scorsese, 1974)	7
1.1	*Italianamerican* (Martin Scorsese, 1974)	29
1.2	*Italianamerican* (Martin Scorsese, 1974)	30
1.3	*Italianamerican* (Martin Scorsese, 1974)	32
1.4	*Italianamerican* (Martin Scorsese, 1974)	36
1.5	*Italianamerican* (Martin Scorsese, 1974)	37
1.6	*Italianamerican* (Martin Scorsese, 1974)	40
1.7	*Italianamerican* (Martin Scorsese, 1974)	41
1.8	*American Boy: A Profile of Steven Prince* (Martin Scorsese, 1978)	46
1.9	*American Boy: A Profile of Steven Prince* (Martin Scorsese, 1978)	47
1.10	*American Boy: A Profile of Steven Prince* (Martin Scorsese, 1978)	50
1.11	*American Boy: A Profile of Steven Prince* (Martin Scorsese, 1978)	51
1.12	*American Boy: A Profile of Steven Prince* (Martin Scorsese, 1978)	52
2.1	*Dont Look Back* (D.A. Pennebaker, 1967)	68
2.2	*Monterey Pop* (D.A. Pennebaker, 1968)	69
2.3	*Woodstock* (Michael Wadleigh, 1970)	70
2.4	*Woodstock* (Michael Wadleigh, 1970)	71
2.5	*The Last Waltz* (Martin Scorsese, 1978)	74
2.6	*The Last Waltz* (Martin Scorsese, 1978)	78
2.7	*The Last Waltz* (Martin Scorsese, 1978)	79
2.8	*The Last Waltz* (Martin Scorsese, 1978)	80
2.9	*Monterey Pop* (D.A. Pennebaker, 1968)	87
2.10	*The Last Waltz* (Martin Scorsese, 1978)	89
2.11	*The Last Waltz* (Martin Scorsese, 1978)	91
2.12	*The Last Waltz* (Martin Scorsese, 1978)	92
2.13	*The Last Waltz* (Martin Scorsese, 1978)	95
2.14	*Shine a Light* (Martin Scorsese, 2008)	97
2.15	*Shine a Light* (Martin Scorsese, 2008)	99
2.16	*Shine a Light* (Martin Scorsese, 2008)	102
3.1	*Feel Like Going Home* (Martin Scorsese, 2003)	116
3.2	*Feel Like Going Home* (Martin Scorsese, 2003)	118

3.3	*Feel Like Going Home* (Martin Scorsese, 2003)	119
3.4	*Feel Like Going Home* (Martin Scorsese, 2003)	120
3.5	*Feel Like Going Home* (Martin Scorsese, 2003)	124
3.6	*Feel Like Going Home* (Martin Scorsese, 2003)	127
3.7	*No Direction Home: Bob Dylan* (Martin Scorsese, 2005)	131
3.8	*No Direction Home: Bob Dylan* (Martin Scorsese, 2005)	132
3.9	*No Direction Home: Bob Dylan* (Martin Scorsese, 2005)	135
3.10	*No Direction Home: Bob Dylan* (Martin Scorsese, 2005)	141
3.11	*No Direction Home: Bob Dylan* (Martin Scorsese, 2005)	142
3.12	*No Direction Home: Bob Dylan* (Martin Scorsese, 2005)	142
3.13	*No Direction Home: Bob Dylan* (Martin Scorsese, 2005)	147
3.14	*George Harrison: Living in the Material World* (Martin Scorsese, 2011)	149
4.1	*A Personal Journey with Martin Scorsese Through American Movies* (Martin Scorsese and Michael Henry Wilson, 1995)	162
4.2	*Il mio viaggio in Italia* (Martin Scorsese, 2001)	170
4.3	*Il mio viaggio in Italia* (Martin Scorsese, 2001)	170
4.4	*Il mio viaggio in Italia* (Martin Scorsese, 2001)	171
4.5	*Il mio viaggio in Italia* (Martin Scorsese, 2001)	175
4.6	*Il mio viaggio in Italia* (Martin Scorsese, 2001)	176
4.7	*Il mio viaggio in Italia* (Martin Scorsese, 2001)	180
4.8	*A Letter to Elia* (Martin Scorsese and Kent Jones, 2011)	186
4.9	*A Letter to Elia* (Martin Scorsese and Kent Jones, 2011)	190
4.10	*Italianamerican* (Martin Scorsese, 1974)	191
4.11	*Il mio viaggio in Italia* (Martin Scorsese, 2001)	195
5.1	*Rolling Thunder Revue: A Bob Dylan Story by Martin Scorsese* (Martin Scorsese, 2019)	202
5.2	*Rolling Thunder Revue: A Bob Dylan Story by Martin Scorsese* (Martin Scorsese, 2019)	205
5.3	*Springsteen on Broadway* (Thom Zimny, 2018)	206

Acknowledgments

Many people have made indispensable contributions to this book. First and foremost, I want to thank Katie Gallof and Erin Duffy at Bloomsbury Press. Katie expressed an immediate interest in this project and was continually supportive throughout the writing process; Erin guided the book to completion. I'm also grateful to Bloomsbury's anonymous reviewer for providing perceptive comments and helpful feedback on the original manuscript. Several of this project's principal ideas were first developed while I was a graduate student at The University of Iowa. As a result, I owe a special debt of gratitude to Rick Altman for his exceptional generosity as a scholar and teacher. Classes with Dudley Andrew, Nicole Brenez, Louis-Georges Schwartz, and Richard Maltby undoubtedly also shaped certain aspects of this work. Iowa City was an exciting place to study film, and the university's faculty and graduate students generated an unparalleled atmosphere of energy and collegiality. My countless conversations with Linda Mokdad, Bjorn Nordfjord, James Tweedie, Gerald Sim, Prakash Younger, Christian Keathley, Chris Babey, Dave Ellsworth, Rufo Quintavalle, and Agnès Mathieu-Daudé reverberate across these pages. The University of Toronto's influence was equally essential to the completion of *Martin Scorsese's Documentary Histories*. Corinn Columpar and James Leo Cahill gave me welcome opportunities to teach documentary film courses to some excellent students at The University of Toronto, and I benefitted enormously from this close correspondence between my writing and teaching. I continue to learn from Charlie Keil, and he remains an example for my ongoing work as a scholar and mentor to students. Lee Carruthers generously offered to read an early version of Chapter 1, and her insights improved the manuscript considerably. I owe an incalculable debt to my parents and sister—their key contributions date back the furthest, and our shared history is rooted deeply in this book. As I was writing, I returned repeatedly to Scorsese's *Italianamerican* and *Il mio viaggio in Italia* for solace and inspiration, and perhaps my parents will see their own story embedded somewhere in my account of these films. Finally, Kaitlyn Kribs deserves special thanks for too many reasons to enumerate here. She has lived with this project every day, reading and re-reading the manuscript, listening as I read sentences and paragraphs to her, and always believing in its value. This book simply couldn't have been written without her.

Introduction
Martin Scorsese's Documentary Histories

In one of the earliest critical synopses of Martin Scorsese's 1970s filmmaking, James Monaco perceives an elementary difference between the director's documentary productions and fiction films. The forty-nine minute "essay" *Italianamerican* (1974), he writes, is attentively "relaxed, broadly humorous, not excessively ambitious," "honest," and "direct," while Scorsese's contemporaneous Hollywood output is unnecessarily hampered by its "self-conscious parody of movies dead and gone" and its creator's "pretentiously anxious film-noir mask" (1979, 161). Indeed, in Monaco's sketch of Scorsese's emergent directorial image, his "less publicized" non-fiction filmmaking constitutes an "important second side to his personality as a filmmaker," yet the director's efforts to "accommodate himself to the system of commercial film production" continually threaten to obscure this other documentary character (1979, 153). Monaco's assessment of Scorsese's work as a documentarian is derived mainly from his viewing of *Italianamerican*, but it refers also to his previous labors as a film editor. *Woodstock*'s (Michael Wadleigh, 1970) success is therefore fully attributed to Scorsese's substantial input in assembling its images and sounds, while a similar technical proficiency in editing is said to have determined the profile of several other early-1970s historical documents: the cooperatively produced *Street Scenes 1970* (Martin Scorsese, 1970), *Medicine Ball Caravan* (François Reichenbach, 1971), and the distended *Elvis on Tour* (Robert Abel and Pierre Adidge, 1972). In the end, Monaco's unsympathetic overview of the Hollywood Renaissance in *American Film Now* equivocates in its evaluation of Scorsese's filmmaking in large part because of the director's varied experiences in documentary production throughout the late-1960s and 1970s. "Documentary," he rightly observes, "provided Scorsese with a second, hidden career" during this period (1979, 153), and *The Last Waltz*'s technical accomplishment and positive critical reception in

1978 simply seemed to confirm the director's longstanding commitment to his non-fiction filmmaking as he approached the 1980s. The production of these films, Monaco implies, could continue to insulate Scorsese from Hollywood's uncertainties, contradictions, and compromises at the onset of a new decade.[1]

Scorsese's documentary film practice would, of course, enter a long period of dormancy after *The Last Waltz*, and when it was finally revived almost two decades later, its methods and foci would be noticeably different. As a result, Monaco's intuitions about the significance of Scorsese's documentary efforts might appear confined to the historical past, that is, to a moment when the director's future course remained relatively undefined; yet the tenor of his short survey of Scorsese's 1970s filmmaking was prescient in at least two important respects. His constructive consideration of Scorsese's various early experiences as a documentarian, uncommon in the first wave of scholarly attention to his 1970s output, unavoidably gives films such as *Italianamerican* the appearance of apprenticeship or diversion, and these descriptions of the director's non-fiction works as "secondary" or "hidden" would be reiterated in many subsequent studies. Robert Phillip Kolker's contemporaneous *A Cinema of Loneliness*, for example, an invaluable auteurist analysis of the Hollywood Renaissance, briefly refers to *Italianamerican*, *The Last Waltz*, and *American Boy: A Profile of Steven Prince* (1978) in the slightly buried form of a single footnote, describing them as "more or less conventional documentaries," and thereby implying their peripherality to a look at the director's output (1988, 166). Admittedly, Scorsese has helped in perpetuating the critical demotion of his non-fiction films by defining them as "smaller projects"; and because the first comprehensive analyses of his filmmaking overlapped with his protracted inactivity as a documentarian in the 1980s and early-1990s, the relegation of these "smaller" (or slighter) films to the sidelines of early auteurist studies is understandable.[2] Similarly, Monaco's characterization of the documentaries' "unpretentiousness" has been repeated in a persistent critical emphasis on their ostensible ordinariness. The films are regularly described as "conventional," and Scorsese's close association with non-fiction production has been framed instead by film studies' formative commitment to modernist aesthetics throughout the 1970s and 1980s.[3] His lifelong participation in documentary filmmaking is accordingly categorized as evidence for a familiar modernist concern with the "blurred boundary" between fiction and non-fiction, but this has only amplified the sense of digression in Scorsese's documentary work.[4] Once again, the non-fiction films—*Italianamerican* and *American Boy: A Profile of Steven Prince* in particular—are essentially viewed as a type of preparation for his well-known Hollywood movies, or defined as a fine-tuning of the latter's techniques and common themes.⁵

The release of *A Personal Journey with Martin Scorsese Through American Movies* (co-directed with Michael Henry Wilson, 1995), however, a commission by the British Film Institute to commemorate the cinema's centenary in 1995, initiated an uninterrupted stream of non-fiction films, videos, and television productions in the years that followed, and the customary inclination to discount this output has now become much too difficult to maintain. Indeed, for more than two decades, Scorsese's resuscitated non-fiction filmmaking practice has matched his Hollywood production, at least in terms of sheer numbers; and describing it simply as a set of "smaller projects" risks misapprehending its meaning in today's diverse documentary settings. *A Personal Journey, Il mio viaggio in Italia* (2001), *Martin Scorsese Presents: The Blues* (2003), *No Direction Home: Bob Dylan* (2005), *Shine a Light* (2008), *A Letter to Elia* (co-directed with Kent Jones, 2010), *Public Speaking* (2010), *George Harrison: Living in the Material World* (2011), *The 50 Year Argument* (co-directed with David Tedeschi, 2014), and Netflix's *Rolling Thunder Revue: A Bob Dylan Story by Martin Scorsese* (2019) have all materialized in this revivified, concentrated moment of documentary activity.⁶ If Scorsese remains known today primarily as the director of fiction films such as *Mean Streets* (1973), *Taxi Driver* (1976), *Raging Bull* (1980), *Goodfellas* (1990), *Casino* (1995), *The Departed* (2006), and *The Irishman* (2019), he is also increasingly recognized as the creator of numerous rockumentaries and wide-ranging histories of cinema on film. Nevertheless, an impression of diversion continues to cling to his non-fiction production, regardless of the films' unmistakable historiographic aspiration, and this is not solely the product of critical indifference. On the contrary, although a popular critical consensus about the films' status as digressions from Scorsese's authentic vocation as a Hollywood filmmaker still delimits their general reception, the close correspondence between this discourse and the director's own promotion of his documentary works has effectively guaranteed their peripherality. Simply put, Scorsese has, in his unassuming way, also helped to determine the films' resistance to sustained critical exploration by continually urging journalists to see them as addenda to his more widely known commercial movies. If his non-fiction film and television productions paradoxically remain "hidden" to some degree, it is principally because viewing them has been overly constrained by the concurrence of such longstanding critical and authorial directives.⁷

As I've indicated, Scorsese typically describes his ongoing documentary production as a "smaller" or subordinate enterprise, and he sometimes situates it as laboratory for his subsequent experiments in fiction filmmaking. Very few contemporary directors are as skillful as Scorsese in encouraging critics to summon a biographical legend with the release of his latest Hollywood movies, but this folklore continues to preemptively misrepresent his documentary personality: on the one hand, his non-fiction films are usually received as placeholders during pauses in his Hollywood schedule; on the other hand, they are seen as byproducts of a different undertaking, whether it be his Hollywood filmmaking, film preservation and restoration, or some other correlated cultural activity. Scorsese has surely benefitted from the popularity and cultural capital of contemporary documentary film, video, and television programs, unprecedented in the genre's long history, but he has also clearly ventured his substantial symbolic capital in the production of his non-fiction works—these assorted films and videos have themselves made a significant contribution to the present-day documentary's elevated status across multiple media platforms. In other words, Scorsese has since the mid-1990s taken advantage of documentary film's growing cultural importance in order to resuscitate his non-fiction filmmaking practice, yet he has at the same time boosted the genre's international reputation with the exhibition of his work. Nevertheless, films such as *Italianamerican, The Last Waltz, Il mio viaggio in Italia, No Direction Home,* and *A Letter to Elia* are seldom considered against the backdrop of documentary history or theory, nor are they positioned within the proximate circumstances of their conception and creation. They are more often cited to corroborate claims about some features of Scorsese's fiction filmmaking—his selection of rock and other kinds of popular music as soundtrack, his cinephilia, his ethnicity, and so forth. In light of the modern documentary's significance to popular—and marketplace—consciousness, several other film directors who alternate between fiction and non-fiction with comparable ease have had their works acknowledged as significant contributions to today's pervasive reality-based media production, but the discussion of Scorsese's documentaries continues to be frustratingly confined by the Hollywood perspective.[8] As a consequence, although he still actively participates in many types of non-fiction filmmaking to this day, both as a director and—increasingly—as a producer, his efforts in this field remain unusually resistant to comprehensive critical scrutiny.

This book examines Scorsese's documentaries, and it begins with a modest analytical proposition: these films and television productions can and should be assessed *as* documentaries, without disproportionate recourse to discussions of the director's Hollywood movies. This is not to disregard the institutional actualities of his present-day position in Hollywood, or the undeniable continuity of concerns across his documentary and fiction films; nor does it neglect the reciprocal relationship between fiction and non-fiction, a central feature of so much contemporary cultural production. But separating Scorsese's non-fiction work from the predominant auteurist frame has substantial heuristic advantages. First and foremost, it permits one to consider how these documentaries participate in a distinct mode of film practice and its lengthy history, while at the same time suggesting a more comprehensive account of their affiliation with various documentary predecessors and proximate contemporary examples. If Scorsese's non-fiction films are often described in terms of their perceived ordinariness, they are also paradoxically received as *sui generis*, and the director's skillfulness in determining their position within a well-known auteurist discourse has obscured how they belong to a much wider documentary tradition—detaching these films, videos, and television productions from his Hollywood work allows for a more exploratory approach to his prolific documentary making. The book's title, *Martin Scorsese's Documentary Histories: Migrations, Movies, Music*, refers to the insistently historical character of Scorsese's many documentaries, and it highlights their core subjects: his immediate family's historical migration from Italy to America and its reverberations across the succeeding decades; his baby boomer generation's deep immersion in the wide variety of popular music, rock music in particular, as a potentially radical force in American society; and his permanent devotion to the history of cinema, but more specifically, his own cinephilia and its connections to otherwise buried strata of historical experience. These are the core emphases in Scorsese's documentary filmmaking, and they each correspond closely with the commemorative and preservationist commitments that have guided his non-fiction work since its revivification in the 1990s. However, in underscoring Scorsese's "documentary histories," this book also seeks to understand how the works formulate practical approaches to the rendering of historical accounts. In other words, Scorsese's documentary films, videos, and television productions are customarily dedicated to interpreting the historical past, and as a consequence, they each develop methods for gathering and arranging their vast materials into original descriptions of history. *Italianamerican* and *American Boy: A Profile of Steven Prince*'s critical engagement with the legacy of American direct cinema, for example, results in a form of commemorative oral history; while *No Direction Home*'s archival excavation and summary of Bob Dylan's journeys through the world of popular music in the early-1960s, like *Feel Like Going Home*'s exploration of the Delta blues' migrations from America's rural southern states to cities such as Chicago and Detroit, generate a collection—of images and sounds—whose historical meaning is derived from editing and its amalgamation of diverse resources. In each of these cases, however, the documentaries devise very different approaches to the rendering of historical accounts, and in the process, they provide viewers with keys for understanding the past's lingering meaning in their present-day reality.[9]

Scorsese's earliest involvement in documentary production was as an editor and assistant director on Michael Wadleigh's epochal *Woodstock*. *Elvis on Tour* similarly recognizes his work as "montage supervisor," and if his particular contribution is ultimately too difficult to discern in this instance, the film's regular recourse to *Woodstock*'s various split-screen techniques positions it securely within the era's succession of concert films. Although he had directed (and edited) the concluding sequence of *Street Scenes 1970*, a collectively produced account of students' anti-war protests in 1970, the making of *Italianamerican* in 1974 truly inaugurates Scorsese's efforts as a documentarian—this forty-nine-minute work introduces an historical orientation that would shape all of his succeeding non-fiction films and videos. Commissioned by the National Endowment for the Humanities (NEH), and eventually broadcast by PBS in an abbreviated form, *Italianamerican* was originally planned within the context of America's Bicentennial observances in 1976 and produced as a tribute to America's early twentieth-century ethnic histories. Ordinarily viewed as the director's most personal and unassuming documentary film, *Italianamerican* would in fact compel Scorsese to participate in the era's inescapable sense of retrospection as well as its developing investment in genealogy, heritage, and history. Indeed, the film's conception alongside this prevailing preoccupation with the past would prove to be pivotal in shaping the meaning of Scorsese's non-fiction output across the succeeding decades. As we'll see, his documentary work takes the era's discovery of a new popular idiom for ethnic recovery and its attendant desire to safeguard assorted brands of cultural heritage as the central frameworks for his own interpretations of history; but the pervasive efforts to generate a new vernacular for historical *reclamation* also established a template for Scorsese's commemorative documentary film practice, and this would become especially apparent after its unexpected revivification in

1995. Simply put, *Italianamerican* was initially formulated with the ethnic revival's language of retrieval, and this would have a long-lasting influence on Scorsese's approaches to documentary production: occasionally nostalgic, but also somewhat resigned in its focused description of an era coming to its end, *Italianamerican*'s tenor would define Scorsese's relationship to history. Although it might have the surface appearance of spontaneity, it is in fact methodical in attending closely to its main subjects (the director's parents) as they deliver their stories, and the film finally functions as an intercessor for the history of Italian immigration to America (Figure 0.1). Scorsese's subsequent documentary films and videos, I want to suggest, need to be reconsidered in terms of their ongoing commitment to this particular vernacular of retrieval and preservation. *Martin Scorsese's Documentary Histories* reassesses the director's essential non-fiction film, video, and television productions within this framework, and it also attempts to explain how each of these works develops its own methods for rendering historical accounts.

In the latter half of the 1970s, Scorsese's documentary work continued to adhere to the template established by *Italianamerican*. *American Boy: A Profile of Steven Prince*, in many ways a despairing sequel to *Italianamerican*, held to the previous film's emphasis on storytelling and storytellers as intercessors

Figure 0.1 *Italianamerican* (Martin Scorsese, 1974).

for the historical past, and *The Last Waltz*'s commemoration of The Band's final concert disclosed a similar commitment to situating its subjects as intermediaries for history. If the director's celebrated documentary about The Band is in part the product of New Hollywood's late-1970s profligacy, it nevertheless remains devoted to the same vernacular of retrieval. Moreover, like its immediate predecessors, *The Last Waltz* is implicitly dedicated to a critical reassessment of its direct cinema inheritance. Direct cinema is a recurrent point of reference in Scorsese's interviews about his non-fiction filmmaking, and it is both an influence on his 1970s documentaries and the subject of thorough reappraisal throughout *Italianamerican*, *American Boy*, and *The Last Waltz*. The observational focus on spontaneity and authenticity is apparent in all three films, of course, and their portraits of distinctive personalities have a qualified relation to classic 1960s works like *Dont Look Back* (D.A. Pennebaker, 1967) and *Salesman* (Albert Maysles, David Maysles, and Charlotte Zwerin, 1969). However, direct cinema's approach usually resulted in the evacuation of social history from its images, and the films' self-described "crisis" scenarios were similarly limited to individual figures whose stories would culminate in a feat of self-realization. *Italianamerican*, by contrast, adjusted itself to the various actualities of historical immigration, and its commission by the NEH guaranteed its connection to the period's obsession with "roots" and ethnic revival. Accordingly, the film merges an emphasis on unplanned conduct before its camera and sound recording devices with a much more interactive method: the director intervenes intermittently, and the film's historical implication is derived from its subjects' varied adjustments to the specific conditions of documentary filmmaking. Yet unlike many other American documentarians in the 1970s, Scorsese isn't especially interested in simply reaffirming subjectivity or personality, nor is his project deterred by the detection of a porous border between the fictitious and non-fiction; instead, *Italianamerican* remains engaged with the legacy of direct cinema, incorporating its substantial insights, while at the same time also modifying various preceding models for its new commission. This culminates in *The Last Waltz*'s ambivalent reckoning with its immediate concert film predecessors. As we'll see in Chapter 2, Scorsese's commemoration of The Band's farewell show revises selected features of its hippie-era concert film antecedents, but it nonetheless remains entangled in direct cinema's core contradiction: its elaboration of the rock concert's collective exhilaration is moderated by an individuated portrait of the musician's freedom and authenticity. In other words, *The Last Waltz*'s emphasis on a cooperatively created rock music ultimately submits to the hippie-era concert documentary's preoccupation with self-realizing rock stars, primarily as embodied by Robbie Robertson's persistent self-assertion in the film, and this incongruity finally discloses Scorsese's equivocal commitment to the legacy of direct cinema and its classic concert documentaries.

I've referred to a long period of dormancy in Scorsese's documentary filmmaking after *The Last Waltz*'s release in 1978, yet he was in fact immersed in a closely related mission during these years. The director's ongoing public sponsorship of film preservation, restoration, and film history has developed into the most recognizable feature of his present-day personality, but in the early-1980s, his nascent efforts in this field incorporated key aspects of his 1970s documentary work. Film preservation, conceived from the beginning as an urgent task, was dedicated to repossessing a cinematic/cultural heritage, and its focus on deteriorating archival holdings narrowed the 1970s films' historical emphases to *film history*. The non-fiction works' familiar themes of retrieval and restoration, however, were easily repositioned in this new undertaking, even if the seriousness of the threat to a cultural past was now intensified. *The Last Waltz*'s farewell show, we should recall, was essentially an act of self-memorializing by guitarist and de facto manager Robbie Robertson, and it was marked by a sense of nostalgia and remorse; but it also implicitly outlined The Band's future in exceedingly bleak terms. For some members of The Band (i.e., everyone but Robbie Robertson), the future simply presented itself as a void in *The Last Waltz*'s concluding images, and this sense of foreboding would carry over to Scorsese's first attempts to expose the hazards of fading color film stock: film preservation, like The Band's sendoff, was conceived as a pressing need in the director's first lectures about these matters, and the annihilation of a cultural heritage, he insisted, would foreclose film's future. In short, something of the director's working experience with Robertson and The Band clearly stayed with him across the succeeding decades, and his various efforts at film preservation—and later, his revivified documentary practice in the mid-1990s—would be defined by a sense of apprehension about the future and an attendant desire to safeguard the past. However, the experiences of film preservation in the 1980s and 1990s, which culminated in The Film Foundation's creation in 1990, would in turn modify Scorsese's approach to documentary. As we'll see, *Italianamerican* resisted the NEH's original commission by using archival materials very sparingly, and though *American Boy* makes recurrent (and ironic) use of the Prince family's home movies, its attention is similarly directed to its principal storyteller and his deportment in the documentary situation. (*The Last Waltz* makes no use of archival resources, relying instead on interviews with Robertson and other members of The Band to complement its farewell concert.) When Scorsese's documentary filmmaking unexpectedly goes silent in 1979, however, it is essentially supplanted by the preservationist's commitment to locating and rescuing archival film prints, and this would decisively transform his renewed non-fiction practice after 1995. Beginning with *A Personal Journey* and continuing with films and television productions such as *Il mio viaggio in Italia*, *Feel Like Going Home*, *No Direction Home: Bob Dylan*, and *A Letter to Elia*, the director's documentaries increasingly made archival mining an essential feature of their production. As a result, *Il mio viaggio in Italia* and *A Letter to Elia* resuscitate the personal ethnic narrative of Scorsese's *Italianamerican* and *American Boy: A Profile of Steven Prince*, yet they substitute a meaningful accumulation of images for the previous films' attentiveness to storytelling subjects; or rather, they discover the last remaining traces of a distant immigrant past in assorted popular film images and the director's supplementary reminiscences about his family members and their communal cinephilia. *Feel Like Going Home*, *No Direction Home*, and *Living in the Material World* similarly reintroduce the past to spectators by reassembling their formerly fragmented historical resources into new totalities. In all of these instances, the films select and compile their assorted archival materials, and editing thereby becomes their principal method for arranging and delivering descriptions of the past.

Martin Scorsese's Documentary Histories registers this passage from Scorsese's 1970s documentary filmmaking to his present-day commemorative compilation work. Although I refer to each of the director's documentary films, videos, and television productions in what follows, I concentrate on what I consider to be Scorsese's core corpus of non-fiction works, that is, the films that provide some interpretation of history. The subjects of migration, movies, and music are brought into clearer focus by *Italianamerican*, *American Boy: A Profile of Steven Prince*, *The Last Waltz*, *Shine a Light*, *Feel Like Going Home*, *No Direction Home*, *A Personal Journey*, *Il mio viaggio in Italia*, and *A Letter to Elia*, and many of the director's later documentary efforts basically rework this material: *Public Speaking* recalls the approach of *Italianamerican* and *American Boy*, although it is noticeably indifferent to their deeper historical foci; *Living in the Material World* is a substantial accumulation of archival possessions, but it ultimately retraces the course taken in *No Direction Home*; *Rolling Thunder Revue* also returns to Scorsese's earlier Bob Dylan film, and its assembly of materials is equally proficient, yet its submission to commonplaces about Bob Dylan's perpetual reinventions produces few new insights. As he continually reminds his interviewers, Scorsese has always embraced the auteurist dedication to "personal" filmmaking, and this individualist focus is arguably more evident—and plausible—within the narrow purview of documentary production. However, the period of his personal non-fiction filmmaking appears to have concluded with *A Letter to Elia*'s critical analyses of Elia Kazan's films and their important place in Scorsese's reminiscences about his childhood and the meaning of his permanent cinephilia. Indeed, the director's ongoing deferral of proposed studies about British and Russian film histories might suggest a rerouting of his substantial cinephilic investments to different types of documentary projects, but it also attests to *A Letter to Elia*'s status as a final critical reckoning with this mission's personal preoccupations.[10] *Martin Scorsese's Documentary Histories* accordingly concentrates on Scorsese's non-fiction films, videos, and television productions from the period 1974–2010: the director's wide-ranging documentary project begins with his decisive discovery of an idiom of retrieval in *Italianamerican*, and it culminates with the unmistakable settling of historical debts in *A Letter to Elia*. As we'll see, the overwhelming sense of retrospection in Scorsese's documentaries develops from their fundamental objective: to reconcile the remote past with the present, but also the individual with much broader historical actualities. The future, however, is a source of apprehension in his non-fiction productions, and this is what ultimately motivates their efforts to preserve selected features of a collective cultural history. In his documentary filmmaking, Scorsese invariably returns to the past, primarily because this is the only way for his films to envision the future as something other than a vacuum.

"Chapter 1: Historical Migrations" examines *Italianamerican* and its sequel, *American Boy: A Profile of Steven Prince*, but it returns these short films to the context of their original conception in order to determine how they devise a shared approach to interpreting ethnic histories. As we'll see, Scorsese's initial reluctance to accept the *Italianamerican* assignment grew from his concern over the NEH's potentially constricting proposals for this commemorative study. Simply put, the NEH directives appeared to confine its commission in an overly predictable manner: an amalgam of archival materials (photographs, moving images, and sounds), contemporary testimonials from first-generation Italian Americans and their descendants, and expository sections would comprise a humble tribute to the nation's twentieth-century immigrants. Scorsese, looking for more autonomy in determining the film's final form, eventually dispensed with most of the familiar iconography of immigration, and decided instead to focus on his parents' various reminiscences and responses to his questions. As a result, an expressive kind of storytelling predominates in *Italianmerican*, and the film finally indicates a *substantial compatibility* between the Scorseses' guileless storytelling—their conduct and idiomatic explanations of their common past—and the larger social history of Italian immigration to America in the early twentieth century. Like so many American documentarians in the 1970s, Scorsese provides a critical reassessment of the contentious legacy of direct cinema in his two earliest documentaries, but the contemporaneous ethnic revival, with its own emerging historiographic conventions and foci, exerted an equally strong influence on *Italianamerican* and its exhausted follow-up, *American Boy*. Together these two short documentaries deliver a critical apprehension of the period's ethnic resurgence by combining particular features of direct cinema with the ethnic revival's essentially participatory affinities. This integration of methods produces what the director calls an "oral history" of America, but Chapter 1 analyses *Italianamerican* and *American Boy* as a distinctive historical project whose roots can be found in the era's developing interest in ethnic retrieval. Viewed as parts in a comprehensive history, these two films provide a despairing account of ethnic assimilation and the destructive meaning of American achievement.

"Chapter 2: Foreclosed Journeys" describes Scorsese's substantial stake in the emergent connection between documentary filmmakers and rock music in the late-1960s, their cooperative creation of the era-defining concert films (*Monterey Pop* [D.A. Pennebaker, 1968], *Woodstock*, etc.), and their outline of popular music's developing social meanings throughout these years, but the chapter's central focus is *The Last Waltz* and its qualified revision of its precursors. *The Last Waltz* remains Scorsese's most distinguished non-fiction film, often mentioned as *the* exemplary concert documentary and a formative influence on subsequent entries in the genre; yet very much like *Italianamerican* and *American Boy*, it has an especially tangled affiliation with the legacy of American direct cinema. This chapter examines the implications of *The Last Waltz*'s inadvertent adherence to the 1960s concert film's core themes: the film's efforts to memorialize a communal experience of music (primarily for its players, but also its listeners) are destabilized by the concert film's habitual focus on the rock star's embodiment of freedom and authenticity. *The Last Waltz* was initially received by critics and spectators as both a celebratory and elegiac summary of rock music in its 1960s countercultural expression, and its paradoxical blend of celebration and regret recalls *Italianamerican* and *American Boy*'s concise oral histories. *The Last Waltz*'s antagonistic production, however, would create long-term reverberations for different members of The Band, and as we'll see, this is largely a result of the film's contradictory effort to fasten direct cinema's preoccupation with musicians' self-realization to its own particular reckoning with a collectively shared experience of rock music during the 1960s. The 1970s saw rock's rapid incorporation by conglomerates and an associated professionalization of popular musicians, and *The Last Waltz*'s close concentration on Robbie Robertson's self-seeking demeanor discloses a developing image of the modern-day musician's work. Combining self-realization with his acquiescence to the concert film's design, Robertson's work frequently neutralizes *The Last Waltz*'s attempt to memorialize the cooperative accomplishments of The Band, and this finally produces an instructive portrait of musician labor as it emerged in the 1970s. The chapter concludes with a look at *Shine a Light*'s rendering of The Rolling Stone's 2006 Beacon Theater concerts because it reiterates *The Last Waltz*'s fundamental observation: the film commemorates Mick Jagger's post-1980s professionalism and describes the group's significance in terms of his resilience and harmonious comportment.

"Chapter 3: Archival Expeditions" continues the analysis of Scorsese's rockumentary output, but it turns to his sketch of the Delta Blues' numerous northward migrations in *Feel Like Going Home* (his lone contribution to *Martin Scorsese Presents: The Blues*), and his wide-ranging portrait of the young Bob Dylan in *No Direction Home*. Scorsese's revived documentary practice began to make extensive use of archival resources in this period, a noticeable modification to his 1970s approach, and the result is an emphasis on the assemblage of materials to create historical meaning. This chapter surveys *Feel Like Going Home* and *No Direction Home*'s combined effort to understand the changing social meaning of different kinds of popular music—the wide variety of American vernacular music (folk, blues, country), the new amalgamations of folk and rock 'n' roll in Dylan's generation defining mid-1960s recordings, and the development of rock music in its late-1960s countercultural expression. *Feel Like Going Home* returns to the Mississippi Delta and Africa to study the blues as modern revolution and ancient folklore, but the film's disclosure of this music's underpinnings is realized in its architectural repositioning of its materials within a broader synoptic design. As we'll see, Scorsese accepts the folklorist's method in unearthing and sharing his various discoveries: a living past is preserved in the blues, and the film presents itself as an audiovisual steward for these cultural artifacts. *No Direction Home* is perhaps the director's most comprehensive compilation about popular music, but the film's accumulation of its resources deliberately interferes with spectators' customary understanding of the 1960s: familiar signposts are filtered through Dylan's unparalleled experiences in this period, and the film's editing works to evade the surplus of mass-mediated images from the mythical "Sixties." The chapter ends with a very brief discussion of *Living in the Material World* and its comparable attempt to filter a late-1960s sense of tumult through George Harrison's self-possessed consciousness. Although *Living in the Material World* seems slightly misaligned with Scorsese's studies of American vernacular music, it reveals the films' common purpose in weaving wider cultural histories with biography.

"Chapter 4: Personal Pilgrimages" turns its attention to Scorsese's elemental cinephile compilations, *Il mio viaggio in Italia* and *A Letter to Elia*, but it closely examines how they both establish deep connections between the director's permanent cinephilia and more obscure strata of historical experience, the experience of migration in particular. *Il mio viaggio in Italia* returns to the immigrant story of departure and arrival, initially told in *Italianamerican* and then alluded to in *A Personal Journey*'s closing passages; but because *Italianamerican*'s principal storytelling subjects are now gone, Scorsese reviews his family's rapidly disappearing past in this collection of venerated popular film images. *Il mio viaggio in Italia* thus selects and compiles its numerous fragments from the familiar corpus of Italian Neorealist films, but refers to them as mobile relics: these movies migrated from Italy to a secondary location in New York City's post-Second World War Little Italy, and in the process allowed Scorsese's family of immigrants to partake again in the original site's value. This rhetoric of transposition is a crucial part of *Il mio viaggio in Italia*'s reckoning with the director's memories and cinephilia, their interconnections and relation to the past, but *Il mio viaggio in Italia* and *A Letter to Elia* both treat their collections of images as repositories for similarly personal recollections and experience. *A Letter to Elia*, however, limits its focus to one director's work and Scorsese's sometimes inscrutable analyses of its import; yet once again, this highly personal missive to Elia Kazan is released in the form of lengthy excerpts and Scorsese's accompanying reminiscences. As we'll see, the recurrence of familiar themes in *A Letter to Elia*—immigration and ethnicity in America, cinephilia, film history—indicates a settling of historical accounts for Scorsese, or rather, his recognition of an obligation to repay debts to an increasingly remote past. In the end, history is embedded in the director's selected images (and sounds), but it can always be summoned once again in the work of documentary compilation.

The book's "Conclusion" briefly considers changes in Scorsese's present-day approach to documentary film production. As he has freely acknowledged in countless interviews, Scorsese's remaining time as a filmmaker is limited, and he is aware of a certain urgency to complete various proposed projects. In terms of his current non-fiction undertakings, however, this sense of resolve has unquestionably increased the rate at which he produces and distributes his documentaries, while simultaneously driving his works into new affiliations and methods of distribution. Longstanding plans for more films about the histories of cinema, for example, have seemingly been abandoned for the ongoing production of documentary profiles, and the latter position themselves in very close proximity to the surplus of similar contemporary reality-based media artifacts. The overabundance of personality profiles on today's inescapable streaming services implies a somewhat restricted range of possibilities in these settings, and Scorsese's qualified excitement over platforms like Netflix suggests an understanding of how they have been both a boon *and* a constraint for directors, documentarians in particular. Indeed, his contributions to documentary since *A Letter to Elia* have been dispersed differently, and this has broadened the remit for his cultural stewardship. Frequently appearing as an interview subject in other filmmakers' studies of movies, music, and history, or adopting the role of executive producer, Scorsese's contemporary documentary character is fully attuned to his position as steward; and while this isn't necessarily an unfamiliar role for him, the context for his documentaries' reception has changed noticeably since *A Letter to Elia* was first broadcast in 2010. The Conclusion therefore provides a brief summary analysis of the director's output since *A Letter to Elia*. It speculates about potential modifications to his work's meaning as it continues to be repositioned in different sites for the production and distribution of documentary films and videos, but it also sketches the broader context for understanding Scorsese's non-fiction filmmaking today.[11]

1

Historical Migrations: *Italianamerican* and *American Boy: A Profile of Steven Prince*

Ethnic Reminiscences: Foundations and Reveries

Commissioned by the National Endowment for the Humanities (NEH), *Italianamerican* (1974) was first conceived within the wider context of America's planned Bicentennial observances in 1976. Indeed, first screened in its familiar forty-nine-minute form at the 1974 New York Film Festival, and then broadcast as an abbreviated twenty-eight-minute contribution to PBS's commemorative *A Storm of Strangers* series, Scorsese's most elemental and "personal" production was envisioned as an unassuming tribute to the period's celebratory ethnic revival.[1] "The mid-1970s," Matthew Frye Jacobson writes, "represented the consolidation" of a revivified ethnicity in America (2006, 17), and Scorsese's intimate short film about his parents and their experiences as second-generation Italian Americans is in many ways a representative historical object—if its everyday backdrop and warm familial accents give it the appearance of a home movie, *Italianamerican*'s deepest roots can surely be found in the period's distinctive political-cultural topography. Jacobson points to the developing interest in "genealogical research" and an associated desire to safeguard assorted types of "heritage" as defining features of the white ethnic revival, and he explains how they would finally generate novel popular idioms for national belonging in the 1970s. Moreover, and more importantly, he describes a pervasive turn to particularized accounts of America's past during this decade, and this would decisively shift critical understandings of history to the more nebulous dimensions of subjectivity and "identity." Jacobson's focus on the convergence of state sponsorship and grassroots ethnic reclamation projects in the 1970s indicates the degree to which Scorsese's documentary was embedded within—and beholden to—these cultural preoccupations. The state's "mounting interest in pluralism" (Jacobson 2006, 54) undoubtedly led it to exploit the energy and activities on view in *Italianamerican*, but ethnically focused films of its kind could in turn authorize a developing commitment to the nation's broader "mosaic" inheritance. Scorsese's provisional plan (eventually abandoned) to follow *Italianamerican* with several more entries in a cycle devoted to American ethnic histories only confirms the perceived appeal of this material to a national audience in the mid-1970s.[2]

Jacobson's wide-ranging analysis of the white ethnic revival in *Roots Too: White Ethnic Revival in Post-Civil Rights America* (2006) includes a very brief and unsympathetic synopsis of *Italianamerican*'s main emphases and methods. "*Italianamerican*," he notes, is among "the most complete fossilized records of [the 1970s'] impulse to recover ethnic heritage," and he derisively compares Scorsese's interviews with his parents to a college student's "heritage hunt" (2006, 53). Because it was sanctioned by the state in the form of its NEH award and proposed by its producers as a contribution to the country's Bicentennial festivities, *Italianamerican* is simply another vehicle for political meaning in Jacobson's account. It establishes more evidence for the regeneration of ethnicity in the 1970s and its critical reversal of America's earlier assimilationist or "melting pot" aspirations, of course; but as a consequence, Scorsese's short documentary, like other popular works of its type, obscures a rather different national history of racial antagonisms and inequalities. According to Jacobson,

> In the years beyond the melting pot there arose a new national myth of origins whose touchstone was Ellis Island, whose heroic central figure was the downtrodden but determined greenhorn, whose preferred modes of narration were the epic and the ode, and whose most far-reaching political conceit was the "nation of immigrants."
>
> (2006, 7)

In the candid and resourceful storytelling of its subjects, *Italianamerican* unreservedly describes this familiar tale of the immigrant's odyssey to America at the turn of the twentieth century. Yet the film's unassuming stories, apparently personal and deeply rooted in the specific details of the Scorseses' historical experiences, also signpost much wider developments in 1970s America. In other words, in the terms of Jacobson's white ethnic revival, an embryonic nation of immigrants would definitively reach its new self-understanding through the reiteration of such ostensibly subjective parables.

Although he is exceedingly dismissive of *Italianamerican*, Jacobson's attempt to situate Scorsese's film in a more expansive historical context is constructive and worth pursuing further. This documentary might indeed appear "fossilized," but only when it is fastened too firmly to the director's ubiquitous "biographical legend" and the predominant terms of an auteurist discourse.[3] Originally conceived as a commemorative endeavor, *Italianamerican*, like so much of Scorsese's subsequent documentary output, was indelibly shaped by the ethnic revival's pervasive language of reclamation: a desire to reconstruct, recuperate, regenerate, or retrieve an historical experience of immigration provided the primary motivation for the film's production. But *Italianamerican*'s approach to its core historiographic commission reveals many meaningful differences from other more orthodox efforts to revivify ethnicity throughout the early-1970s. According to Les Keyser, Scorsese "wanted to nothing to do with a mundane, stereotypical account of Italians pouring off ocean liners, encountering Ellis Island, then crowding into Lower Manhattan" (1992, 1), and he would accept the NEH assignment only if he was permitted more latitude in determining *Italianamerican*'s form.[4] One can easily imagine a version of the NEH's projected documentary: abundant voice-over exposition, assorted archival moving images and photographs, retrospective testimony from a wide assortment of anonymous Italian immigrants, a narrative of hardships and eventual success, and so forth. But *Italianamerican* chooses instead to have its director's second-generation Italian American parents respond to his questions and simply tell their life stories to a camera and crew of filmmakers in their Little Italy apartment, and the finished film makes only fleeting use of the iconographic imagery alluded to by Keyser. As a consequence, an especially expressive type of storytelling predominates throughout the film, as do the conspicuous repetitions of ceremonial undertakings (the telling of stories, cooking, eating, and talking at the dinner table) and the extemporaneous movements of subjects within the restricted space of the family's apartment. *Italianamerican* might intermittently have the appearance of a "home movie gone mad" (Keyser 1992, 2), but its approach, that is, its conscious choices and circumvention of the ethnic revival's fundamental prescriptions, should be understood in terms of its inception as an historical project: these choices are effectively interventions in the period's broader commemorative activities; they are ultimately attempts to activate different historical materials within the setting of the decade's wider ethnic revival.

Scorsese's unwillingness to, as he puts it, "go back to 1901 with stock footage and a narrator saying, 'In 1901' ..." (Kelly 1991, 17), implicitly acknowledges the disproportionate dispersion of certain kinds of images and movies during the 1970s, but it also indicates a deeper engagement with the assorted questions or problems of historiography, particularly as they relate to his documentary assignment. Indeed, his abandonment of the period's accumulating iconography of European immigration should compel us to precisely distinguish *Italianamerican*'s perspective on the era's widespread sense of ethnic renewal. Can we, for example, more accurately characterize this film's originality as an account of Italian American history? Should we in fact understand *Italianamerican* as a commemoration *and* assessment of the 1970s ethnic revival? If conventionalized photographs in this period typically dispensed vernacular knowledge about the histories of immigration to America, Scorsese's short film pointedly interrupts the immediacy of such imagery by concentrating on a substantially different task: it attends closely to its present-day storytellers' embodied recollections; it highlights the smallest changes in their comportment, storytelling, and the velocity, intonation, and sound of their voices because these are keys to comprehending several less apparent features of the history in question. In this respect, *Italianamerican* resists one prevailing aspect of the ethnic revival, namely, its developing rendition of the immigrant experience as a set of archival images, and replaces it with another of the era's characteristic historiographic tendencies: the construction of social "histories from below" and their attendant reliance upon oral accounts of the past. According to Alessandro Portelli, the tonality and "volume range and the rhythm of popular speech carry implicit meaning and social connotations" (1998, 65), and these should be differentiated from other modes of conveying historical experience such as writing or the abundant "stock footage" mentioned by Scorsese. In other words, the "tone," "volume range," and "rhythm" of idiomatic communication establish a foundation for any oral history. *Italianamerican*'s methodical attentiveness to popular speech and storytelling, the deportment of its principal storytellers, and the self-reflexive conduct of its interviews indicate how the film's final form comprises a *critical* apprehension of the era's ethnic renaissance. In Jacobson's brief account, *Italianamerican* seems to be little more than an ossified relic, but the film can be more usefully understood as an active reassessment of the ethnic revival's central predispositions as well as its accompanying historiography. Although it is not the director's first experience with documentary filmmaking, *Italianamerican* effectively represents Scorsese's true "beginning" as a documentarian dedicated to rendering accounts of the historical past. In many ways, the film initiates the director's longstanding preservationist efforts, but only insofar as it apprehends such work in the identifiable idiom of "recovery." Edward Said has helpfully distinguished "beginnings" from "origins," describing the former as "first step[s] in the intentional production of meaning" (1975, 5). *Italianamerican*'s perceptive and focused participation in the period's ethnic resurgence, I want to suggest, establishes precisely this kind of meaningful "beginning" for Scorsese's documentary production.

In what follows, I return to *Italianamerican* and its exhausted follow-up, *American Boy: A Profile of Steven Prince* (1978), and I closely examine their shared approach to meeting the various challenges of rendering historical accounts on film during this period. Collected in sense memories and storytelling deportment, history in these two films is consistently drawn from their narrators' lucid documentation of a wide range of retrospective signposts. Effectively dispensing with the iconographic archival resources alluded to above, *Italianamerican*'s approach implies a substantial compatibility between the Scorseses' artless storytelling—their natural comportment, gestures, and vernacular rendering of historical accounts—and the larger social history of Italian immigration to America at the onset of the twentieth century. *American Boy: A Profile of Steven Prince*, in many ways an extended and apprehensive epilogue to *Italianamerican*, assumes this same approach in order to register the termination of the Scorseses' optimistic stories of arrival—and cautious assimilation—in the new world. As a consequence, the films' storytellers come to function as conspicuous intercessors for the historical past: their particular narration of assorted anecdotes intervenes decisively in the films' interpretations of the histories in question. In other words, the Scorseses' and Prince's increasingly communicative storytelling grasps a meaningful dimension of the past and discloses a very different generational attunement to the films' broader story of migration to America. As we'll see, *Italianamerican* and *American Boy* finally catalog a set of externalized thoughts and emotions whose source is a substantial relation to the historical experience of immigration to America. In Antonio Gramsci's familiar formulation, the "starting point of critical elaboration" is a developing self-consciousness, or an awareness of oneself "as a product of the historical process to date which has deposited in [oneself] an infinity of traces, without leaving an inventory" (1971, 324). In Scorsese's *Italianamerican* and *American Boy: A Profile of Steven Prince*, we can perceive the framework for this type of self-consciously critical inventory, and our attendant efforts to clarify and characterize each figure's unique storytelling, that is to say, our determination to recognize the films' accumulating assemblage of historical traces, are what ultimately direct our comprehension of their perspectives on the past *as* history. Simply put, *Italianamerican*'s (and *American Boy*'s) adoption of this amalgam of observational and participatory methods distinguishes it from the NEH's projected expository approach, and it is the key to understanding Scorsese's particular rendering of historical accounts.[5]

Emotions in the Emulsion: *Italianamerican* and American Documentary in the 1970s

Although it was plainly conceived as the first of Scorsese's self-described "smaller projects" (Christie and Thompson 2003, 113), *Italianamerican* continues to figure prominently in interviews with the director. He has on occasion provocatively called it "the best film I ever made" (Kelly 1991, 17), but more often he describes this unpretentious short documentary as an experimental laboratory for his subsequent fiction filmmaking explorations. In other words, *Italianamerican*'s permanent value is repeatedly said to reside in the instructive solutions it establishes for the close cognate problems of fiction filmmaking:

> We shot medium shots of people talking [in *Italianamerican*], and intercut with some music over stills of them. To me it seemed very, very strong. It smashed all those preconceptions about what a film should look like and how a film should be presented. It also freed me in a sense. It streamlined the style for *Taxi Driver*. And in *Raging Bull*, we didn't give a damn. We didn't care about transitions, really. What I should say is, we didn't care about *artful* transitions.
>
> (Kelly 1991, 18; emphasis in original)

In this and many other similarly retrospective assessments, Scorsese values the *Italianamerican* experiment primarily for its embryonic challenges to conventional filmmaking—its unvarnished compositions, its recourse to a small number of set-ups and simple editing strategies, its informal deployment of music and sounds—and the apparently easy transferability of such methods to his fiction work.[6] The renewal of Scorsese's non-fiction film practice since 1995, however, has been accompanied by intermittent reflections upon these same issues, along with several unexpectedly speculative assertions about the blurred boundary between documentary and fiction filmmaking, their typically knotted reciprocity, and most significantly, *Italianamerican*'s pivotal influence on his approach to working with actors in the much more familiar Hollywood setting.

For example, in a wide-ranging interview about documentary filmmaking with longtime collaborator, Raffaele Donato, Scorsese further develops his previous ideas about *Italianamerican*'s long-lasting lessons, particularly those gleaned from the experience of watching real people who appear, with varying degrees of self-consciousness, before a camera and filmmaking crew:

> It's those moments when the defenses are down, where [people] get so comfortable that they really let themselves show, that are so precious. That's what I discovered when I made *Italianamerican*. And that's what I'm always trying to find with actors in a dramatic film.
>
> (Donato 2007, 204)

Scorsese once again reiterates his description of *Italianamerican*'s direct methods ("a medium two-shot of two people talking, some close-ups" [Donato 2007, 202]), but the persistent renewal of his non-fiction filmmaking seems to have encouraged him to clarify the consequences of such interactions with social actors in the documentary situation. *Italianamerican*'s "style," he asserts, "was very simple," yet it nevertheless permitted an unprompted delineation of what he now calls this film's "key event": "ultimately, the human being, the human face, had to become the event" (Donato 2007, 202). Formal simplicity resulted in the "human being, the human face," *having to become* the film's essential event. This novel critical conception, with its elusively metaphysical implications, describes the appearance of something like an apparition, the primary documentary "event" unexpectedly making itself perceptible to film spectators only through *Italianamerican*'s human conduits. But what constitutes an *event* in these strategically nebulous formulations? Is it a uniquely documentary experience? What features of the human being are "directly transmitted" (Donato 2007, 202) by the camera's scrutiny of interviewees, their expressions, movements, and general demeanor? Given the film's emphasis on an Italian American experience of immigration, does the guileless storytelling in *Italianamerican* reveal something meaningful about "the human being's" relationship to the past? In other words, is there a discernible connection between the putative documentary event ("the human being, the human face") and the concrete *historical events* being summoned unpretentiously by the film's two principal storytellers and their assorted anecdotes?[7]

At first glance, Scorsese's responses to these kinds of questions seem overly equivocal, but his reflections upon such matters indicate a continuing search for pragmatic solutions to the primary problems of documentary filmmaking.

As we've seen, *Italianamerican*'s inception as a commemorative project, and Scorsese's immediate resistance to the NEH's orthodox directives, resulted in one elemental decision in the film's subsequent production, namely, the substitution of several present-day discussions with the director's parents for the rudiments of an expository documentary. Scorsese, however, persistently explains this foundational adjustment in focus and method simply as an effort to "stick to the emotions" (Kelly 1991, 17), and these "emotions," he claims, establish something other than ordinary "plot information" (Kelly 1991, 18) or the basic requirements of a traditional historical account (the weighing of evidence, a close examination of historical traces, determining the truth and meanings of past events, etc.). In other words, a documentary adherence to "the emotions" is meant to indicate *Italianamerican*'s connection to another stratum of truthful descriptions, one which the deployment of "stock footage" might not reach. Indeed, although the archive of standard images to which Scorsese refers is defined by its anonymity, "sticking to the emotions" by contrast designates a responsiveness to subjectivity and consciousness: *Italianamerican*'s techniques highlight its storytellers' capacity to retrospectively *interpret* their many experiences and the latter's *meaningful* relation to concrete historical events. In the director's often-repeated accounts of documentary method, "the emotions" thus refer to the varied psychological expressions of a subject, and *Italianamerican* attends to this same subject's articulate interpretations of assorted past experiences because these ultimately disclose an original form of historical understanding—for the film's central storytellers *and* its viewers. If Scorsese's attempts to clarify *Italianamerican*'s methods customarily seize upon the commonplace connotation of terms like "the emotions" and "key event," such expressions should nevertheless be understood first and foremost as idiomatic descriptions of the film's fundamental adherence to subjectivity, consciousness, and interpretation in its rendering of historical accounts.

The phrase "stick to the emotions" is, of course, distantly implicated in a long history of philosophical thinking about emotions, cognition, perception, consciousness, and understanding. Nonetheless, Scorsese's vernacular explanations of *Italianamerican*'s commitment to its primary storytelling subjects—or more accurately, its willing *participation* in the film's "key event"—are best understood in relation to much more proximate and pragmatic resources.[8] *Italianamerican*, I want to suggest, purposefully modifies its commemorative documentary assignment according to two closely connected and complex 1970s phenomena:

first, developing tendencies in American documentary filmmaking, and more precisely, their entanglement with the contentious legacy of direct cinema; and second, the concurrent ethnic revival and its own emergent documentary and historiographic conventions, many of which intersect in meaningful ways with the period's non-fiction filmmaking. *Italianamerican* is an especially noteworthy artifact because it refocuses its documentary commission in the same terms as these developing—and intertwined—features of the period's cultural production. As several scholars have rightly noted, American documentary filmmaking during the 1970s was defined by its increasing concern with affirming the value of subjectivity, both personal and collective, and critics have usually framed this as a progressive—or remedial—reaction to the predominance of observational techniques in the preceding decade. Bill Nichols, for example, consistently characterizes this widespread shift to "subjectivity" as an unequivocal repudiation of direct cinema, its supposed commitment to "objectivity," and its need to excise any evidence of people's inevitable self-consciousness before a camera and sound recording devices:

> Reacting against the small-scale, observational qualities of documentaries in the 1960s that began to shift attention from the state to facets of everyday life and lived experience [...], work in the 1970s returned [...] to the use of the interview to recount historical events and personal experience. [...] With this shift the form and style of documentary representations expand to encompass a breadth of perspectives and voices, attitudes and subjectivities.
>
> (2001, 607–8)

Simply put, the "personal" and "subjectivity" paradoxically narrow *and* expand the purview of documentary filmmaking in the 1970s, and in the process, they apparently displace the previous decade's "observational qualities." This historical account is commonly accepted in present-day documentary studies, but it has had the unfortunate consequence of diminishing direct cinema's continuing significance to American non-fiction filmmaking throughout the 1970s.[9] Arguments in favor of such a decisive shift to subjectivity, customarily characterized as the introduction of novel pluralized idioms for documentary representation (a breadth of perspectives, voices and attitudes), often neglect the degree to which direct cinema was itself already implicated in this ideological formulation. Indeed, 1960s observational cinema's concentration on acts of self-realization and self-actualization, frequently performed by musicians or actors, shares an individualist or liberal alignment with 1970s documentaries, and both moments are undoubtedly delineated by the perennial American fixation on character or subjective disposition. There is, in other words, a great deal of continuity between direct cinema of the 1960s and developing trends in 1970s documentaries. The emphasis on particularism of various kinds clearly stretches across the two decades, and each period understands "subjectivity" as a type of refuge from America's broader homogenizing forces—for example, the increasingly powerful intrusions of mass media, consumption, and commodification into everyday life.[10] According to William Rothman, American non-fiction filmmaking in the 1970s can in fact be more usefully understood as an "extension" and "transformation" of 1960s direct cinema (2000, 418); that is to say, it should be seen not as a complete disavowal of direct cinema's practices and embedded philosophy, but rather as an ongoing modification of the earlier films' preoccupation with subjectivity.[11] Scorsese's *Italianamerican* is an instructive 1970s work precisely because it clearly derives many of its methods from direct cinema, yet it renews this controversial inheritance according to documentary filmmaking's experiments and critical developments throughout this period.[12]

Direct cinema's principal practitioners—Robert Drew and his associates, Richard Leacock, Albert and David Maysles, and D.A. Pennebaker—were frequently taken to task for the perceived anti-intellectualism of their filmmaking and its accompanying theoretical pronouncements. As Stephen Mamber observes, a commitment to "emotions over reason" (1974, 47) was seen as the defining quality in classic works such as *Primary* (Robert Drew, 1960), *Dont Look Back* (D.A. Pennebaker, 1967), *Salesman* (Albert Maysles, David Maysles, and Charlotte Zwerin, 1969), and *Gimme Shelter* (Albert Maysles, David Maysles, and Charlotte Zwerin, 1970), and as a result, the films—and their makers—often appeared to be equating emotions with a heightened sense of truthfulness. Indeed, one could adopt Scorsese's language and argue that these observational documentaries routinely "stick to the emotions," insofar as they conspicuously sidestep any overt exposition or historical contextualization, and their representative effects are in turn derived from the sight and sounds of people's inadvertent candidness before a camera and crew of filmmakers. Paula Rabinowitz isolates this type of uncontrolled "access to emotion" (1994, 133) as a potential advantage in direct cinema's observational approach, while Thomas Waugh critically identifies the films' "highly charged emotional statements" (1985, 235) as an unavoidable—and politically unreliable—consequence of their methods. In his sketch of documentary history, Bill Nichols similarly classifies direct cinema as an "affective form" because of its persistent concentration on this narrow register of experience:

> It affords the opportunity for the viewer to look in on and overhear something of the lived experience of others, to gain some sense of the distinct rhythms of everyday life, to see the colors, shapes, spatial relationships among people and their possessions, to hear the intonation, inflection and accents that give a spoken language its "grain" and that distinguish one native speaker from another.
>
> (1991, 42)

According to Nichols, direct cinema in this way underscores the "historical specificity" of the observed world, and more importantly, renders it in terms of an "emotional geography" (1991, 41). Scorsese's retrospective explanations of how documentaries continue to influence his own work return persistently to this foundational moment in the 1960s, and American observational filmmaking is invariably the touchstone in his efforts to establish a theoretical underpinning for his own non-fiction project. Significantly, however, *Italianamerican* has prompted the director's most consistently suggestive assertions about his documentary techniques and their intended effects. If Scorsese's theoretical observations about his non-fiction filmmaking are sometimes articulated in overly broad terms, *Italianamerican* nonetheless reveals how the director extends and transforms direct cinema's focus on emotional and historical specificity. And it does so within the context of 1970s documentary production and its developing emphases—its confirmations of individual and collective subjectivity, a rehabilitated commitment to participatory interviews, its increasing self-reflexivity, and a renewed preoccupation with history. In other words, Scorsese's descriptions of method, that is, his claims for the historiographic import of *Italianamerican*'s close adherence to its storytelling subjects' "emotions" and consciousness, demarcate a technique inherited from the primary practitioners of American direct cinema, and his initial reluctance to incorporate stock images into his film suggests an association with the observational documentary's concentration on the present. The "human being, the human face" therefore had to become the film's "key event" because of this humanist emphasis, but the "event" in *Italianamerican* is in fact the unique experience of being filmed while thinking and speaking about the historical past. Simply put, *Italianamerican*'s recourse to direct cinema explains its determined focus on "the emotions," while its participation in the basic documentary event indicates the film's meaningful elaboration of its direct cinema inheritance. In this respect, the film navigates between competing movements in 1960s and 1970s documentary filmmaking in order to arrive at its historiographic approach: it revitalizes direct cinema's traditional concentration on unplanned speech and action by attending closely to its two storytellers and their everyday expression of distinctive perspectives on the historical past.

If American direct cinema establishes one of the analytical frames for comprehending *Italianamerican*'s methods, the film's commemorative undertaking compels it to also make use of practices that one ordinarily associates with historians, oral historians in particular. This unmistakable shift to historical preoccupations, Jonathan Kahana writes, was common in 1970s American documentaries (2006, 200), but in Scorsese's *Italianamerican* it is interwoven with corresponding concerns in the concurrent ethnic revival, and these ultimately transform the direct cinema inheritance outlined above in significant ways. In other words, this additional influence impels *Italianamerican* to rely upon participatory interviews and the other basic methods of oral historians, and this purposefully recalibrates direct cinema's emphasis on discourse and "person-sized spaces": the film accommodates the renewed attentiveness to history amongst 1970s documentarians; yet at the same time, it critically reassesses the ethnic revival's developing oral renditions of the past.[13] Alessandro Portelli characterizes these resurrected forms of oral history (testimonies, present-day interviews, audiovisual recordings, folkloric storytelling, biography, etc.) in terms of their indispensable "narrative functions," and his classification helpfully illuminates the primary features of *Italianamerican*'s historical account. Such narrative functions "reveal the narrators' emotions," Portelli contends, "their participation in the story, and the way the story [has] affected them" (1998, 65–6), and as a consequence, they present a "unique and precious element" to the oral historian: "the speaker's subjectivity" (1998, 67).[14] As I've already indicated, *Italianamerican*'s approach to its historical assignment seeks to renew direct cinema's comparable concentration on emotions and subjectivity, but it only does so by subtly readjusting its filmmaking conduct and making its interactions with the film's primary storytelling subjects a fundamental part of its commemorative undertaking. And as we'll see, such a candid approach to filmmaking finally convinces the film's two reluctant interviewees to serve as *Italianamerican*'s conspicuous conduits for the historical past: their meaningful storytelling *in the present*, always closely observed by the filmmaker, intercedes definitively for the history in question.

Storytelling as Intercession: *Italianamerican*'s Oral History

Italianamerican begins with a self-consciously presented white-on-black title card, "FILM IS ABOUT TO START," but this is immediately followed by several similarly self-reflexive signs of filmmaking sincerity: a handheld shot of sound recording equipment and its hunched operator; an accompanying zoom-in to this same figure as he clutches a light meter (Figure 1.1); and finally, a leftward pan to a medium shot of Martin Scorsese as he stares first at the light meter and then its operator, promptly asking, "is that the light?" Scorsese walks from right to left between the camera and his parents, and then rapidly moves offscreen to engage in the first of several extemporaneous verbal interactions with these visibly nervous people.[15] Catherine and Charles Scorsese are seated at the couch in a medium-long shot, and in an effort to ease the evident tension, Catherine calmly—and repeatedly—tries to coax her husband into moving closer to her. Her good-humored invitation is directed at her husband, but also assorted members of the film crew who gradually gather around the couch

Figure 1.1 *Italianamerican* (Martin Scorsese, 1974).

and the Scorseses during these unsettled preparatory moments. Indeed, the director and his collaborators reposition themselves in precisely this manner throughout *Italianamerican*, and as a result, they constitute the principal audience for the Scorseses' artless storytelling. Catherine in turn looks offscreen at her interlocutors often during this short conversation, quickly assessing their reactions and intentionally provoking additional responses to her behavior. Her storytelling deportment in *Italianamerican* is defined by a growing sense of ease in these interactions and is critical to understanding the film's approach to rendering its historical account. Charles, on the other hand, merely listens attentively and speaks only with considerable circumspection (Figure 1.2).

However, when Catherine moves to the kitchen to explain how she makes meatballs and tomato sauce, Charles looks offscreen at the director and crew to impatiently complain about his wife "trying to put on, I don't know why." She should be "talk[ing] natural" rather than adopting the expressive gestures and unhurried speech of her cooking lesson—"you're not an actress," he says dismissively. To Charles, Catherine seems to be behaving like something other than herself throughout the sequence in question. After catching her in this

Figure 1.2 *Italianamerican* (Martin Scorsese, 1974).

act, he attempts to undermine her "performance" and return the production to what he considers a more appropriately sincere form, namely, the commonly acknowledged conventions of documentary filmmaking. Like the aimless and tangential discussion that directly precedes it, this exchange purposefully brings an unsettled performance directly to the foreground: Catherine's equivocal conduct is framed (by Charles) as an obstacle to what really needs to be said about *Italianamerican*'s putative subject matter, yet it is also unmistakably—and paradoxically—an unavoidable and necessary condition for its saying. Charles is largely concerned with *how* he and his wife should express their stories, and he wants their storytelling to be shorn of any inaccuracy and pretension; while the camera instead lingers willfully on this puzzling moment of awkwardness because it establishes the basic conditions for *any* storytelling in *Italianamerican*. In other words, if Charles understands Catherine's undefined cooking "act" as an obstruction in the film's search for truthfulness, *Italianamerican* nonetheless positions it as an indispensable point of departure for the ensuing tales about immigration and its aftermath. Scorsese claims to have initially intended to eliminate this prefatory material from the finished film, but he finally decided to include it as evidence for the "very human adjustment people make when they're in front of a camera" (Donato 2007, 203). *Italianamerican*'s stuttering introductory passages are unquestionably comical depictions of people in this discernible state of adaptation before a film's camera and sound recording equipment. One watches as Catherine and Charles persistently reposition themselves against the simple backdrop of the family living room during these preliminary moments of hesitation, and one senses their discomfort as they now find—or perhaps momentarily lose—themselves in a new documentary setting. In an instance of what Stanley Cavell has elsewhere suggestively called "opaque self-consciousness" (1979, 205), these two conspicuously anxious people unexpectedly appear to us—are on view for us—as they must appear to themselves at this very moment: they are suddenly aware of observing themselves from the inside, that is to say, from an uncharacteristic and possibly perplexing point of view (Figure 1.3).

Yet it would be inaccurate to claim that this intentional process of human adjustment somehow disappears with the conclusion of these passages.[16] On the contrary, as viewers we are constantly aware of the Scorseses' ongoing need to make small, deliberate modifications to their demeanor, speech (inflections of their voices, a recourse to vernacular language in their folkloric tales), and their general approach to their roles as the film's primary storytellers. Social

Figure 1.3 *Italianamerican* (Martin Scorsese, 1974).

actors, of course, are typically impelled to accommodate themselves—with varying degrees of discernment—to the material impositions of documentary filmmaking. But *Italianamerican* is itself rendering an account of the historical experience of adjusting oneself to new circumstances. In other words, the Scorseses' consistently absorbing stories about immigration are shaped by their memories of having made modifications within a new American setting, by reminiscences about the numerous deprivations that provoke adjustment regardless of one's willingness to change in the new world, and by their commemoration of the assorted minor victories that ensure their immigrant family's survival in an inflexible and unfamiliar environment. This is how the director's parents come to function as conspicuous intercessors in *Italianamerican*'s rendering of historical accounts. They evidently resuscitate this historical condition; or rather, they reenact a past irrevocably marked by periodic adjustments and the increasing clarity of self-consciousness. In short, these two figures disclose a characteristic manner of being in the new world, and in their distinctive storytelling, they exemplify a manner of continuous modification to the demands of their historical world. If we return to Scorsese's statement of methodological principles, this is how *Italianamerican* finally transposes "human being" into an "event." An historical condition and disposition are revealed by these two figures, in what they say and mean, and in their determined efforts to discover the right tenor for meaningful speaking and conduct throughout this short film.

Paula Rabinowitz has described certain kinds of documentary filmmaking in terms of their "graphing [of] history in and through the cinematic image and taped sound" (1994, 16). Such documentary histories are always perceptibly shaped by the medium's formative materials, but in *Italianamerican*, the historical past must also migrate through its two main subjects, or rather make its mark on the film by being sifted through two storytellers whose self-consciousness before the camera and crew of filmmakers is evident. As I've indicated, *Italianamerican*'s interpretation of history involves closely examining the Scorseses' self-consciousness and, more importantly, its progressively intelligible connections to a remote historical past, but the film still lingers meaningfully over images of these two people as they thoughtfully assess themselves and their newfound apprehensiveness before the camera and filmmakers. Indeed, this is the principal conundrum of *Italianamerican*'s extended introductory passages, and it recalls countless discussions about documentary "performance," the "matter of camera influence" in direct cinema (Mamber 1974, 179), and the associated worry over people's defensive need to adjust themselves to the circumstances of non-fiction filmmaking. In various efforts to understand and theorize photography, one sees a corresponding—and especially instructive—preoccupation with this same type of self-awareness and the always imminent prospect of pretense. Roland Barthes's *Camera Lucida: Reflections on Photography*, for instance, a commonly canonized example in film studies, explicitly ponders how the subjects of photography can "work on [their] own skin from within" to counterbalance this initial sense of camera-induced nervousness and self-awareness (1981, 11).[17] According to this formulation, "the skin" is somehow pliable and can be "worked on" from within; its malleability presumably graphs one's increasing sense of self-consciousness at this very instant:

> I have been photographed and knew it. Now, once I feel myself observed by the lens, everything changes: I constitute myself in the process of "posing," I instantaneously make another body for myself in advance into an image. The transformation is an active one: I feel that the photograph creates my body or mortifies it, according to its caprice.
>
> (Barthes 1981, 10–11)

Further on, Barthes narrows his focus to the possibility of artifice in portrait photos:

> In front of the lens, I am at the same time: the one I think I am, the one I want others to think I am, the one the photographer thinks I am, and the one he makes use of to exhibit his art. In other words, a strange action: I do not stop imitating myself, and because of this, each time I am (or let myself be) photographed, I invariably suffer from a sense of inauthenticity, sometimes of imposture.
>
> (1981, 13)

Scorsese has spoken in very similar terms about his own experience of self-awareness before the film camera:

> I find that as soon as the camera is on me I become conscious of where I'm sitting, where I'm looking, the way I'm walking. I get up and start to walk, and suddenly I'm aware of putting one foot in front of the other, not to mention everything else I'm doing. That's why I have so much admiration for actors who can pour themselves out, just cleanse any trace of self-consciousness, as if the camera didn't exist.
>
> (Donato 2007, 204)

In many ways, this is the essential challenge—and foremost fiction—of 1960s American direct cinema. In D.A. Pennebaker's landmark *Dont Look Back*, for example, Bob Dylan's noticeable evasiveness and dissembling suggest a need to counteract the camera's persistent intrusions into his everyday life as he tours across England. If the camera is simply another active variable in the documentary situation, Dylan's continuous self-awareness and persistent "working on his own skin from within" belie direct cinema's most deeply held fiction; namely, that its primary subjects' increasing comfort with the camera's presence somehow allows them to, in Scorsese's terms, "cleanse any trace of self-consciousness" from their ordinary behavior. Attempts to theorize photography once again provide a valuable point of comparison here. Michael Fried has revealed how Barthes's preoccupation with the inescapable experience of inauthenticity and self-consciousness before a camera does not produce a preference for "the large class of photographs of persons who are unaware of being photographed" (2005, 548), that is, for the type of candid photography consistently promoted by the original practitioners of direct cinema in America. On the contrary, *Camera Lucida* is finally possessed by photos that look one "*in the eye*" (Barthes 1981, 111; emphasis in original), and the so-called *punctum*, a photograph's piercing or wounding element, is only palpable if seen against the backdrop of this artificial situation. According to Fried, the *punctum* in fact both requires and "overcomes" the uncomfortable "theatricality" of these instantaneously adopted positions before a camera (2005, 571). In *Italianamerican*, the Scorseses' developing storytelling acts are similarly directed to the creation of effects; their persistent invocation of historical realities both requires and permeates the self-consciousness on view throughout the film's hesitating opening moments. Such storytelling is, of course, invariably emphatic (it has a plain purpose in this film), but the continuously dynamic exchange between these two figures and the camera (as well as the film's director and his crew) nevertheless establishes the ground from which their rendering of historical accounts can emerge.[18]

The comparison to photography is particularly useful in this case because it sheds light on *Italianamerican*'s critical relation to the period's ethnic resurgence. According to Jacobson, the ethnic revival relied on an extensive visual iconography of immigration: powerful images of steerage passengers in flight; the countering weight of the Statue of Liberty's presence and promise; chaotic scenes of arrival at Ellis Island; and abundant photos of turn-of-the-century Manhattan tenements with their despair, scarcity, over-crowdedness, familial warmth, and so on. This basic iconography was deftly deployed in numerous Hollywood films from the period, and its pervasiveness during the 1970s (and beyond) gave it a generic, easily understandable function in emergent narratives about America's new mythic origins.[19] But the photographic foundations for such images are worth reconsidering here because *Italianamerican* only intermittently—and only by implication—relies upon their authority as archival objects or legitimate "recordings" of the past. Jacobson identifies the Jewish Museum in New York's 1966 exhibit "Portal to America" and the publication of its catalogue the following year as signal events in the recovery and consolidation of this immense archive of images. By collecting and displaying so many soon-to-be iconic photos by figures such as Jacob Riis, Lewis Hine, and Joseph Byron (among others), the exhibition and its catalogue endowed the immigrant experience with "a newfound immediacy in visuality and inaugurated a new genre, the immigration photo-epic, within that ascendant mode of 1960s cultural production called heritage" (Jacobson 2006, 79). As Jacobson rightly notes, however, these photographs are marked by an implacable "emotional distance" (2006, 80) from their immigrant subjects, many of whom are stereotypically framed as *objects* of social concern. If such photos occasionally look their spectators in the eye, more often they choose to avoid contact with the people on view and instead establish an air of "impenetrable exoticism and foreignness." As a consequence, the photographs' imagining of the immigrant's everyday experience, Jacobson concludes, predictably positions it as "a curiosity, a symptom of the rising social ills attending industrialization" (2006, 80–1).

Italianamerican occasionally borrows the visual power of such imagery when it cuts briefly to turn-of-the-century stock footage of anonymous, indistinguishable faces and figures. Determined and unfathomable, these people simply appear fleetingly and silently as perceptible evidence for the Scorseses' assorted assertions about the past, yet they are not individuated and generally remain unidentifiable (Figure 1.4). *Italianamerican*, however, effectively sidesteps the well-known pictorial lexicon of contemporaneous popular immigration narratives. In Jacobson's description, 1970s Hollywood had a clear advantage over contemporaneous photo exhibits when employing the ethnic revival's predominant visual iconography because its fiction films routinely gave such images a "familiarizing" quality. Engaging characters like

Figure 1.4 *Italianamerican* (Martin Scorsese, 1974).

Figure 1.5 *Italianamerican* (Martin Scorsese, 1974).

Vito Corleone in *The Godfather Part II* (Francis Ford Coppola, 1974), for instance, allowed an easily deciphered form of subjectivity to permeate scenes of early twentieth-century squalor and misery. One might plausibly claim that *Italianamerican*'s collection of the Scorseses' abundant family photographs serves a comparable purpose: it establishes a palpable sense of familial contentment and folksy firsthand subjectivity, while at the same time appearing to reinforce an affiliation with the ethnic revival's more widely disseminated imagery (Figure 1.5). *Italianamerican*'s commitment to an oral history, however, results in a palpable resistance to the period's mass-mediated interpretations of the immigrant's subjectivity, even complex and fully formed examples like *The Godfather Part II*. In other words, by refusing to make these images a fundamental element in its own historiography, Scorsese's film unassumingly repudiates the era's prevailing turn to photographic archives and their promise of distance and impartiality. Indeed, *Italianamerican* avoids the temptation to flatten its storytellers' expressive speech for the period's predominant visual iconography, preferring instead to have these people look viewers directly in the eye. Yet it does so only by sticking to the Scorseses' present-day oral testimony and attentively observing these two storytellers as they intercede for history, as they sift through the facts of the past while also grappling with this particular history's place in their imaginations, its symbolic resonance in their assorted reminiscences, and its relation to their evident nostalgia for the Italian American past.

Anamnesis in Acts: Relocations and Revivals

The stories that follow *Italianamerican*'s hesitating introductory passages share a number of particularly meaningful characteristics. When Catherine and Charles speak about their parents' arrival to America in the early twentieth century, for example, their reminiscences return repeatedly to discernibly physical experiences: their mothers arduously washing clothes by hand; their fathers' similarly strenuous winemaking, somehow accommodated by their constricted family residences; childhood friends who engage in petty thievery; the arrival of additional boarders to their already overcrowded Little Italy apartments; and recurrent scenarios devoted to food and eating, "always eating," as Charles puts it. These reminiscences are persistently sensorial, for as Fredric Jameson has noted in a slightly different context, "it is the senses that remember, not the 'person' or personal identity" (1990, 2). As a consequence, the Scorseses' shared recollections about their neighborhood's street vendors tellingly seize upon the latter's tendency to set up push-carts on a shaded side of the street during hot summer mornings, only to then dutifully move them with the sun (and shade) to the other side in the afternoons. Similarly, Catherine's affectionately delivered tales about her parents' Staten Island property include seemingly insignificant information about her father's "certain kind of gravy and tomato paste," yet she nonetheless stops to emphasize this pasta sauce's "dark and dry" quality. Indeed, her impressionistic account of her father's dying fig tree emerges directly from this sequence of sense memories: she moves effortlessly from detailed observations about her parents' property and her father's dark and dry tomato sauce to a virtually mythic concluding scene of her mother's unexpected death. The film fittingly acknowledges this symbolic terminus with a black-and-white freeze-frame of Catherine's pensive expression as she stoically concedes, "and that was that."

But all of these stories assume a relatively precise shape as *Italianamerican* unfolds, and they can thus be characterized in three ways. First, the film's main storytellers, customarily shot in medium scale, repeatedly complete each other's thoughts and sentences, and in so doing, they share the burden of recollection with one another. When Catherine, situated directly to Charles's left on the couch, eagerly describes how their mothers would wash clothes with a washboard and cold stove, Charles leans his head back, looks briefly to the ceiling, and then promptly interjects with crucial additional details and forceful emphases: "in *cold* water," he says, "they would *boil* the clothes." Similarly, when Charles calmly provides details about the exploits of neighborhood children who would steal from street vendors, Catherine instantly attempts to soften the image of wrongdoing or criminality by looking repeatedly at her interlocutors, self-consciously shrugging her shoulders, and then finally adding with laughter, "from hand to hand, you know, kid's stuff." Second, Catherine insistently looks at her immediate audience when Charles is speaking, rapidly nodding in agreement, laughing with approval, or biting her lip in mock fear as she looks first at her son and then at other members of the crew. At such moments, one is made aware of a shared or universal past; or rather, one senses the thoughtful corroboration between these two people as they recall their varied historical experiences. Finally, the film frequently lingers on single shots of either Catherine or Charles when they are *not* speaking (Figure 1.6). During these instances, the historical past, summoned by a succession of energetic and artless acts of storytelling, clearly encompasses the complete documentary situation: "the emotions," it would appear, are collective, and it hardly matters which of the Scorseses expresses them. On the contrary, storytelling itself is the foremost matter in *Italianamerican*; that is, storytelling is significant throughout this documentary because it indicates a communal turn toward thinking about the historical world. And in its uninterrupted effort to revivify various events and people, such storytelling ultimately intervenes decisively for the history in question. In other words, the film's narrowly conceived historiography posits a substantial link between this particular mode of description and the historical past.

This quality of intercession is especially pronounced in *Italianamerican*'s concluding sequence. Suddenly declaring that she has had "enough for today, Marty," Catherine rises and moves away from the dinner table; she walks quickly

Figure 1.6 *Italianamerican* (Martin Scorsese, 1974).

to the distant background, turns on an air conditioner, and then impatiently asks her son when the living room can be returned to its pre-filmmaking orderly state. The director stands for a few moments, but he immediately steps from right to left and swiftly seats himself again at the edge of the frame in an effort to allow the zooming camera lens unimpeded access to his mother's movements. The filmmaker's continuing—and deliberate—laughter has encouraged Catherine to revisit an earlier story about her father's embarrassing experiences with American immigration officers. Unable to speak anything but a Sicilian dialect, Catherine's father was finally persuaded to apply for American citizenship with the assistance of another daughter/interpreter. According to Catherine's comic account, however, officials scolded her father for his inability to "speak American," although he had already lived in the new world for more than thirty years. Not surprisingly, he instantly took exception to being reprimanded in this manner, and the tale's accelerating comedy is derived largely from Catherine's reiteration of his stubborn responses. When she returns to this short anecdote, however, Catherine does not simply repeat her previous oral rendition of the story; instead, she reconsiders and revivifies the scene for her interlocutors. Now standing in long shot, she supplements her verbal descriptions with a physical demonstration of what purportedly took place at the immigration offices all those years ago, first stepping back to lightly mutter and half-deliver her father's essential obscenity, and then moving forward, bending her body slightly at the waist and mimicking his conduct as he allegedly leaned over the offending officer's desk for a final remonstration (Figure 1.7). The filmmakers, evidently amused by this extemporaneous addition to the film, now allow Catherine to experience her own amusement and satisfaction with this new extended version of the story. After concluding her comic reenactment, however, Catherine looks directly at the camera and asks her son with mock irritation, "Is he still taking this? I'll murder you! You'll never get out of this house alive." The verbal story, it would appear, can be "taken," but not this particular rendition; not this comic performance which might seem to test the limits of her tale's reliability.

According to Scorsese, Catherine and Charles's "everyday personalities" (Donato 2007, 203) emerge at such moments, primarily because these passages reveal the storytellers' renewed comfort with themselves and the camera. As we've seen, the formative conditions of documentary filmmaking in *Italianamerican* are a potential obstacle to the rendering of historical accounts, insofar as they initially seem to make these two figures exceedingly self-conscious and possibly

Figure 1.7 *Italianamerican* (Martin Scorsese, 1974).

distant from the historiographic task. But Scorsese is right to claim that this sense of apprehensiveness eases as the film proceeds: his parents' ordinary dispositions unquestionably reveal themselves, and their growing relaxation and openness with the filmmakers are among *Italianamerican*'s longest lasting impressions. Nevertheless, the Scorseses' evident self-consciousness during the film's tangential preliminary passages is never entirely abandoned, and it in fact remains an integral part of *Italianamerican*'s approach to composing its account of history. The Scorseses might gradually feel free to be themselves as the film progresses, yet they nonetheless remain distinctly self-conscious beings as they recount their historical experiences—their basic self-awareness pervades each of their reminiscences and stories in *Italianamerican*. In other words, the camera ultimately reveals self-consciousness to be an essential part of the Scorseses' "everyday personalities": the combination of guilelessness and reticence, sincerity and submissiveness, candidness and circumspection that inscribes itself upon the film's introductory moments never disappears completely, and as viewers we inevitably find ourselves trying to parse the significance of the Scorseses' expressive storytelling deportment. In precisely this way, *Italianamerican* shrewdly discovers how the history of Italian immigration to America has been irrevocably marked by such an experience of self-consciousness and continual adjustments. And the Scorseses' distinct style of storytelling—their voices, gestures, deportment, vernacular speech—in turn reveals itself to be a storehouse for this historically determined attunement to the world. By the time *Italianamerican* arrives at its concluding passages, Catherine and Charles have, to once again borrow Stanley Cavell's apt formulation, undoubtedly achieved a heightened everyday "lucidity" (1979, 205): Catherine is now visibly prepared to engage with every incursion into her living room, that is to say, any potential challenge to her understanding of the Scorseses' historical experience of immigration.

In his wide-ranging study of American Catholic arts, Paul Giles reminds us that Alexis de Tocqueville found American Catholics both submissive and sincere, but ultimately "unwilling to challenge established authority" (1992, 42), and this disposition discloses something essential in the apparently elusive logic behind Catherine Scorsese's rephrased tale about her father's ordeal. *Italianamerican*'s concluding scene sees Catherine resisting the temptation to add an implausible happy ending to her father's immigration story, yet its reenactment for comic effect reframes the purported conflict in significant ways. If his behavior cannot be characterized as simply docile or fully compliant,

Catherine's father's defensive relation to the institutions of American citizenship should nevertheless be described as slightly ironic, maybe even parodic. His discomfort and self-consciousness manifest themselves in his strategic isolation from America (he evidently does not want to learn the language or become an American citizen), but his allegedly obstinate response to the immigration official's reprimand was less a challenge than a sardonic rejoinder. (According to Catherine, her father did eventually receive his American citizenship.) The comic embellishment in Catherine's second delivery of her anecdote carefully diffuses the actual anger in this episode, but more importantly, it thereby reenacts a very specific reality in the Scorseses' immigrant history. In the end, these present-day images cannot—and should not—be "taken" because Catherine is self-consciously aware of what they reveal about the past and her father's experiences. With "skill and effort," Bill Nichols has noted, "the pressure of the past on the present moment of recounting [...] can become as much a subject of [a given documentary's] story as the history ostensibly recounted" (1994, 5); and at this instant, spectators are aware of how Catherine Scorsese's present-day storytelling demeanor has resuscitated a critical aspect of this historical reality. Like so many other moments in *Italianamerican*, this brief coda discloses how storytelling finally intercedes in the film's interpretation of historical actualities: its plainly physical qualities are paradoxically joined to highly particularized past experiences.

Time Fades Away—*American Boy: A Profile of Steven Prince*

Italianamerican is commonly interpreted as an objective addendum to Scorsese's previous fiction film, *Mean Streets* (1973), and its position as a "postscript" to the director's Hollywood output is meant to highlight this documentary's unpretentiousness. Both works are essentially preoccupied with Italian American life, of course, but *Italianamerican* provides a convivial, comic, and much less apprehensive understanding of this ethnic story.[20] *American Boy: A Profile of Steven Prince*, in many ways a despondent sequel to *Italianamerican*, is similarly framed by critics as a conventional supplement to Scorsese's contemporaneous fiction filmmaking, in this case *Taxi Driver* (1976).[21] Once again, the predominant auteurist discourse describes this short film about Scorsese's friend and working associate, Steven Prince, as an unassuming exercise: its meaning ultimately derives from its connection to a far more widely known Hollywood movie. However, while *Italianamerican* remains an important point of reference for Scorsese's ongoing thinking about documentary filmmaking and history (its significance has continued to grow steadily since 1974), *American Boy: A Profile of Steven Prince* appears to be a disorderly object by comparison. As we've seen, *Italianamerican*'s historiographic aspirations were encouraged by the close convergence of state sponsorship and a developing grassroots interest in ethnicity throughout the 1970s. But *American Boy*'s production lacked a comparable institutional justification, and as a result, its relation to the period's commemorative ethnic revival is not immediately evident. Neil Young biographer Jimmy McDonough provides a cursory but illuminating assessment of the film, and his equivocation on the value of Scorsese's work speaks directly to this impression of *American Boy*'s waywardness: he rightly lauds the director's inventive use of Young's "Time Fades Away" during the film's introductory credits sequence (the "single best filmic use" of the Canadian songwriter's music, he claims), yet at the same time abruptly dismisses *American Boy* as a "little-seen sleazebag documentary" (2002, 505). If Scorsese's unruly film nonetheless continues to be cited by confirmed cinephiles like Richard Linklater and Quentin Tarantino, it is primarily because of its impassive collection of Steven Prince's many drug-related anecdotes and reminiscences about psychotic gun violence. In other words, *American Boy*'s limited currency today is drawn mostly from its correspondence with the fundamental attributes of *Taxi Driver*'s cosmos.[22]

American Boy's inescapable association with *Taxi Driver*, however, has obscured its original conception as an oral history about ethnicity in America and diverted attention away from the film's tentative relation to the contemporaneous ethnic revival.[23] Indeed, *American Boy* somehow continues to be misrepresented as a "lost film," and this has only amplified its sense of intractability and distance from any concrete historical context.[24] Yet *American Boy: A Profile of Steven Prince*, I want to suggest, is more usefully seen as an exhausted and apprehensive coda to *Italianamerican*'s verbal history of immigration. The Jewish Steven Prince and his anecdotes are important to the filmmakers principally because of their *generational* representativeness, and *American Boy* is in this respect best situated as *Italianamerican*'s disconcertingly distant sequel. In other words, *American Boy* adopts the white ethnic revival's most generic qualities in order to *universalize* an American ethnic experience and explain a much broader generational division—*Italianamerican* affectionately recalls the generative beginning to the Scorseses' expansive immigration narrative, while *American*

Boy progresses instead to the incongruous, terminal, present-day moment of this same history.[25] The films' relation to one another accordingly assumes a familiar historiographic pattern described by Eric Hobsbawm in *On History*:

> For the greater part of history, we deal with societies and communities for which the past is essentially the pattern for the present. Ideally each generation copies and reproduces its predecessor so far as it is possible, and considers itself as falling short of it, so far as it fails in this endeavor.
>
> (1997, 10)

In *Italianamerican*'s stories, the Scorsese family appeared to have successfully survived with a social strategy of minimal, cautious assimilation in the new world. By contrast, *American Boy*'s anecdotes indicate that such a survival tactic has now been discarded: the film's lone storytelling figure has been incorporated—admittedly, with a lingering sense of uneasiness and detachment—into a number of American institutions, the music/entertainment business foremost among them. Steven Prince therefore offers show biz stories, that is to say, recognizable tales of mobility and ethnic incorporation; but his concluding embrace of "success" hardly seems celebratory, and the film ironically portrays the related phenomena of ethnic assimilation and American achievement as wholly destructive.

Originally envisioned as part of a "projected six-film cycle on American ethnics begun with *Italianamerican*" (Friedman 1997, 112), *American Boy* deliberately revivifies the preceding film's method for its more pointed interpretation of history. Like Catherine and Charles Scorsese in *Italianamerican*, Steven Prince is surrounded by his receptive audience of filmmakers, friends, and interlocutors throughout *American Boy*, and the whole crew is again conspicuously confined to a narrow household space (Figure 1.8). As a consequence, Martin Scorsese, Julia Cameron, Mardik Martin, and George Memmoli are each visible at various moments, purposefully crowding around Prince as he delivers his comical monologues, yet they all actively embrace their roles as spectators and participants; while the film's lone location, Memmoli's unpretentious Los Angeles home, loosely resembles the Scorseses' Little Italy apartment space. (In this case, of course, the implied distance between these two everyday domestic settings is substantial.) However, *American Boy*'s relationship to its predecessor is more complex than these immediate similarities might indicate. For example, both films refine American direct cinema's adherence to "the emotions" and its sharp focus on speech and the ordinary deportment of its subjects, yet they

Figure 1.8 *American Boy: A Profile of Steven Prince* (Martin Scorsese, 1978).

each also make their filmmaking conduct an important part of what viewers understand, and imply that what one comes to learn about history in these works cannot simply be separated from the circumstances of documentary filmmaking.[26] Therefore, as in *Italianamerican*, *American Boy*'s basic procedure involves closely following its principal storytelling subject as he intervenes for the historical past with his anecdotes. At certain decisive moments, the camera observes Prince apprehensively as he stands and delivers his most disturbing monologues; at others, it impassively registers his storytelling as he visibly modulates the rhythm, volume, and speed of his speech for effect, or to make meaningful disclosures about the incidents and experiences in question. If Prince is ultimately a much more skillful—and less evidently self-conscious—performer than the Scorseses, he is nevertheless also seen coping with the circumstances of documentary making, and these establish the parameters for his descriptions of past events. In other words, the particularity of Prince's storytelling develops from this visible filmmaking situation. It is a medium for our comprehension of the past, but more importantly, it implicitly alerts us to

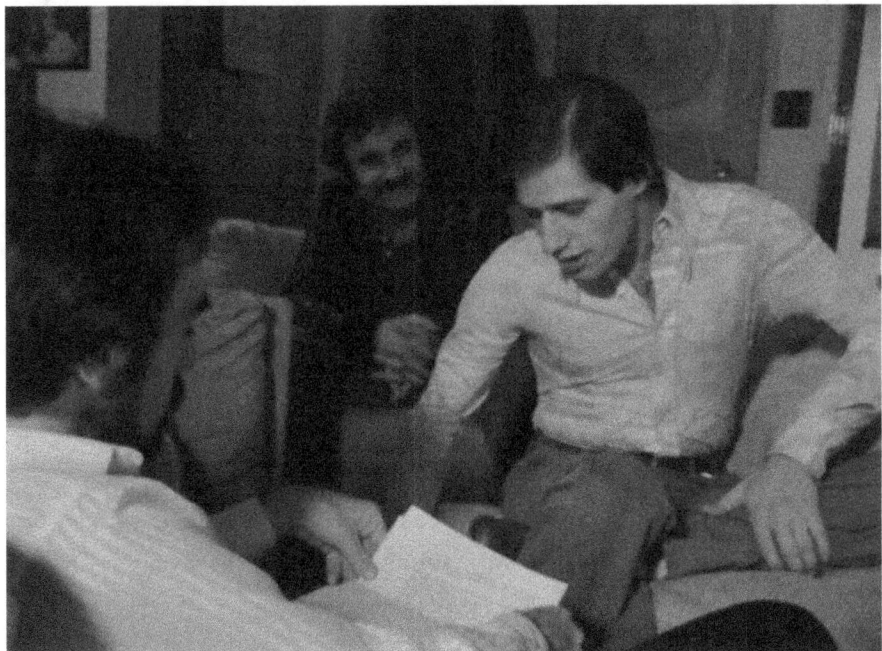

Figure 1.9 *American Boy: A Profile of Steven Prince* (Martin Scorsese, 1978).

American Boy's determined effort to continue and conclude the history set forth in *Italianamerican* (Figure 1.9).

The first half of *American Boy* therefore consciously returns to *Italianamerican*'s family emphases, but now they are all refracted through deadpan and mordant title cards such as "Dad," "Mom," "Aunt Bessie," and "On the Sound," as well as the increasingly sardonic deployment of grainy home movie footage to introduce Prince's assorted stories. Furthermore, *American Boy*'s details pointedly reverse *Italianamerican*'s narrative trajectory—they travesty the former film's sympathetic history of familial warmth and ethnic accomplishment in the new world. As a result, although we listen to Prince dutifully describing his mother with the same unequivocal language employed by Charles Scorsese in *Italianamerican* (she was a "very strong lady," they each note), his frequently comic tale about his parents concludes with a farcical scene wherein his father and mother cling helplessly to a tree during a blizzard as their children watch through the living room window. *Italianamerican*'s noble, occasionally sentimental family story, is in this way repeatedly reconfigured as caricature in *American Boy*. Indeed, Prince begins this anecdote by wholeheartedly characterizing his mother's cooking as "bland," while Martin Scorsese stares into the camera and comically shakes his head with horror at Prince's assertion ("he's saying this about his mother"). But this comical sense of derision ultimately demarcates the wide historical passage that divides the Scorseses' Little Italy apartment from this new and strangely remote Los Angeles world. The recollections in both films are equally detailed, of course, but *American Boy*'s approach involves recasting historical incidents from *Italianamerican* in the very different terms of Prince's progressively bleak and rootless journey to the present.

American Boy's conspicuous resurrection of *Italianamerican*'s self-consciously stuttering preliminary passages is especially revealing, in this respect. As the small crew of filmmakers and friends awaits Prince's delayed arrival, Scorsese sits impatiently on a sofa at the left-hand side of the frame; Memmoli is seated to the right and directly faces the camera, while a few other figures simply shuffle around without purpose behind him. The director then sluggishly announces, "roll it, I guess," and after a few seconds repeats his instructions with uncharacteristic exhaustion. The film's central figures are marked by a strange aimlessness and lethargy throughout this sequence, with Scorsese in particular moving like he's submerged in water—he pivots slowly to address his director of photography, Michael Chapman, and his sagging eyelids and slurred dialogue perhaps indicate the filmmakers' substantial share in Prince's stories of drug use and addiction.[27] Finally, the doorbell rings. Memmoli opens the front door to reveal a rail-thin Steven Prince in long shot, his arms outstretched and partially engulfed by the exterior's darkness; he stands in the doorway momentarily and offers a self-satisfied smile (he seems pleased by his delayed appearance in the film), but then enters the house and unexpectedly pretends to strangle Memmoli. An inexplicably protracted wrestling match follows, and whenever Prince breathlessly concedes defeat, he comes back to life and resumes his combat with Memmoli. Like *Italianamerican*'s stammering opening moments, this extended sequence could have easily been cut from the finished film, but it clearly foregrounds an unstructured form of role-playing ("role it, I guess"), and is similarly projected as both an immediate obstacle (in its bizarreness and interminability) *and* a necessity ("we're going to start now," the director says wearily) to the film's ensuing interpretation of the historical past. Once again, if the very experienced performer Steven Prince is less visibly apprehensive than the Scorseses during these introductory passages, his self-consciousness is nonetheless perceptible in the way that he continually forces the scene's mounting chaos, thereby delaying the film's proper beginning.

Prince's emaciated physical appearance at this stage—visibly rotting teeth, dark circles around his eyes—and his repeated returns to life throughout his opening skirmish with Memmoli reverberate symbolically across *American Boy*'s subsequent account of the historical past: Prince the ex-drug addict is lifeless on arrival, but the film deliberately exhumes this frail figure to have him explain his belatedness within the context of a broader story about ethnicity and generational succession in America. Indeed, at the film's midpoint Prince eagerly explains the physical effects of heroin as the equivalent of "the tana leaf" and "life juice," to which Scorsese immediately and perceptively responds, "ah, the Mummy's tomb." *American Boy* accordingly frames its historical report in these fatalistic terms: Prince is resuscitated only to provide a final series of recollections about history, that is, to share his dwindling memories of an ethnic narrative that appears to have definitively reached its terminus here. As a result, the film's early comic tenor predictably yields to an escalating sense of desolation with the "In the Park" anecdote and its introduction of *American Boy*'s fascination with inadvertent violence and death. Prince's story about a young person's accidental electrocution at an outdoor concert venue is quickly followed by progressively unsettling recollections about robbery and gunplay ("Jack the Cop"), drug busts ("Cocoa Jacks"), overdoses and cadavers ("Shooting Gallery"), and finally, crime and suddenly murderous violence ("Ethyl and Regular"). "Ethyl and Regular," Prince's extended tale about a violent, gun-related episode at a Barstow gas station, fittingly functions as *American Boy*'s centerpiece, and Scorsese noticeably underlines its meaningful departures from the film's customary approach to Prince's storytelling. Prince stands and delivers his lines for the majority of this sequence, while Scorsese stands to his left, hovering silently at the frame's edge, then moving apprehensively to the background when Prince abruptly produces a handgun to reenact the murderous events (Figure 1.10). Shot from a low angle and followed by cast shadows as he anxiously shuffles before the camera, Prince recollects and reenacts a nightmarish scene, but at this point his ironic utterances can no longer ease his audience's discomfort. Indeed, the concluding close-up of Prince's face provides no meaningful insight about these experiences, and instead implies that the deadly episode remains confusing to Prince himself: he seems shell-shocked after his reenactment is completed, nodding repeatedly as though awakening from a bad dream.

Figure 1.10 *American Boy: A Profile of Steven Prince* (Martin Scorsese, 1978).

American Boy, David Kehr writes, "takes place almost entirely in isolating close-ups," and this is undoubtedly the overwhelming impression created by the second half of the film, its final sequence in particular.[28] As Prince's stories increasingly fixate on puzzling acts of violence, his immediate audience gradually drops away from the screen, and he is left irretrievably alone to contemplate the frustrating experience of disintegration ironically described as "Surviving" in the film's final title card (Figure 1.11). *American Boy*'s closing sequence purposely borrows the key attributes of *Italianamerican*'s short epilogue, but this is merely the last in a series of considered reversals of the preceding film's formal values: dark for light; Los Angeles for New York City; an isolated storyteller for *Italianamerican*'s shared reminiscing; and an incongruous, rather than continuous, connection with the historical past. Just as Catherine Scorsese ends *Italianamerican* by comically reprising one of her earlier anecdotes, so too does Prince reiterate a story about his last telephone conversation with his father, transforming it with each take to accommodate Scorsese's emphatic request that he change its tenor (Prince is "too matter of fact," the director says). Scorsese is surprisingly insistent at this moment,

Figure 1.11 *American Boy: A Profile of Steven Prince* (Martin Scorsese, 1978).

particularly when compared to his uncertain appearances as an interviewer in the simultaneously produced *The Last Waltz* (1978), but his methodical direction undoubtedly punctures Prince's flippancy and equivocations. As Prince is encouraged to recount his tale three times in progressively closer framings, an air of self-doubt gradually emerges as the inverted counterpart to the nostalgic freeze-frame of Catherine Scorsese's stoic expression as she ends her allegorical tale about her parents' dying fig tree in *Italianamerican*. Indeed, Prince's third and final "take" begins with a momentary view of the filmmaker's light meter, yet another expedient and self-conscious reference to—and reversal of—the earlier film: this story, it seems, will also be "taken" by and before a camera, that is to say, with the camera and filmmaker in view as principal catalysts (Figure 1.12). But in the broader context of the films' description of generational succession, these parallel passages should be understood historically. *Italianamerican*'s cautious, successful adjustment to the new world has now turned into self-delusion and disappointment in *American Boy*. In the final analysis, Scorsese purposely frames ethnic incorporation as a dismal experience across these two documentaries, and Prince's tentative storytelling

Figure 1.12 *American Boy: A Profile of Steven Prince* (Martin Scorsese, 1978).

comportment at this particular moment implicitly discloses an imminent end to the Scorseses' extended historical passage.

Scorsese's critical emphasis upon a sense of generational succession in Prince's narrative transforms *American Boy* into an extended coda to *Italianamerican*: difference is ultimately subsumed by universality in this historical account's broader trajectory and synoptic aspirations. The film's unconvincing concluding tale of "survival" finally discloses an ill-fitting WASP-ish adherence to notions such as individual integrity and determination, and an empty investment in the cherished American ideals of self-reliance and self-sufficiency. These attributes, of course, are irretrievably disconnected from the Scorseses' communal storytelling in *Italianamerican*. Although Catherine and Charles Scorsese remain tightly bound to the immigrant's unshakable sense of outsiderhood, they also derive a shared strength from it, and their collective stories indicate small victories and a genuine wisdom about "survival" in the new world. By contrast, Prince's disorienting experience of incorporation and isolation is wholly destructive. "And that was that," Catherine says stoically after she ends her story about her mother's unexpected death, and *Italianamerican* and *American*

Boy graph this historical narrative about immigration with a comparably calm inevitability. They may both elect to closely observe their storytelling subjects as they intercede for an ordinary and experiential history, but the subjects' categorization of remembered incidents and emotions, like the films' corresponding inventory of these matters, appears to be complete at this point—there can be no sequel to *American Boy: A Profile of Steven Prince*. According to Pam Cook, *Raging Bull* (1980), Scorsese's subsequent Hollywood production, characterizes the "assimilation of the Italian immigrants" as a "negative blessing," that is, as an event to be "mourned": adjustment to America involves the "loss of the integrity and the unity of that [immigrant] community, and the breakdown of the traditional Italian family" (2005, 144). One might understand *American Boy*'s narrowing of its ethnic narrative to an isolated, solitary, and bewildered storyteller as a comparable lament over the experience of assimilation: nothing good appears to come from the complete incorporation of *Italianamerican*'s immediate descendants. However, unlike the despairing *Raging Bull*, *Italianamerican* and *American Boy* collectively offer a relatively resigned and dispassionate interpretation of this specific history's conclusion. To be sure, they describe ethnic incorporation in America as a regrettable phenomenon, yet when taken together *Italianamerican* and *American Boy* are unusually stoic about this condition. If the contemporaneous ethnic revival repeatedly positioned ethnic particularity as a new assimilative norm, *American Boy*'s impassive concluding account of "survival" mercilessly undercuts the characteristically celebratory tenor of 1970s ethnic renewal. In the terms of *Italianamerican* and *American Boy*'s surprisingly resigned interpretation of this history, ethnic incorporation is finally followed by nothingness—"and that was that."[29]

Public Speaking: From Intercession to Substitution

I've repeatedly characterized the Scorseses' and Prince's storytelling as moments of "intercession." On the one hand, I'm utilizing the term in its everyday meaning, that is, "mediation": as in any oral history, the films' principal speakers are conspicuous intermediaries between the remote past and the contemporary moment of their testimonies. On the other hand, however, I've also intended to invoke "intercession" in a more narrowly (though correlated) theological sense because it indirectly refers to how Scorsese gives these instances of guileless storytelling a broader historiographic purpose.[30] *Italianamerican*'s method originated in the director's decision to substitute a series of interviews with his parents for the NEH's more orthodox recommendations, and *American Boy* purposefully resumes this approach by focusing intensively on Prince's abundant tall tales, his memories, and interpretations of his various experiences. In these foundational acts of exchange, Scorsese's documentaries indicate a substantial compatibility between the idiosyncrasies of storytelling (the speaker's deportment, use of voice, etc.) and assorted historical realities: a significant dimension and experience of ethnic histories are in this way apprehended—or manifested—in what Scorsese calls "a particular way of being American" (Michael Henry Wilson 2011, 88). In the end, the increasingly lucid storytelling on view in these films reveals the Scorseses' and Prince's very different attunement to the facts of a rapidly receding ethnic history, and in Prince's case, it also exposes an ostensibly foreclosed future. More importantly, however, one's efforts to describe, clarify, and interpret such storytelling are evidence of a growing comprehension of these assorted anecdotes *as* oral histories. In other words, in both *Italianamerican* and *American Boy: A Profile of Steven Prince*, spectators learn about the past solely through human intermediaries—each of these films summons its subjects to tell their stories, which in turn intercede decisively in one's understanding of a much wider ethnic history.

Scorsese's 1970s documentaries' characteristic approach to framing these various filmic intercessions has seemingly receded into the distant past along with the director's parents, Steven Prince's generation, and their ethnic representativeness. The director's present-day documentary output has returned repeatedly to *Italianamerican* and *American Boy*'s concern with generational succession and "survival," but Scorsese's current preservationist dedication to archival resources has been combined with the ethnic revival's most important legacy, namely, its popular idiom of recovery, and this has modified the director's approach to matters of cultural heritage and historical preservation. Indeed, although interviews continue to feature prominently in several of Scorsese's contemporary documentaries, they no longer permit subjects to engage in the kind of expressive storytelling that one witnesses throughout his 1970s films, nor do they instinctively disclose the meaning of a speaker's evident need to adjust to the different circumstances of documentary filmmaking. In the cinephilic compendia *A Personal Journey with Martin Scorsese Through American Movies* (co-directed with Michael Henry Wilson, 1995), *Il mio viaggio in Italia* (2001), and *A Letter to Elia* (co-directed with Kent Jones, 2010), Scorsese appears as a lone storytelling subject, but these three films typically highlight a coordination between the director's colloquial voice-over narration and his assemblage of obsessively remembered moving images and sounds instead of the participatory interview approach of *Italianamerican* and *American Boy*. In short, in his recent documentaries, the historical past is typically summoned in the methodical matching of speech and collected archival images. Although *Il mio viaggio in Italia* and *A Letter to Elia* both return to the ethnic narrative of Scorsese's central 1970s documentaries, they conspicuously substitute a meaningful compilation of moving images for the previous films' close adherence to storytelling subjects; that is to say, these documentaries discover the remaining traces of an immigrant past in various popular film images and the director's accompanying interpretations of his cinephilia and family history.

There have been a few exceptions to this first-person practice. Scorsese's tributes to New York City's cultural history, *The 50 Year Argument* (co-directed with David Tedeschi, 2014) and *Public Speaking* (2010), make abundant use of retrospective interviews to create their chronicles of the city's recent past. *The 50 Year Argument* locates *The New York Review of Books*' legacy in its public dissemination of reason and enlightenment, and the film's relatively orthodox approach to interviews with co-founder Robert Silvers and assorted other contributors allows these figures to provide a rationale for the magazine's ongoing existence as a public forum for thought. *Public Speaking*'s portrait of Scorsese's friend, Fran Lebowitz, is likewise focused on discourse, critical thought, and the public sphere, and like *The 50 Year Argument*, its title proposes a possible return to the director's 1970s films' focus on storytelling, language, and their meaning in oral histories. Unfortunately, if *Public Speaking*'s portrayal of Lebowitz's abundant monologues is intended to position her as Steven Prince's storytelling successor, its prearranged interviews rarely reproduce *American Boy*'s unexpected humor and perceptiveness. Instead, Lebowitz's speeches devolve into self-consciously cantankerous, yet nonetheless monotonous complaints about cell phones, young people, and the contemporary world's innumerable other deficiencies. In certain ways, these cranky protestations recall the emphatically antimodern perspective of Catherine and Charles Scorsese's numerous asides in *Italianamerican* ("people today ... they got it easy," "back then there was no such thing as 'tired,'" Charles says), but their nostalgia for a refuge from the contemporary world could be firmly positioned within the era's ethnic renewal: they undoubtedly perceived a lifeless "modern" Americanism as a threat to what Charles calls New York City's "Italian people."[31] By contrast, too many of Lebowitz's laconic observations in *Public Speaking* seem simply self-congratulatory or largely insignificant ("Here's what news used to be—information!"), and they unwittingly reveal a potential shortcoming in Scorsese's present-day historiographic emphases. The director's current documentaries review and commemorate the 1960s (its canonical moving images, music, culture, etc.), and by his own account he has made these films to enlighten "young people" about an important period in American history (Donato 2007, 206). The menace of baby boomer triumphalism is always lurking in this type of formulation, of course, and *Public Speaking*'s interviews sometimes succumb too easily to an air of self-satisfaction. But *Public Speaking* is an uncharacteristic example of Scorsese's current documentary practice, and its atypicality only serves to underscore the wider and decisive shift in his historiographic approach since the 1970s. The ethnic revival established an analytical context for *Italianamerican* and *American Boy*'s oral histories, and like any serious historiography, these two short documentaries ultimately sought to safeguard a sense of the "pastness" of the past, even as they acknowledged a continuing dialogue between past and present. Rather than simply projecting a set of contemporary concerns onto the past, *Italianamerican* and *American Boy* attempted to understand what recent—and not so recent—history could tell their viewers about 1970s America. Scorsese's contemporary non-fiction film and television documentaries similarly attempt to discern the historical significance of the 1960s, the era's pastness and present-day meaning, but they typically do so by shifting their attention to a vast archive of popular images and sounds. The growing indirectness of Scorsese's approach to interviews in these films (generally conducted by someone other than the director) only confirms how such interviews have been reconfigured as another kind of archival material to be sifted through, rearranged, and then displayed in a novel setting and for a new audience.

By his own admission, Scorsese was "fascinated" by Bob Dylan's inscrutability as an interview subject in *No Direction Home: Bob Dylan* (2005), and in many ways this wide-ranging documentary exemplifies his post-1990s approach to surveying the lasting legacies of migration, popular movies, and music. "The interview *fascinated* me," Scorsese observes, "the way he [Dylan] was on camera—it's ultimately more important than what he's saying. You see him searching for the words, and what's going on behind his eyes is fascinating" (Donato 2007, 207; emphasis in original).[32] Not surprisingly, this image of a figure persistently adapting himself to the conditions of documentary making reminded Scorsese of his earlier approach to producing an oral history in *Italianamerican*: "it's not about the technique, it's not about the style. It's the *people*, and what's revealed the moment they lose their self-consciousness and let you in" (Donato 2007, 207; emphasis in original). Because of his essential role in the production of *Dont Look Back* (and in a very different way, *Eat the Document* [Bob Dylan and Howard Alk, 1972]), Dylan's extensive interviews in *No Direction Home* are uniquely interwoven with the history of American documentary filmmaking, and Scorsese's description of the singer's elusive comportment reveals the weight of this inheritance. Dylan's present-day position as the key intermediary for the Sixties and its history undoubtedly informs the director's assessment of these interviews and the meaning of Dylan's searching public speech throughout *No Direction Home*.[33] However, we can also see how Scorsese's longstanding engagement with direct cinema continues to guide his thinking about documentary filmmaking in important ways. *No Direction Home*'s look back at Dylan's 1960s work and life is immersed in the worlds of American folk and rock music, and it ultimately seeks to provide a comprehensive portrait of the decade's most significant popular songwriter, but the film can also be usefully seen as a retrospective examination of direct cinema and its contentious legacy. Indeed, *No Direction Home* inevitably reminds us of Scorsese's earlier collaboration with Dylan on *The Last Waltz*, and it should encourage us to reconsider the meaning of their common commitment to direct cinema's most durable contribution to American documentary: the concert film. Scorsese, like many other filmmakers of his generation, has had a far-reaching involvement with popular music, but his formative experiences coincide closely with rock music's developing connections with American documentary during the 1960s.[34] *The Last Waltz* is customarily seen as both a celebratory and elegiac summary of rock music in its 1960s countercultural expression, and its paradoxical combination of commemoration and regret closely resembles *Italianamerican* and *American Boy*'s oral histories. However, *The Last Waltz*'s highly contentious creation would eventually produce long-lasting reverberations for members of The Band, and as we'll see, this acrimonious history can be traced back to the film's contradictory effort to fasten direct cinema's characteristic preoccupation with self-realization and self-actualization to its own reckoning with a collectively shared experience of rock music in the 1960s. The Band's very existence discloses this tension between self and collectivity in an especially resonant way, and the commemorative *The Last Waltz* effectively outlines the fundamental thematic quandary in Scorsese's subsequent documentary work: how to reconcile the past and present, the individual with historical realities, when the future presents itself as a vacuum.[35]

2

Foreclosed Journeys: *The Last Waltz* and *Shine a Light*

Nothing Was Delivered: *The Last Waltz* and Its Contested Legacy

Like *Italianamerican* (1974) and *American Boy: A Profile of Steven Prince* (1978), *The Last Waltz* (1978) was originally envisioned as an effort to preserve historical accounts for posterity. Jonathan Taplin, a co-producer on *Mean Streets* (1973) and The Band's onetime tour manager, approached Scorsese with the prospect of documenting The Band's farewell concert on November 25, 1976, and the director eagerly accepted the commission, promptly—and perhaps predictably—describing his newest undertaking in the insistently preservationist language of his previous non-fiction work, *Italianamerican*. The Band's celebratory sendoff should be recorded, Scorsese said, because the resulting footage would comprise indispensable, unadorned "archival" evidence for subsequent generations. Indeed, many of the concert's invited performers had made substantial contributions to the growth of rock music in its countercultural expression throughout the Sixties, and because this "last waltz" was also being characterized as the mournful "end of an era," simple audiovisual documentation of the event would undoubtedly be valuable to historians at some point in the future.[1]

Scorsese's intensive preparations, however, soon supplanted these elementary "archival" aspirations, and his approach to filming *The Last Waltz* was reshaped by an expansive 200-page shooting script. Rather than producing an unembellished record of The Band's farewell concert, the director and his close collaborators now imagined a far more intricate cinematic rendering of the event. In addition to their exhaustive coordination of the November 25 show, the filmmakers eventually decided to supplement The Band's onstage work with several post-concert interviews as well as purposefully planned, studio-bound performances of "The Weight," "Evangeline," and "Theme from The Last Waltz."[2] In this way, *The Last Waltz* exchanged its archival mandate for the filmmakers' broadening conception, and as the film continued to develop during a lengthy postproduction process of approximately eighteen months, it assumed a distinctive, if somewhat paradoxical historiographic shape. The completed movie would attempt to reconcile The Band's distinguished past with their apparently inescapable terminus on the Winterland Ballroom's stage in November 1976; yet at the same time, Scorsese's perspective on this historical material could only envision the future in incongruously bleak terms, namely, as a void for certain members of The Band and their generation's rock music.

The Last Waltz remains Scorsese's most celebrated documentary, but in some ways it is also an atypical work: unlike any other of his subsequent non-fiction films, videos, and television productions, this meticulous chronicle of The Band's farewell concert has gathered the weight of a forcefully challenged legacy.[3] Shortly after *The Last Waltz*'s theatrical release in 1978 and The Band's attendant disintegration, Levon Helm, the group's drummer, vocalist, and original leader, unequivocally rejected the film's authenticity, dismissing its account of The Band's leave-taking and history as equal parts fabrication and economic opportunism. In *This Wheel's on Fire: Levon Helm and the Story of The Band* (2013), Helm offers an emphatically negative reevaluation of Scorsese's collaboration with Robbie Robertson, describing it as "a real scandal" (277) and "a disaster" (274): they "edited the movie," he claims, simply "to please themselves" (275). Helm's objections to the director's partiality in assembling *The Last Waltz*, like his recurrent complaints about Robertson's deceitfulness in devising The Band's departure, recall the grievances of many working musicians in the rock era: onerous and unfair publishing contracts, shrewd and thieving managers who eventually vanish with songwriting royalty checks, recognition and rewards given (and received) when they aren't justified, financial wrongdoing or betrayal by former bandmates, and so forth. These stories about fiscal misconduct and duplicity in the music business are much too familiar today. But Helm looks directly to *The Last Waltz* for the most damning evidence of Robertson's dishonesty, and in each of his critical descriptions, Scorsese's film is the emblematic demonstration of Robertson's willingness to betray The Band and their shared past. Indeed, in the drummer's forthright first-hand account, *The Last Waltz*'s perspective on history was effectively determined—and ultimately disfigured—by a set of intensely antagonistic working relationships, and these fraught affiliations, he contends, are clearly on view throughout Scorsese's film should one simply care to look for them.

Levon Helm is the lone apostate among *The Last Waltz*'s key players, but his dissenting opinion about the film's production and insider's knowledge about The Band's bitter dissolution establish a credible reassessment of Scorsese's most distinguished documentary.[4] In other words, although his personal stake in diminishing the film's substantial achievements is apparent in *This Wheel's on Fire*, Helm's stubborn interpretation of *The Last Waltz*'s meaning requires additional parsing: his plainspoken assertions point to bigger issues in the film's representations of popular music-making, myth-making, and history-making. Stephen E. Severn's reevaluation of *The Last Waltz* on the occasion of its "25th anniversary" examines Scorsese's work in exactly these terms.[5] *The Last Waltz*, he argues, certainly does disclose its director's one-sidedness and Robertson's central role in determining the film's final form, but it is best comprehended as "a crucial turning point" for Scorsese: *The Last Waltz* "stands as [the director's] first exploration of the manner by which image may be manipulated as a means for eliminating risk" (2002, 26). The threat or anticipation of "risk" in *The Last Waltz* refers, of course, to Robertson's attempts to "establish himself as a star within the Hollywood community and launch his post-Band career," and Severn explains how the director tacitly authorizes Robertson to foreground his developing, "identifiable public persona" at the expense of his bandmates (2002, 26–7). (Throughout his memoir, Helm justifiably complains about the disproportionately high number of images of the guitarist in Scorsese's film.) In this respect, *The Last Waltz* is finally an exercise in self-mythologizing. The film's true subject is "without question" Robertson, not The Band or the farewell concert's numerous guests (Severn 2002, 31), and its primary focus is effectively a form of self-directed accomplishment rather than communal creation.

Severn's interpretation of *The Last Waltz*'s preoccupation with "risk" and "image-making" is perceptive and persuasive, yet his emphasis upon this theme's place in Scorsese's succeeding *fiction* filmmaking sometimes overlooks *The Last Waltz*'s complex affiliations with its concert film and documentary predecessors. Moreover, readers encounter a recurring concern with the meaning of *work* throughout Helm's *This Wheel's on Fire*, the labor of rock musicians in particular, and the centrality of this framework in his down-to-earth "story of The Band" casts the notion of risk in a substantially different light.[6] To put it simply, Helm's grievances about *The Last Waltz* constantly grasp at the significance of his lifelong work as a popular musician and its paradoxical representation in Scorsese's concert film: how is such work characteristically undertaken? Is it cooperatively done by the members of a group? Or, are their contributions and accomplishments individuated? Does the work of musicians rely upon a distinctive sense of exchange between individuals and collective entities (i.e., rock 'n' roll bands)? Is the value of The Band's *labor*, that is to say, their exertions—and subsequent exhaustion—on the Winterland Ballroom's stage, finally distorted by *The Last Waltz*'s particular rendering of historical accounts?[7] If Helm's many misgivings about the film's producers have the surface appearance of personal grudges, they nonetheless emphatically ask these questions about musician labor. Indeed, such questions reverberate insistently throughout *The Last Waltz*, particularly during Scorsese's brief interviews with the unusually taciturn Helm and the other—equally reticent—members of The Band (bassist Rick Danko, vocalist/pianist Richard Manuel, and keyboardist Garth Hudson). Although Robertson is fully at ease in the film, these figures are noticeably uncomfortable with the broader documentary task.

The Last Waltz was shaped by The Band's discordant understandings of their work, so in what follows I re-view Scorsese's film as an exemplar of the "golden age" rockumentary's often contradictory representation of rock musicians and their labor.[8] Because the 1970s witnessed the culmination of rock music's incorporation by conglomerates and a correlated professionalization of popular musicians, *The Last Waltz* has been described as "a portrait of the big business rock music had become during the 1970s" (Baker 2015b, 248).[9] The film's representation of musicians as they work, however, ultimately submits to the concert documentary's fundamental paradox: its elaboration of a collective euphoria is continually moderated by an individuated image of the rock star's freedom and authenticity. I begin with a brief consideration of the hippie-era concert films' illustration of rock music's communal rituals, that is to say, their utopian commitments to popular participation and spontaneous expression. I focus on the era's prototypical products of American direct cinema, but I resituate their overriding preoccupation with self-actualizing musicians as an analysis of the latter's labor. These self-described "observational documentaries," I want to suggest, implicitly establish models and prescriptions for an emerging, modern brand of work; or rather, having been conceived within the individualized frame of direct cinema's longstanding obsession with self-expression and self-realization, the prototypical 1960s concert documentaries consistently emphasize an image of self-directed, autonomous musician labor. As a consequence, they quickly established a durable site for subsequent filmic figurations of this type of expressive work.

The Last Waltz's contentious post-production history indicates a set of contradictions in its conception as a concert documentary, and these are a result of the film's critical engagement with its direct cinema inheritance: the effort to memorialize The Band's collective achievements sits uneasily beside Robbie Robertson's concurrent attempts to reposition himself as an aspiring solo artist. As I've already indicated, critics have long acknowledged this aspect of the film, but they've frequently explained it in terms of Robertson's personal shortcomings, namely, his self-importance.[10] The rock music industry, however, required self-assertion *and* compliance from its artists in the 1970s, and this is crucial to comprehending the guitarist's—and *The Last Waltz*'s—rather restricted interpretation of The Band's history.[11] In other words, Robertson's plainly self-seeking endeavor in *The Last Waltz* is instructive because it discloses a developing image of the modern-day musician's work. Matt Stahl has described such work as an amalgamation of "self-actualization, discipline, freedom and authenticity" (2013, 74), and these individuated qualities neutralize *The Last Waltz*'s efforts to memorialize The Band's shared accomplishments. I conclude with a brief look at Scorsese's *Shine a Light* (2008) because The Rolling Stones have, to borrow one of the director's favorite notions, "survived" as rock remnants from the 1960s, but they have done so by incorporating an analogous set of contradictions into their continuing work as a legacy act. *Shine a Light* chronicles two shows by The Rolling Stones at the Beacon Theater in 2006, and like *The Last Waltz*, it visualizes the concert stage as a largely self-enclosed utopia: the rock group's sense of achievement is restricted to their labor in this live setting. However, if The Stones and their disruptive rock 'n' roll music were once vehicles for direct cinema's unexpected breakdown in *Gimme Shelter* (Albert Maysles, David Maysles, and Charlotte Zwerin, 1970), their present-day image is instead based entirely on the promotion of proficiency and control. Mick Jagger, of course, is the exemplar for such attributes, and *Shine a Light* is effectively a commemoration of the musician's post-1980s professionalism. Although it consciously refers to The Stones' unruly place in the history of documentary filmmaking, Scorsese's film ultimately portrays the band's significance in terms of their contemporary resilience and harmonious deportment.

Across the Great Divide: The 1960s Concert Film and Rock Music's Collective Rituals

Scorsese began filming *American Boy: A Profile of Steven Prince* a mere two weeks after The Band's Thanksgiving Day farewell concert, and *The Last Waltz*'s interview sequences, shot after the director's wide-ranging conversations with Steven Prince, would overlap in many ways with *American Boy*'s engrossing storytelling. Both films are explicitly set against the backdrop of the entertainment industries (1970s rock music, but also New Hollywood), and they each knowingly revel in tales of dissipation and the musician's precarious life on the road, while at the same time anticipating a decisive release from show business and its abundant dangers. Prince is credited as Associate Producer on *The Last Waltz*, and he is also listed as an Assistant Director on the MGM studio shoots of "The Weight," "Evangeline," and "Theme from The Last Waltz." (He makes an appearance in the extended final shot of "Evangeline.") One therefore shouldn't be surprised by the existence of loosely corresponding elements in these concurrently produced documentaries.[12] Indeed, *American Boy* and *The Last Waltz*'s historical subjects all appear to surrender completely to the period's prevailing sense of post-1960s exhaustion, either suddenly diminishing (Prince) or gradually vanishing (The Band) in the films' concluding sequences. As we've seen, however, Prince's consistently comic stories about mobility and ethnic integration into the worlds of entertainment intersect with the period's wider white ethnic revival, and if *American Boy* purposely renders his tale of achievement in ironic terms, the familiar contours of a generations-long Jewish-American odyssey are nonetheless on view throughout this short documentary. *American Boy* is noticeably uneasy about the experience of assimilation, of course, and it is also ambivalent about the price paid for discarding ethnic "insularity" in favor of the more worldly—that is to say, "American"—entertainment industries; yet its social portraiture continues to be articulated in the period's unmistakable ethnic accents. In short, *American Boy: A Profile of Steven Prince* establishes, in Scorsese's own words, an "oral history of America" (Wilson 2011, 82), but its America remains a nation of immigrants.

Although *The Last Waltz* describes them somewhat nostalgically as renegades on the road, the members of The Band were not immigrants or exiles in this same sense—they were brought together by a youthful embrace of early rock 'n' roll, rockabilly, blues and soul, and they sought this music's deepest roots in the American South. Composed of four Canadians (Danko, Hudson,

Manuel, Robertson) and the Arkansan Helm, The Band logged a long period of apprenticeship in the early-1960s as Ronnie Hawkins's backing group, The Hawks, and they toured continuously across the Southern states and Canadian provinces of Ontario and Quebec. A vital second phase in their education began when Bob Dylan recruited Levon and The Hawks (the group's new name after a split with Hawkins) for a set of groundbreaking concerts in 1965–6; yet even in these singularly raucous circumstances, The Hawks persisted in developing their distinguished ensemble playing, and their special alchemy as Dylan's short-lived backing band can be heard in various recordings from the era.[13] In his indispensable study of The Band's contributions to popular American music, Greil Marcus recognizes the road-tested qualities of cohesion and collaboration as keys to the group's subsequent accomplishments in the late-1960s. "[T]heir music and their stories," he maintains, "were not only a version of America, but a reflection of their own unity," and their songs and recordings permitted them to deliver "what was special about themselves to something bigger than any of them" (2015, 57). Marcus's focus on the internal workings of rock 'n' roll bands parses these mutual exchanges between individual voices and a more collective vision of production, and in his account, The Band's *Music from Big Pink* (1968) and *The Band* (1969) are benchmarks for such reciprocity in American popular music-making.[14] Rock 'n' roll songs, but also dispatches to new listeners in search of comparable affinities (with these records, but also with each other and America), The Band's first recordings revealed the group's internal unity while at the same time suggesting new possibilities for parallel experiences in an emergent rock audience.[15]

These attributes—unanimity, cooperation, an essentially democratic sense of give-and-take—should have made The Band ideal subjects for one of the decade's numerous concert films, but their unconventionality and modest popularity left them at the periphery of these developments.[16] Indeed, unlike other countercultural partisans such as Jefferson Airplane, Jimi Hendrix, The Rolling Stones, and The Who, The Band were not featured in documentaries before *The Last Waltz*.[17] They had performed at the Woodstock Music and Art Fair in August 1969, but Albert Grossman, the group's manager and a major player in the era's expanding music industry, ultimately prohibited Michael Wadleigh from including their work in *Woodstock* (1970).[18] They were headliners on the following year's torpid Festival Express Train Tour, performing alongside the Grateful Dead, Janis Joplin, The Flying Burrito Brothers, Delaney & Bonnie & Friends, and several others, yet this condensed expedition across Canada was a commercial catastrophe for its organizers, and a proposed documentary was abandoned to prevent further losses.[19] The Festival Express Train Tour's abbreviated itinerary and discarded film project predict rock music's—and the rockumentary's—accumulating contradictions in the 1970s: hopeful for a new utopian social order, but providing only a brief glimpse of a disconnected culture in transit, the Festival Express Train Tour's surrender to various fiscal realities anticipates rock musicians' increasing alienation from their own work in the coming decade. Regardless, the relationship between rock music and documentary filmmaking would continue to derive its energy from the counterculture's utopian aspirations. The Band, however, would remain at the margins of these cinematic developments, even though their music clearly shared the hippie-era concert movie's preoccupation with rock's emergent communality.[20] Scorsese's *The Last Waltz* would be shaped decisively by this paradoxical inheritance. Although it refers self-consciously to its many concert film antecedents, its repositioning of The Band and their music at the center of a novel (for this group) documentary endeavor would produce a meaningful reconfiguration of the preceding decade's rockumentaries and their customary meanings.

The earliest concert documentaries developed alongside popular music throughout the 1960s. "Rock 'n' roll," David E. James reminds us, was "the most important art in the period of resurgent populist politics in the two decades after the mid-1950s," and "no other industrialized medium matched music's capacity for popular participation and popular control" (2016, 9). As a result, commercial cinema—and Hollywood cinema in particular—appeared antiquated once rock 'n' roll began to make its "unalienated utopian promises" to youthful audiences in the mid-1950s (James 2016, 9). Even if such promises were soon rivalled by the dystopian determination to incorporate and mass-produce this new music's popular energies, rock 'n' roll's instigation of revolutionary changes in American culture proved to be too much for the cinema to immediately comprehend or withstand. Hollywood's inclination to subsume rock 'n' roll within fictions about juvenile delinquency, like its recurrent affirmations of the cinema's principled superiority to such recalcitrant cultural production, undoubtedly betrayed an awareness of this newcomer's potential to dislocate its sizeable adolescent audiences.[21] By the mid-1960s, rock music had indeed largely supplanted commercial movies as the foremost popular medium in America's conspicuous youth culture. Hollywood's misunderstanding of the Sixties counterculture's implications, James notes, would repeat its fundamental confusion at the initial appearance of rock 'n' roll in the mid-1950s (2016, 21), but contemporaneous documentary filmmaking instantly developed noticeably different associations with the period's popular music. Accordingly, cinematic representations of the counterculture's rock music could be found in independently produced documentaries such as *Dont Look Back* (D.A. Pennebaker, 1967), *Monterey Pop* (D.A. Pennebaker, 1968), the epochal *Woodstock*, and the hippie-era comedown *Gimme Shelter*, and these works acknowledged the participatory dimension of autonomously staged concerts by highlighting the period's music festivals and their imagining of a new youth "nation."

In this respect, the elaboration of the concert documentary's forms and themes closely paralleled rock music's foundational blending of folk music with rock 'n' roll in the mid-1960s. If the early-1960s folk revival had encouraged audiences and performers to connect in a variety of collective rituals (at performance venues, political protests, and other associated events), folk music's subsequent amalgamation with rock 'n' roll broadened the scope of these social unions substantially: the era-defining music festival would become an emblem for the counterculture's corresponding gatherings and utopian aspirations. Bob Dylan, an admittedly reluctant figurehead for the consolidation of folk music and rock 'n' roll as "rock music," was the first subject of this developing alignment between documentary and popular music.[22] D.A. Pennebaker's pioneering depiction of Dylan, *Dont Look Back*, covers the artist's tour of England in the spring of 1965, his final journey as a "folk singer" before the following year's historic "gone-electric" concerts with The Hawks. Throughout the film, brief fragments of Dylan's solo performances are embedded in a succession of offstage scenes and happenings in hotel rooms, backstage spaces, assorted public places, cars, and trains, and these extemporized settings promise to uncover the "real" Bob Dylan for viewers (Figure 2.1). An atmosphere of spontaneity predominates in these segments, yet *Dont Look Back* returns repeatedly to its examination of Dylan's committed sense of self-direction as he disagrees with suspicious journalists or engages in several more relaxed conversations with fans who were resisting his music's incorporation of electric guitars, drums, pianos, and Hammond organs. Not surprisingly, the film's emphasis on Dylan's independence and apparent rejection of all pretense is very closely aligned with direct cinema's initial articulations of its own filmmaking principles: these new documentaries sought a similar spontaneity in terms of technique, and they also aimed to eliminate any evidence of pretense or self-consciousness from their images. Unlike most other hippie-era concert documentaries, however,

Figure 2.1 *Dont Look Back* (D.A. Pennebaker, 1967).

Dont Look Back's focus remains wholly fixed on its singular, inscrutable subject, and the film's intermittent views of fans and audience members are ultimately superseded by the paradoxical display of Dylan's self-realization *and* elusiveness.

Pennebaker's subsequent *Monterey Pop* would go further in affirming the significance of music festivals and their audiences to the Sixties counterculture's developing self-understanding, and along with *Woodstock*, it would determine hippiedom's defining iconography. *Monterey Pop* basically highlights an assortment of captivated audience members at the Monterey International Pop Festival (June 16–18, 1967), and the event's utopianism is plainly aligned with Pennebaker's attempts to integrate his film's spectators into an expanding sense of communion. As James notes, *Monterey Pop* overturns the fundamental organizing principles of *Dont Look Back*. Except for a few brief introductory images of The Mamas and The Papas' John Phillips and his fellow concert organizers making telephone calls to prospective performers, backstage scenes are mostly excluded, and this film instead "takes place entirely in the festival's public spaces" (James 2016, 215). The significant reduction of any distance between producers and consumers gives audience members an "unprecedented prominence" in the festival's numerous happenings: their hippie clothing and peaceful comportment emphasize "the counterculture's visual aesthetics" and mostly inchoate objectives (James 2016, 215–16). Nevertheless, although the intensifying sense of give-and-take between musicians and spectators is undoubtedly a primary focus throughout *Monterey Pop*, images of the constant collaboration amongst the performers onstage are underscored as equally utopian moments of expression for concertgoers. This is especially evident in Otis Redding's rendition of "I've Been Loving You Too Long (To Stop Now)." The singer's appeal to Monterey Pop's "love crowd" as he begins his song ("We all love each other, right?") comprises another instance of the festival's idealized union of audiences and musicians, but the ensuing performance culminates in the singer's confident improvisations with Booker T. and the M.G.s ("Can you do that one more time, Al [Jackson Jr.]," he asks after one such moment), and the sequence's increasingly abstract images implicitly connect the band members' spontaneous interaction to the crowd's perceptible enthusiasm and commitment.[23] In this way, *Monterey Pop* continually underscores the audience's important contributions to the festival's increasing sense of collaboration, while simultaneously positioning the performing musicians as representative models for such cooperation (Figure 2.2).

Scorsese, of course, had a substantial share in direct cinema's elaboration of the concert documentary's style and content in the late-1960s. Indeed, *The Last Waltz*'s methods can be seen as belated adjustments to direct cinema's axioms, but its determined revisionism is also rooted in Scorsese's filmmaking experiences during this period. Credited as an editor and assistant director on

Figure 2.2 *Monterey Pop* (D.A. Pennebaker, 1968).

Michael Wadleigh's *Woodstock*, Scorsese's input was instrumental in creating one of the film's most representative sequences: Santana's euphoric daytime performance of "Soul Sacrifice."[24] In this influential visualization of the music festival's continuing self-realization, *Woodstock*'s split screens are closely aligned with *Monterey Pop*'s visual abstraction of Otis Redding's "I've Been Loving You Too Long (To Stop Now)." Utilizing the film's widescreen format, "Soul Sacrifice" stresses Santana's capacity for ensemble playing, yet it also features a lengthy percussion break as well as Carlos Santana's two ascending guitar solos. Once again, spectators are able to see the festival's crowd and musicians merge gradually as assorted split screens bring them together in a novel audiovisual assemblage, but the group members' improvisatory back-and-forth establishes a prototype for the festival's broader idealistic commonality: distinct moments of self-expression and extemporaneous soloing (on drums, organ, guitar, etc.) invariably bring the band back to their cohesive playing, and the audience's increasing commitment to this music is coordinated with the scene's rapidly edited crescendo and conclusion (Figure 2.3).

"Soul Sacrifice" is followed by an equally impressive rendering of Sly and The Family Stone's "I Want to Take You Higher," and together these two extended sequences exemplify the Woodstock festival's—and film's—utopian aspirations.

Figure 2.3 *Woodstock* (Michael Wadleigh, 1970).

In this case, the dimly lit split screens reiterate the earlier scene's general effect. Sly Stone and his band guide their audience through a climbing call-and-response repetition of the word "higher," and editor Yeu Bun Lee (Scorsese's collaborator on *The Last Waltz*) deploys a variety of split screens to unite the massive crowd and performers. At the same time, however, the sequence is immersed in The Family Stone's skillful assimilation of their expressive soloing (on trumpet, saxophone, organ, and harmonica) and their collaborative creation of the song's stretched rhythmic figure.[25] A culminating leftward pan from the stage to an ecstatic audience formulates the festival's vision of popular participation, and the uninterrupted rightward pan back to Sly Stone fully confirms the musicians' role in creating this sense of collectivity. In other words, the audience-musician configuration is again underscored—and idealized—in *Woodstock*'s refinement of *Monterey Pop*'s survey of the autonomous concert, but the sense of cooperation onstage assumes an equal importance in Wadleigh's film because it helps to shape the festival's emergent social relations. Although such collaborative rituals may have been established slowly over the course of the 1960s, they were decisively represented in these new amalgamations of the rock music festival and documentary filmmaking in America (Figure 2.4).

Figure 2.4 *Woodstock* (Michael Wadleigh, 1970).

It Makes No Difference: The Self-Enclosed Utopia of *The Last Waltz*

Woodstock was the hippie-era concert documentary's apotheosis: it definitively envisioned the generation-defining music festival as an incipient model of utopianism. And although its deeply contradictory post-production and exhibition history would eventually demonstrate capitalism's voraciousness and prefigure the counterculture's disillusionment, the film nevertheless managed to sketch a substantial portrait of rock music's nascent collective rituals.[26] The Band, residents of Woodstock since 1966, performed at the festival in nearby Bethel on the evening of August 17, 1969, but their relationship with the Woodstock generation was apprehensive—if not actively antagonistic—from their inception as "The Band" in 1968. Shortly after "Woodstock," and at the peak of their popularity, The Band appeared on the cover of *Time* magazine as hand-drawn faces placed vertically beneath an unfortunately chosen title, "The New Sound of Country Rock." The cover's graphic design resembles the era's ubiquitous concert posters and album covers (it could be a "rustic" and "traditional" version of Love's *Forever Changes* [1967] cover art, for instance), and the designation "country rock" is an attempt to describe the counterculture's incorporation of a broad variety of American vernacular music. However, the accompanying profile story, "Down to Old Dixie and Back," describes The Band as distinct from the splintering hippie movement, its psychedelic rock, and formative generational animosities and feelings of dissension. The group's music exemplifies "pure sentiments," an "unidealized look into yesterday" or "a consideration of the old," and *Music from Big Pink* and *The Band* are accordingly positioned at the vanguard of a substantial shift in popular music-making:

> Though The Band calls it "just music—everything we've ever heard or done," the convenient label is country rock. However labeled, it is a turning back toward easy-rhymed blues, folk songs, and the twangy, lonely lamentations known as country music. Country rock is also a symptom of a general cultural reaction to the most unsettling decade the U.S. has yet endured.[27]

Critics often highlighted The Band's indifference to the hippie counterculture as a sign of their individuality, but the group's fondness for summoning distant historical periods and ways of life had the same surface appearance as much of the era's popular music-making. The "country rock" identified above was generally nostalgic and pastoral in its imagery, yet even "psychedelic rock" loyalists like Jefferson Airplane could share these same "every hand in the land" preoccupations (see *Volunteers*' "The Farm" [1969], for example). Nevertheless, in spite of *Time*'s claims to the contrary, The Band were never truly folkie sentimentalists.[28] And although their fascination with an imperceptible and remote North American history would soon swerve too close to self-parody (*Cahoots*' "Last of the Blacksmiths" [1971]) and self-imitation (*Northern Lights—Southern Cross*' strained epic, "Acadian Driftwood" [1975]), their first and best recordings readily conveyed what Greil Marcus has called a "rough moral drama" about the country's broader purpose and promise (2015, 41). If such familiar accents seemed to be aligned with *Woodstock*'s simultaneous imagining of a rustic utopia, songs like *The Band*'s "King Harvest (Has Surely Come)" indicated an effort to unearth some grimmer strata of America's past (and present). As Marcus puts it, The Band in this way "consciously" presented themselves as an alternative to the "instant America of the sixties"; their early music "was fashioned as a way back into America" after a very turbulent period of self-estrangement and failure (2015, 40–1).

The Last Waltz implies this historical context, but The Band's unsettled relationship with the hippie counterculture is obviously a pretext for Scorsese's significant reshaping of the classic concert documentaries—if *Woodstock* can best be described as the concert film's apotheosis, *The Last Waltz* represents its apostasy. As a consequence, *The Last Waltz*'s opening images promptly refer spectators to the preliminary segments of *Monterey Pop*, *Woodstock*, and other exemplars of the hippie-era concert documentary, but they also noticeably differentiate themselves from those foundational—and largely self-validating—sequences. After a short passage dedicated to Rick Danko's explanation of "cutthroat," a mercenary's vision of every-man-for-himself billiards, *The Last Waltz* moves to the Winterland Ballroom for a predictably charging rendition of The Band's "Don't Do It," and each player is closely framed—and effectively isolated—as his name appears momentarily onscreen. "Don't Do It" was actually the final song played at the Thanksgiving Day concert in 1976, and Robbie Robertson introduces it at this instant as a farewell gift, a reward for the audience's commitment and stamina ("you're still there, huh?"). Despite the song's persistent progression, however, these opening images are permeated with a sense of irrevocability ("we're gonna do one more song, that's it," Robertson announces lethargically); and while "Don't Do It" suggests a familiar rock/pop song theme of supplication, its repositioning at this early juncture in the film reveals how *The Last Waltz* proposes to overturn the classic concert film's conception of its central events. In *Monterey Pop*'s rendering of the audience-musician relation, Otis Redding's "I've Been Loving You Too Long (To Stop Now)" is a celebratory appeal to the "love crowd" of white bohemians, while *Woodstock*'s parallel conception of such exchanges reaches its crescendo during Sly and The Family Stone's "I Want to Take You Higher." In *The Last Waltz*, by contrast, "Don't Do It" registers a more ambivalent meaning: it effectively indicates expiration rather than exhilaration; the song's lyrics are at once committed and repentant, yet there can be no future for the sentiments that they express. Coming at the *end* of The Band's valedictory concert, "Don't Do It" might have seemed like an acknowledgment of the audience and its central participation in the evening's proceedings, but its repositioning at the *beginning* of *The Last Waltz* essentially signals the termination of this crowd's involvement. Commonly characterized as an "elegy" for the rock era and its fundamental social rituals, Scorsese's film is surprisingly unsentimental in its instantaneous unseating of the concert film's requisite scenes of beseeching performers and their audiences (Figure 2.5).

The following credit sequence continues to subtly underline *The Last Waltz*'s impassive abandonment of the hippie-era concert film's imagery, or more precisely, its predominantly pastoral iconography. Starting with a sequence

Figure 2.5 *The Last Waltz* (Martin Scorsese, 1978).

of six travelling shots taken from the interior of a vehicle, Scorsese's film delivers detached images of the city's decrepit fringes—dirty streets, dented and deserted cars, discarded people, and a feeling of disrepair predominate in this particular series of images, and each vision is accompanied by Robertson's incongruently ceremonial "Theme from The Last Waltz." The closing shots frame a winding, waiting line of the concert's attendees, and the segment concludes with a low angle shot of the Winterland's dilapidated exterior sign, a slow tilt down reaffirming the general implication of decline and exhaustion: the rundown sign's only functioning lights spell the words "win and," and they resonate unexpectedly with Rick Danko's earlier description of the mercenary "cutthroat." *The Last Waltz*'s opening credits directly follow these assorted urban visions. "A Martin Scorsese Film," "THE BAND," and a vertically scrolling adaptation of *The Last Waltz*'s promotional poster appear in a succession of three images, each accompanied by the repeated entry and exit of a studio-bound waltzing couple. Names of invited performers then materialize briefly over select scenes from the pre-concert formalities: Thanksgiving dinner served to the entire Winterland audience, a live orchestral performance, several images of figures waltzing, and so on. (The same couple is seen in both the studio-bound and Winterland locations, briefly blurring the fictional and non-fictional, planning and spontaneity.) An extreme long shot of the concert stage and full auditorium completes the credit sequence, and its view of dining tables, candles, and chandeliers discloses this "last waltz's" extravagance and exhaustive preparation. The hippie-era concert documentary's introductions customarily attended closely to the festival crowd's developing capacity for spontaneous self-expression and its association with onstage events, but in *The Last Waltz* the credit segment's combination of planning and pre-show decorum neutralizes such autonomy, and the apparent constraints placed upon audience members during these formalized moments restrict any potential for popular participation. The filming and editing of the concert's first number, "Up on Cripple Creek," confirm the opening credits' wider implication: *The Last Waltz*'s stage is a wholly self-enclosed utopia, and the concert's crowd will be confined to its perimeter, effectively concealed from view throughout the film.

The filmmaker's decision to expel The Band's Winterland audience has been highlighted frequently as one of *The Last Waltz*'s most significant stylistic and thematic innovations, and the crowd's circumscribed involvement certainly recalibrates the concert film's usual connotations.[29] Whereas the hippie-era festival documentary tended to underscore the extemporary contributions of audiences and musicians alike, *The Last Waltz* focuses exclusively on The Band, their playing, collaborations, and the tension between unity and individuated moments of expression. The Band in many ways epitomized rock music's decade-long incorporation of American vernacular music (Chicago blues, country, gospel, folksong, Memphis soul, Motown, Dixieland jazz, rock 'n' roll—a comprehensive synthesis of black and white forms is present in the group's music), and their technical proficiency made them especially adept at assembling their songs from these abundant fragments and resources.[30] As a consequence, the group's music could appear instantly colloquial and complex, recognizable and new, but their expertise in such a wide variety of expressions also allowed for an unpredictable type of collaborative playing to emerge:

> In most blues or rock bands, each musician has to give something up in order to make a performance work; the men in The Band played and sang with second sight, and they made no concessions at all. The beat is tough, but open; fast little riffs shoot out from behind vocals without warning; vocals twist around seemingly random chords. The parts combine to pull listeners into a labyrinth, with no idea what might be lurking around the next turn.
>
> (Marcus 2015, 44)

If *The Last Waltz* immediately delineates the Winterland stage as a self-enclosed utopia, it is primarily because it seeks to commemorate this aspect of The Band's shared work, while at the same time memorializing the present-day concert event as a summation of the group's history. Indeed, directly before the performance of "Up on Cripple Creek," a brief conversation between Robertson and Scorsese formulates the Thanksgiving Day show's purpose in exactly these terms: the farewell concert (and by extension, *The Last Waltz*) is a "celebration" of The Band's history and an expansive range of American vernacular music. But The Band's name, immodest yet also designating an anonymous and self-effacing form of accompaniment, lends itself naturally to this basic feature of the concert's conception: in addition to performing their own set, The Band serve as a backing group for their musical guests, and *The Last Waltz*'s best scenes concentrate on this specific scenario's inherent potential for spontaneous collaborations.

The film's visual approach therefore emphasizes the players' oscillation between their attentiveness to the songs' structures/constraints and an ongoing effort at extemporary invention: synchronized multi-camera shooting, a relatively restricted framing of onstage musicians (mostly medium shots and close-ups), and the calculated use of zooming and rack focusing all function to isolate moments of intuitive give-and-take between players. At times, these can be transitory (an alternating shift in focus from Robertson's guitar solo and Hudson's saxophone work at the end of "It Makes No Difference," for example), while other interactions progress gradually over the course of a single tune, or in a few exceptional instances across several songs. The Band's work with Ronnie Hawkins and Bob Dylan, important mentors from their earliest days, fully discloses the group's easygoing adaptability when Hawkins and Dylan both make impromptu additions to their songs. Hawkins's intentionally loose "Who Do You Love," one of his earliest recordings with The Hawks, contains several instinctive interpolations: a few band members' names are inserted into Bo Diddley's lyrics; he waves his hat comically in front of Robertson's pick hand, impelling him to "burn" as he plays his guitar solo; the measured movement of Hawkins's left hand directs the group to dramatically lower its volume during the performance's final passage; and he clearly takes pleasure in silently extending the song's latter verses by several bars, prompting The Band to pause and watch him diligently for any additional changes. *The Last Waltz*'s multiple cameras frame these figures in a variety of medium shots and medium close-ups throughout the sequence, emphasizing their proximity and long-established bonds, yet simultaneously revealing how each musician pushes *and* follows the song's dynamic modifications. Dylan's performance of "Forever Young" captures an analogous moment of understanding and improvisation when he forces The Band to linger over a clearly unrehearsed modulation (Dylan plays a prolonged, arpeggiated D7 chord as everyone onstage stops and stares at his hands and guitar) before changing keys and launching into a short reprise of "Baby, Let Me Follow You Down" (Figure 2.6). The two segments essentially commemorate The Band's long pre-history as The Hawks, but they're also excellent examples of how *The Last Waltz* creates visual counterparts for the onstage exchanges between this seasoned group of musicians and their guests: camera movement, framing, and editing repeatedly establish audiovisual equivalents for these intuitive collaborations. Once again, *The Last Waltz* might choose to visualize the Winterland stage as a self-enclosed utopia, but it does so because such interactions are uniquely possible in this space and solely under these particular conditions.

The Last Waltz's focus on this collaborative ideal is best represented in a lengthy passage through the blues at the movie's midpoint. Paul Butterfield's "Mystery Train" begins with a long shot of The Band, Butterfield (situated at a microphone to Levon Helm's immediate left), and the song's resonant opening

Figure 2.6 *The Last Waltz* (Martin Scorsese, 1978).

notes played by Robertson on guitar, but the unplanned—yet opportune—malfunctioning of the stage's overhead lights during the shot's concluding zoom-out forces the film to narrow its concentration to Butterfield and Helm's vocal back-and-forth in the sequence's subsequent images. (Richard Manuel is intermittently visible as he plays a second set of drums behind Helm, and The Band's other members are mostly absent after these opening images.) Illuminated by a lone spotlight and flashing camera bulbs, closer views of Butterfield and Helm's singing capture the song's careening choruses as they develop into Butterfield's more completely formed harmonica soloing. The shot selection here is reduced to over-the-shoulder reverse views of Butterfield and Helm and a few embedded close-ups of each figure, but an overriding sense of rhythmic give-and-take predominates throughout "Mystery Train" (Figure 2.7). If the metronomic potency of Muddy Waters's subsequent "Mannish Boy" initially appears to prohibit this kind of instinctive interaction, it actually comprises a highpoint in *The Last Waltz*'s close scrutiny of how musicians work in concert with one another. Butterfield remains onstage to add his characteristic harmonica playing to Waters's performance, and their common understanding is unmistakable: an extended, narrowly framed medium-long shot presents the whole group huddled together around Waters as they produce the song's precision rhythm and refrains. Yet even within this constrained structure and setup, the musicians reveal their readiness to push the song in different directions: Robertson interjects occasionally with screams and

Figure 2.7 *The Last Waltz* (Martin Scorsese, 1978).

his spontaneous soloing, to which Waters's guitarist, Bob Margolin, responds with a look of surprise and approval.³¹ Although *The Last Waltz* has noticeably different origins and aims than Scorsese's *Italianamerican*, its approach to documenting The Band's final concert nonetheless resembles the earlier film's methods in decisive ways. The basic documentary situation, wholly designed and coordinated for projected effects, furnishes the necessary circumstances for intuitive work; and while The Band and their guests are undoubtedly more practiced performers than *Italianamerican*'s main storytelling subjects, they too have to work at overcoming the documentary pact's constraints if they are to arrive at the collaborative moments documented by *The Last Waltz* (Figure 2.8).

Paul Butterfield's presence in *The Last Waltz*'s winding movement through America's blues is especially instructive, however, because it reveals this farewell concert's historiographic purpose. Various incarnations of the Butterfield Blues Band had played at the Monterey Pop and Woodstock festivals, yet their work was not included in the originally released versions of either *Monterey Pop* or *Woodstock*.³² Butterfield's relatively prominent place in *The Last Waltz*, though surely determined in part by a shared professional path (he was also a resident of Woodstock and would continue to collaborate with members of The Band after *The Last Waltz*), finally serves as a reminder of The Band's effort to excavate a specific version of their history in this concert and Scorsese's film, a story with only indirect connections to the 1960s counterculture. The Band were momentarily at the center of the decade's popular upheaval, especially during

Figure 2.8 *The Last Waltz* (Martin Scorsese, 1978).

their brief working association with Bob Dylan; yet as we have already seen, from the release of *Music from Big Pink* in 1968 they insisted on their musical and philosophical differences from the wider hippie counterculture. Nevertheless, their valedictory concert and Scorsese's *The Last Waltz* clearly remain modeled on celebrity-filled, hippie-era precursors such as George Harrison's *The Concert for Bangladesh* (Saul Swimmer, 1972), that is to say, on previous concerts and documentaries whose procession of 1960s-era special guests reconfirmed the music industry's growing economic heft and influence during the 1970s. But if the philanthropic purposes of Harrison's concert and film (and triple album soundtrack) worked to alleviate the inevitably self-validating features of such representations, *The Last Waltz*'s concert and documentary (and triple album soundtrack) disclose no immediately comparable rationale. In other words, a film like *The Concert for Bangladesh* could easily justify its "all-star" conceit, but as J.P. Telotte rightly notes, *The Last Waltz* somehow leaves viewers to wonder "precisely what is being celebrated" (1979, 12) or eulogized in this film's exhaustive set-up. In 1971, Harrison's charity event could still draw some of its sustenance and sense of self-belief from the disintegrating counterculture, but The Band's original conception for their farewell performance promptly disconnected itself from such affiliations, even though the concert and film remained situated within a very familiar generational framework. The Thanksgiving Day concert's emphasis on collaborative work is without question being celebrated in *The Last Waltz*, but the impermanence of these collective accomplishments is also lamented—this is "the last waltz," after all. Telotte offers a compelling interpretation of *The Last Waltz*'s overriding stress upon this sense of irrevocability. The film's thematic trajectory, he argues, encompasses a passage from expression to expiration, culminating in the show-closing "I Shall Be Released" and its intimation of reprieve from both individual "limitations" and "our far from expressive world" (1979, 13). But for *The Last Waltz*, such "release" is in the end a form of self-directed accomplishment rather than collective achievement, and this elusive shift in the film's priorities is best exemplified in Scorsese's interviews with Robbie Robertson. At these moments, The Band's common history "on the road" is rerouted through the guitarist's persistent self-assertion, and this in turn reframes the musicians' work as a solitary and precarious endeavor.

The Shape I'm In: Direct Cinema, *The Last Waltz*, and Working Musicians

The Last Waltz seeks to distinguish itself from the prototypical hippie-era concert movies. Its comprehensive prearrangement of the documentary event restricts the potential for spontaneous expression and popular participation, that is, the utopian promise in films like *Monterey Pop* and *Woodstock*, and this is most evident in its detachment from The Band's Winterland audience; the interpolation of interviews similarly guides such an interpretation of the final concert's meanings by repeatedly affirming the priority of Robertson's—and to a far lesser degree, The Band's other members'—subjectivity in this scenario. On their surface, these qualities appear to be methodical rejections of American direct cinema's primary axioms and premises, yet *The Last Waltz* remains bound to the central paradoxes of its concert film predecessors. Indeed, its focus on collaboration evokes the hippie-era concert film's emphasis on musicians and their extemporary onstage work, and it matches *Monterey Pop* and *Woodstock*'s efforts to establish visual equivalents for the rock band's collective efforts. But as a self-enclosed utopia, *The Last Waltz*'s stage is not portrayed as an exemplar for its audience. If the hippie-era concert documentary was finally preoccupied with the music festival's envisioning of a new utopian communality, and if this position encompassed both musicians *and* festival audiences, *The Last Waltz* restricts itself instead to representations of musicians and the wide variety of their expressive labor. In the process, however, Scorsese's film foregrounds one of the hippie-era concert movie's fundamental contradictions: in *Monterey Pop* as well as *Woodstock*, the elaboration of a collectively shared excitement is consistently neutralized by images of the individuated rock star's freedom and authenticity. When it confines its vision of working musicians to the Winterland stage, *The Last Waltz* closely details several instances of spontaneous, collaborative interaction; but as I've indicated above, its view of musician labor is ultimately redirected by Robertson's self-interested interviews, and as a consequence, such work is reconfigured as a type of autonomous self-realization. This critical conundrum is a long-lasting inheritance from American direct cinema; and despite its determination to modify and develop the classic 1960s concert documentaries, *The Last Waltz* is fastened securely to this framework. Like its many predecessors, Scorsese's concert film continually moderates its study of musicians' collaboration according to the much more limited terms of Robertson's sense of self-direction.

In retrospect, direct cinema—as both theory and practice—seems like an inescapable counterpart to the communal energy of the counterculture and its rock music, and their conjoined missions were eventually undermined by comparable contradictions. In his indispensable "Jargons of Authenticity (Three American Moments)," Paul Arthur reminds us that American direct cinema succeeded as a modestly popular foray in the 1960s because its rhetoric of immediacy specified a critical relation to Hollywood's contemporaneous production. Although its predisposition toward "intimacy, physical proximity, [and] an isolated focus on 'personality' struggling for self-definition" (Arthur 1993, 121) was in fact shared by many Hollywood films during this period, the particular effects derived from direct cinema's unobstructed scrutiny of faces, gestures, and demeanour were intended (at least in theoretical pronouncements by filmmakers and other proponents) to replace an inferior and artificially dramatic form.[33] Prototypical films like *Primary* (Robert Drew, 1960), *Crisis: Behind a Presidential Commitment* (Robert Drew, 1963), and *Happy Mother's Day* (Richard Leacock and Joyce Chopra, 1963) purportedly freed viewers to closely consider a figure's embodied emotions and the unprompted inner stirrings of "character," and such sights were said to exceed the truths to be found in Hollywood's fiction films. Charged with understanding a narrowly framed aspect of America's postwar reality, direct cinema sought to offer its spectators unrestricted access to person-sized spaces and the spectacle of individual crises (not entirely unlike its Hollywood foil, in this respect), but in so doing, it shaped the world according to its subjects' strong sense of self-direction and desire for self-realization. Indeed, the resolution of direct cinema's so-called "crisis" scenarios typically turned on a decisive moment of self-actualization, and the spontaneous discovery of individuality quickly became a trademark of the new documentaries.

Scholars have underscored the many parallels between such emphases and the main tenets of American liberalism. Arthur, for instance, situates the techniques and philosophy of direct cinema within the "undulations of American liberalism" (1993, 121), while Robert C. Allen and Douglas Gomery's *Film History: Theory and Practice* (1985) describes the Drew Associates' primary need for portable, lightweight 16-mm cameras and synchronized sound recording devices in similar terms.[34] The filmmakers' fundamental faith in technology's emancipatory potential is certainly consistent with a liberal ideological position, and as Allen and Gomery convincingly demonstrate, this disposition partially explains direct cinema's essentially "reformist" theoretical pronouncements and practice (1985, 233–7). When observed with circumspect "neutrality" by a documentarian, Richard Leacock would say, the facts of a particular situation should be directly revealed to viewers who can in turn make reasonable judgments about their world.[35] Leacock's invaluable summary of his cohort's 1960s output returns repeatedly to such far-reaching descriptions of individual audience members who are at liberty to evaluate images and sounds in the new documentaries. As he bluntly puts it, with the advent of direct cinema, spectators were at last free to "figure out what the hell is really going on" in the world around them.[36] In their principal statements of purpose, Leacock and other Drew Associates consistently prioritized this spectatorial situation because it promised to facilitate the incremental, judicious, and democratic transformations of extra-cinematic realities by the films' viewers; yet according to this same liberal/individualist alignment, direct cinema's unimpeded rendering of visible facts could not support more drastic or "revolutionary" efforts at improving society (Allen and Gomery 1985, 234). In short, within the ever-present Cold War context of its conception, direct cinema would swiftly dismiss any desire for systematic change as the symptom of a "Marxist hangover," and its practitioners could thereby claim to be humbly providing tools for spectators to deliberate rationally—and act appropriately—within the public sphere.[37]

Critical accounts of direct cinema have customarily focused on its preoccupation with the mainstream media's obfuscation of this public sphere. According to Jonathan Kahana, *Primary* "seeks to teach its audience something about how popular images are constructed and how they function in the democratic process" (1999, 101), and like Jeanne Hall and Paul Arthur, he rightly emphasizes the tacitly self-validating motivation for this variety of pedagogical image-making.[38] "*Primary*'s argument," Kahana writes, "consists largely of [a] critique of image; against the various manifestations of technologically induced charisma, the film posits cinema's ability to present a true picture of personality" (1999, 102). This demystifying filmic rhetoric and the attendant valorization of authentic personalities are familiar features of the period's Cold War political posturing and liberal ideology, and they are essential to the earliest direct documentaries' journalistic goals; but the films made by Leacock, Pennebaker, and the Maysles brothers after their break with Robert Drew begin to reshape these emphases in subtle ways. Burrowing more deeply into a variety of intimate spaces while simultaneously engaging with the counterculture's growing collective aspirations, these documentaries offer contradictory sights of people situated uneasily within an assortment of workplaces. Although seldom described as such, the public spaces and stages occupied by musicians in the hippie era's numerous concert films were notable examples of workplaces, yet this emergent focus covered the broader range of direct cinema's output throughout the 1960s. The Maysles brothers' *Salesman* (1969), for example, provides a sharp outline of fundamentally competitive individualism amongst its door-to-door Bible peddlers, and the film discloses the increasingly negative effects of its central subject's inability to maintain his very small network of customers and supports. *Salesman* extends and transforms the Maysles's earlier concentration on celebrities considerably, devoting itself instead to a close observation of working-class life. In so doing, however, it perceptively redirects its brand of observational documentary filmmaking's attention to different forms of interaction between these new subjects and their immediate surroundings. In other words, in these late-1960s films, the camera's focus is increasingly trained on the workplace itself as a site for meaningful self-actualization and self-expression.

Direct cinema was first conceived in a very specific post-Second World War socio-political and cultural setting. Galvanized by the concurrence of postwar individualist attitudes and a widely disseminated critique of mass cultural production, the direct cinema associates could confidently stress their rejection of previous documentary conventions (the routine, the clichéd, and most importantly, the carefully managed or staged), while at the same time placing their trust in the film viewer's capacity for critical deliberation. These closely conjoined emphases, however, had a significant influence on the filmmakers' approach to representation, especially when it came to their images of working people: left largely to their own devices and frequently isolated, these archetypes for what observers today would call "creative workers" were paradoxically the embodiment of both competitive individualism and "American liberalism's prosocial agenda" (Stahl 2013, 74). On their surface, the hippie era's abundant concert documentaries, direct cinema's primary output during this period, might appear to be significant exceptions to this attention to self-direction, but as Matt Stahl has argued, such films also "model and prescribe" (2013, 74) a conspicuously modern form of work, even if their subjects achieve a level of personal expression that would have been unthinkable for *Salesman*'s Paul "the Badger" and his colleagues. In this important respect, Pennebaker's *Dont Look Back* is the prototypical creation of 1960s direct cinema: Bob Dylan's calculated commitment to self-invention and its accompanying autonomy perfectly exemplifies an emergent form of self-directed work. Throughout *Dont Look Back*, one watches Dylan as he shifts apprehensively between a principled sense of 1960s-style unanimity and a contradictory devotion to competitive individualism. During his often-discussed condescending response to Donovan's musical tribute to him, for example, Dylan is surrounded by sympathetic beatniks and fledgling hippies, yet his competitiveness quickly transforms the general camaraderie into a lopsided competition between singer-guitarists. At these moments, we witness direct cinema tacitly participating in what Stahl calls "the production and proliferation of new and future working subjects" (2013, 74), and the emerging features of their work make themselves fully apparent in Dylan's deportment: he is a model for the authentic life and highly valued virtues like independence, expressivity, and self-realization. *Dont Look Back*, however, shrewdly exposes a certain pretence in this narrowly self-seeking conception of work. According to David E. James, Pennebaker's film in fact reveals "Dylan's apparent autonomous authenticity [...] to be sustained by a battalion of road and stage managers, journalists and reviewers, friends and hangers-on, all watched over by his aggressively avuncular manager," Albert Grossman (James 2016, 207). Whereas Dylan had sometimes presented himself as a "non-commercial" artist during his early folk-protest incarnation, *Dont Look Back* continually implies the songwriter's turn to an expanding rock sound and its set of closely associated business commitments. Nevertheless, one's lasting impression is of Dylan's unique capacity for self-mythologizing and perpetual self-invention ("I'm glad I'm not me," he says while quickly scanning a newspaper story about his smoking habits), and whatever one might ultimately think about these particular aspects of his personality, they give his labor the surface appearance of independence and self-sufficiency.[39]

The hippie-era concert films that followed *Dont Look Back* were far more circumspect in their representations of the music business and its assorted behind-the-scenes economic realities, yet they invariably preserved Pennebaker's emphasis on self-direction and self-realization.[40] Indeed, the films' highlighting of utopian participation was consistently fitted to more focused images of self-expression. In *Monterey Pop*, Pennebaker's attempt to situate his film completely within the festival's public spaces is visibly moderated by a close observation of individual performers, and this recalibrates the concert event's collective ritual in meaningful ways. As a result, a band such as Canned Heat remains relatively anonymous during their rendition of Muddy Waters's "Rollin' and Tumblin,'" and the West Coast's most significant music-making and social entities—Buffalo Springfield, The Byrds, and the Grateful Dead—are altogether eliminated from the original film. *Monterey Pop* is instead perceptibly committed to groups with less democratic constituents (Big Brother and the Holding Company, The Jimi Hendrix Experience), and the film's visual fabric is finally woven with tightly framed images of an energized individuality: Janis Joplin's stomping feet during "Ball and Chain," the programmed commotion of Jimi Hendrix's "Wild Thing," and Otis Redding's raucous performance of Sam Cooke's "Shake!"—each of these sequences defines an exceptional moment of self-realization. But The Who's anarchic "My Generation" establishes an instructive point of comparison, insofar as it reveals how *Monterey Pop* tends to trade its images of spontaneous participation for more narrowly directed feats of self-expression (Figure 2.9). Not necessarily marked by the anonymity of a Canned Heat, but lacking the instant recognizability of the various San Francisco groups, The Who appear remote from the crowd of American bohemians gathered in front of them; and while their ritualistic instrument smashing is received enthusiastically (with a trace of disorientation), it is promptly cleaned away by the professionalism of a small cadre of stagehands: this act's potential meaning to the festival's audience is quickly curtailed, completely restricted to the stage, and then dismissed. The band's performance in *Woodstock* is defined by a similar detachment, regardless of the song lyrics' implicit deliberation on the concert's participatory utopianism. "We're Not Gonna Take It" (cut to its "See Me/Feel Me" coda) is introduced as a slow motion abstraction, essentially silent in its rendering, and the subsequent images and editing situate The Who in an onstage space that

Figure 2.9 *Monterey Pop* (D.A. Pennebaker, 1968).

closely resembles *The Last Waltz*'s self-enclosed utopia in important ways. The band members all appear to respond instinctively to one another's playing, but several of the split screens separate the musicians from each other, isolating them as well as their audience, and the effect is particularly pronounced when compared to other moments in the movie (like Santana's "Soul Sacrifice," for example). In The Who's "See Me/Feel Me," collaborative work is obfuscated slightly by the same self-realizing exploits on view in sequences dedicated to more fully individualized performers such as Hendrix and Joplin.

The Last Waltz inherits this underlying contradiction from 1960s concert documentaries and combines it with *Dont Look Back*'s vision of an elusive solo musician and his self-directed creative work, but in so doing, it transforms its onstage foci in meaningful ways. The addition of interviews to *The Last Waltz* was surely intended to both complement the farewell concert's images of collaborative work and provide a more complete picture of The Band's inner dynamics. Viewers would presumably witness these exchanges and understand the rock band as a social unit, as an entity formed by agreements (both formal and informal) and finally exhausted by an assortment of recriminations and distortions; The Band as a cooperative unit defined by the initial desperation of endless failures and the exhilaration of unexpected achievement, and so on. Scorsese's interviews with Robertson occasionally investigate these historical realities, but more often they permit the guitarist to reformat The Band's past according to a small number of well-rehearsed topoi: the struggles and hazards associated with the rock musician's "life on the road"; the entertainment world's frequently comic intersections with organized criminality; and rock 'n' roll's origin myths, situated within America's southern states, yet nonetheless encompassing The Band's mostly Canadian members. The first of these interviews, however, quickly sets the stage for Robertson's concerted effort to retrofit The Band's history to his present-day requirements. It begins with a brief close-up of Robertson as he relates The Band's past ("OK, look, we've been together sixteen years," he says as the credit sequence fades to black and *The Last Waltz* turns its full attention to his interview), and then expands its perspective to include Scorsese as he listens, nods approvingly, laughs, and occasionally intervenes to encourage the guitarist to elaborate upon important details. The sequence appears to progress as a plainspoken explanation of the farewell concert's structure and broader purpose, but its relatively swift editing and revealing changes of shot scale subtly specify a different story. The addition of new details is repeatedly accompanied by renewed close-ups of Robertson, and this eventually has the cumulative effect of rearranging his references to The Band as a collective "we" into a series of first-person statements about the past.

Robertson is seated comfortably in front of a large Canadian flag as he recalls The Band's winding passage from "eight years in bars, dives, dancehalls" to "eight years of concerts, stadiums, arenas," and he unequivocally positions the Thanksgiving Day show as a terminus for the group and its existence as a touring act (Figure 2.10). However, when Scorsese asks him to say more about the concert's assorted invited guests, Robertson offers an immodest assessment of the musicians' historical and generational import: he tells the director that "some friends showed up and helped us take it home," but continues by describing these players as "some of the greatest influences on music, on a whole generation." The camera lens promptly begins to zoom-in as he says, "greatest influences," and the movie's perspective on its historical subject slowly comes into sharper focus for viewers. The Band clearly have a stake in this generational legend, of course, but Robertson's position as the group's principal spokesman places him uniquely amongst the contingent of influential solo artists (except for The Staples, The Band's invited players are all solo acts), and the group's other members will remain confined to their storied past. In short, for Helm, Danko, Manuel, and Hudson, the future presents itself here simply as a void, while Robertson's close alignment with the cadre of solo guests implies his

Figure 2.10 *The Last Waltz* (Martin Scorsese, 1978).

ongoing significance as a working musician. The subsequent close-up brings us to Robertson's familiar explanation of the farewell concert as "a celebration," and the sequence ends with what sounds like an outtake from *Dont Look Back*. "A celebration of the beginning or an end," Scorsese excitedly asks. The "beginning of the beginning of the end of the beginning," Robertson answers, evidently pleased with his evasive formulation, and *The Last Waltz* shares in the guitarist's self-presentation as the concert's sole conductor and, as Steven E. Severn convincingly argues, its main beneficiary (2002, 27). A mere minute and twenty-three seconds in length, this sequence quietly introduces Robertson as separate from The Band, even though he is recounting a well-known version of their collective history.

In this way, *The Last Waltz* shifts from the polyphony of its concert performances to the distinctly monophonic properties of Robertson's interviews. The Band's earliest recordings and concerts were driven by the unexpected blending of Helm's, Manuel's, and Danko's individual voices, and this has customarily been underscored as the group's most distinctive attribute. For Greil Marcus, songs like "We Can Talk," "Rockin' Chair," "King Harvest (Has Surely Come)," and "The Weight" disclose how the amalgamation of dissimilar voices was The Band's essential contribution to American popular music. The expansive sounds of their vocal interplay, he notes, designate "room for friends and strangers, room for escape and room for homecoming" (2015, 48). Although this interweaving of voices would gradually fade on The Band's subsequent records, several of *The Last Waltz*'s interviews attempt to resuscitate this cooperative quality by gathering The Band together to answer Scorsese's questions. Unfortunately, the film's priorities are fixed during Robertson's brief opening exchange with the director, and as a result, succeeding interviews with the whole group are either truncated and inconsequential, or they are composed principally of images of Robertson speaking as the others sit and silently listen to him. Robertson's lone interview voice—the sound of an engaging narrator, but seldom a featured singer on The Band's recordings—consistently climbs over any interjections by his bandmates, and his storytelling predominates during all of these noticeably strained get-togethers. A lengthy tale about the young Hawks' short residency at a Texas nightclub owned by Jack Ruby; Manuel, Danko, and Robertson's ragged acoustic performance of "Old Time Religion," which concludes with Robertson's admission that "it's not like it used to be"; and the remarkable anecdote about The Hawks' drunken evening with Sonny Boy Williamson II in 1960s Arkansas—each of these segments, with the partial exception of "Old Time Religion" (Robertson's voice tellingly deserts him at this moment), is seized by the guitarist as he purposefully guides our understanding of the past.[41] Typically, he reinterprets the meaning of The Band's historical experiences as a series of moral lessons gathered from their years together on the road, mostly comic tales that signpost the group's journey from youthful recklessness to their—or more accurately, Robertson's—present-day self-possession. In these cases, The Band's story is subtly overhauled by the guitarist and set definitively in the past, but by attending so closely to Robertson's exertions as a lone storyteller, *The Last Waltz* continually reaffirms his particular presence, his special place in the present, and it tacitly authorizes his future as a working musician (Figure 2.11).

The foremost exception to all of this, of course, is Levon Helm. Although Robertson is seated beside him during each of his interviews, Helm approaches the documentary task with a mixture of wariness and control. His authoritative account of rock 'n' roll's origins in America's southern states ("near Memphis, cotton country, rice country") is undoubtedly one of *The Last Waltz*'s highlights, yet his reticence has a palpable influence on the director's conduct throughout these conversations. Scorsese was a resourceful interviewer in both *Italianamerican* and *American Boy: A Profile of Steven Prince*, but in *The Last Waltz* his questions often appear tentative and self-conscious, and he is noticeably overmatched by Helm's caginess across these segments.[42] For example, Helm's relaxed description of the south's original blending of various

Figure 2.11 *The Last Waltz* (Martin Scorsese, 1978).

kinds of vernacular music ("country, bluegrass, blues music") is quickly met by Scorsese's naïve, though not necessarily unknowing, "what's it called then?" ("Rock 'n' roll," Helm calmly tells him.) Helm's later explanation of the "Midnight Ramble" is equally easygoing and confident in its knowledgeable account of southern musical idioms and popular customs, but it is instantly diminished by Robertson's interpolation of a familiar description of rock 'n' roll's early reputation as "the devil's music." These two brief exchanges, seemingly slight and serving principally to telegraph the concert sequences that immediately follow them (Muddy Waters's "Mannish Boy" and Van Morrison's "Caravan" respectively), establish forceful evidence for the unbridgeable distance between Helm and Robertson, or rather, between their incompatible ideas about the work done by musicians. When asked by Scorsese for the names of seminal performers from "cotton country, rice country," Helm offers only Muddy Waters ("king of country music") and Carl Perkins, while Robertson immediately supplements this short list with the more readily recognizable Elvis Presley, Johnny Cash, and Bo Diddley. Waters and Perkins were indisputably influential musicians (this is especially true in Waters's case), but they are regional figures when compared to Presley, Perkins's contemporary at Sun Records in the 1950s. Robertson calls upon Elvis in both fragments, yet the second segment of this interview is permeated by an exceptional awkwardness. Helm shifts undecidedly in his chair, looks away momentarily as he finishes his cigarette, and remains serious throughout Robertson's sketch of the conventional "devil's music" legend. For Helm, the "Midnight Ramble" is a popular tradition of "tent shows" and "traveling shows," a wide-ranging collection of southern customs; although he refers knowledgeably to rock 'n' roll's important place in this folklore (its "duck walks, steps and moves"), his descriptions make no mention of individual performers, nor do they attempt to diminish the traveling shows' everyday qualities. Robertson, on the other hand, purposefully reroutes the Ramble, making it a first step on the road to rock 'n' roll stardom in the 1950s. Chuck Berry, Jerry Lee Lewis, and Bo Diddley are summoned as evidence, but Elvis's name is again invoked as the personification of rock 'n' roll's mythological expeditions from America's southern states to the rest of the country—and world—in the mid-1950s. Robertson turns to these figures because they were instrumental in commercializing the southern tent shows' most common elements, but Elvis's achievement is evidently of another order: his originality indicates an exceptional form of self-realization, a type of self-expression that appears to have transcended its origins and contexts, the contributions of collaborators, and perhaps the music business' substantial influence. Interwoven throughout the film, these interviews with the guitarist continually refocus our view of the onstage segments and their emphasis on collaboration, compelling us to instead concentrate on an aura of individuated harmonious deportment and self-directed achievement (Figure 2.12).[43]

Figure 2.12 *The Last Waltz* (Martin Scorsese, 1978).

Elvis's death in 1977 is registered as an instructive moment by Robertson, and his final interview in *The Last Waltz* explicitly connects Presley to the film's broader reckoning with The Band's history as a touring act. Elvis, Robertson tells us, is yet another weary victim of the road, and he is situated in a long succession of rock casualties. In a medium close-up, his head covered by a fedora, Robertson once again offers his interpretation of the touring life's inevitable toll and threats, while Scorsese, seated and reflected in a mirror, listens attentively, sometimes appearing to direct his subject with slight motions of his hands. "The road has taken a lot of the great ones," Robertson says ponderously, "Hank Williams, Buddy Holly, Otis Redding, Janis [Joplin], Jimi Hendrix, Elvis." He then continues in a tightly framed close-up, smiling at the irrevocability of his observation: "It's a goddamn impossible way of life … no question about it."[44] According to Severn, Robertson's efforts to align himself with Elvis in *The Last Waltz* are aimed at burnishing his own mythology (2002, 29–30), but the implied correspondence between the guitarist, Elvis, and these other victims, though admittedly self-aggrandizing, appears to be calculated for a substantially different effect. What is the *meaning* of his short inventory of rock star mortalities? Why does it emerge at such a late stage in the film? The pietistic litany of rock 'n' roll music's casualties is commonplace, and would have been so even in 1976–8, but Robertson's account is deliberately inaccurate, emphasizing the impossibly hazardous "road" when almost every one of the figures in question died for reasons other than touring. Although Holly and Redding—and in a different way, Williams—could be described plausibly as casualties of their road work, Elvis died in his Graceland home, a victim of assorted overindulgences, while Joplin and Hendrix both also succumbed to accidental drug overdoses. Robertson's enumeration of dead musicians comes directly after The Band and their invited guests have concluded a reverential rendition of "I Shall Be Released," and at this moment, the guitarist's purpose appears obvious: the road itself is—or has become—yet another form of confinement, and Robertson's interviews (but not The Band's) assure us that he has now blocked its numerous risks. If the concert's utopian features remain set within the self-enclosed stage area, the road's dangers are similarly cordoned off in this account; yet Robertson's future seems to be guaranteed wholly by the film's illustration of his autonomy. Liberated from both the stage and road, the guitarist is now in possession of an exceptional sense of self-sufficiency and control. This independence, however, is conspicuously denied to the group's other members.

It's tempting to see *The Last Waltz*'s incidental disclosure of this essential disagreement between Helm and Robertson as an anticipation of Helm's post-Band dissension and its continuing reverberations. According to the prevailing view, Helm, born and raised in the American South, was an authentic rock 'n' roll musician, and he was ultimately concerned with The Band's integrity, while the outsider Robertson was always an interloper, a shameless self-promoter whose every decision was determined by self-interest. This is one possible interpretation of the Helm/Robertson feud and Scorsese's film, and it accurately acknowledges Robertson's pivotal role in The Band's difficult demise; but in *The Last Waltz*, the often slippery notion of authenticity does not align itself so simply with either of these figures, and the film's close adherence to Robertson's perspective bestows an unusual authority on the guitarist's reflections, casting them as authentic—and substantial—insights into the touring musician's life and labor. In his memoir, Robertson's attempts at self-exculpation emphasize his former bandmates' abundant drug-taking as the principal reason for The Band's drawn-out dissolution in the 1970s. This particular subject, like so much else in *Testimony*, offers a reevaluation of The Band's past, but it also seeks to confirm the correctness of Robertson's viewpoint on a range of events, the contentious production of *The Last Waltz* foremost among them. Like the simultaneously produced *American Boy: A Profile of Steven Prince*, *The Last Waltz* celebrates its principal subject's absorbing storytelling, especially when it turns to the wilder aspects of the rock 'n' roll musician's existence, but Robertson's collection of rock star casualties does much more than merely reinforce his myth-making. The guitarist's standard complaint about his bandmates in *Testimony* insinuates their destructive, inharmonious comportment—endless automobile accidents, excessive drug and alcohol consumption, a lack of the discipline required for songwriting and recording, their unreliability on the road, and so forth. In short, Manuel, Danko, and Helm (but not Hudson) are portrayed as professionally inadequate, and their risk-taking while on tour indicates how their professional trajectories will eventually diverge from Robertson's. In this respect, the guitarist's affiliation with his catalogue of rock star victims is unexpectedly shifty. Rather than bolster his place in this lineage, Robertson's account underlines his distinction from such discordant personalities, especially the purportedly crisis-ridden members of his own group. *The Last Waltz*'s commitment to the guitarist's perspective on The Band's past as well as their foreclosed future allows his definitive assessment of "life on the road" to linger over the film's concluding studio-bound image, a ceremonial tracking shot away from the group as they disappear into a self-sustaining legend of their historical achievements (Figure 2.13).

"Successful artists," Matt Stahl writes, "often appear to us as paragons of autonomous self-actualization" (2013, 2), and Robertson's presence as a solo interview subject throughout *The Last Waltz* casts him an exemplar of such self-sufficiency: he presents himself as the wiser for his various experiences with The Band, but this knowledge is finally the product of his self-realization and therefore cannot be shared by anyone else in the group. American direct cinema's ostensibly self-reliant heroes were customarily situated in informal working environments (door-to-door Bible peddling, music-making, etc.), and in the particular case of the concert film, these artist-protagonists were invariably engaged in a form of value-added symbolic production. If the ostensible autonomy of their onstage efforts was consistent with the counterculture's constructive revolt against routine daily labor, much of what might have once been regarded as liberating or self-actualizing comportment in the hippie-era documentaries has in subsequent decades badly deteriorated in the hands of various "corporate managers" (Ross 2009, 5).[45] With the benefit of hindsight, of course, the malady of self-expression can be easily diagnosed in the counterculture and its concert films (and their countless descendants), but the representation of a conspicuously self-seeking type of work is one of direct cinema's enduring legacies. In American documentary after the 1960s, even in those modes of film practice that steadfastly position themselves

Figure 2.13 *The Last Waltz* (Martin Scorsese, 1978).

against "observational" precepts, this individualist emphasis would—perhaps predictably—drive the rediscovery of "voice" and "subjectivity."[46] In *The Last Waltz*, Robertson's numerous interviews embody this particular paradox in the hippie-era concert film; if such interviews seem to be departures from direct cinema orthodoxy, they in fact manifest the hippie-era concert documentary's entrenched conception of musician labor. Seemingly self-realizing and self-directed, work in these films is imagined in relatively restricted terms, and Robertson's attempt to retrofit The Band's collective history to his growing aspirations as a solo artist splits *The Last Waltz* between the group's and guitarist's plainly incompatible professional trajectories. Scorsese's film seeks to revise and refine its concert film antecedents, but this residual contradiction structures its representations of The Band's music-making and history-making.[47]

Sole Survivor: *Shine a Light* and the Pillars of Harmonious Professionalism

Shine a Light, Scorsese's rendering of two shows by The Rolling Stones at New York City's Beacon Theater in 2006, purposefully resuscitates several aspects of *The Last Waltz*'s approach to representing the rock concert (Figure 2.14). The stage, for instance, is once again envisioned as a largely self-enclosed utopia, and The Stones' audience makes only intermittent appearances in the film. At certain moments, the crowd is condensed into a congregation of nondescript hands, arms, and heads pushing through the bottom of the frame, or it swells as a dimly lit backdrop for the band's work; in other instances, audience members assemble around Mick Jagger's and Keith Richards's feet as they suddenly advance to the stage's perimeter, though even at these moments the film remains entirely absorbed in the group's performance. The Rolling Stones' longstanding cultivation of a noticeable—and ultimately insurmountable—distance from their audiences lends itself naturally to Scorsese's stage-as-enclosure strategy here, and their habitual detachment from the rock concert's rituals of supplication authorizes the film's thorough analyses of their onstage cohesion.[48] In this respect, *Shine a Light* simply renews *The Last Waltz*'s focus on musicians and their intuitive collaborations, although the dynamically—and quickly—interpolated close-ups of The Stones' guitars, hands and fingers, harmonicas, microphones, and faces describe the group's substantial differences from The Band and their routinely rigid onstage deportment.[49] That

Figure 2.14 *Shine a Light* (Martin Scorsese, 2008).

said, if *The Last Waltz* constitutes a crest in the "second wave" of "golden age" rockumentaries in the 1970s (Baker 2015b, 246), *Shine a Light* appears slightly misaligned with contemporaneous documentaries about popular musicians and the music industry. Indeed, Matt Stahl has identified a meaningful shift in present-day rockumentaries: the hippie-era films' celebratory vision of the music festival and its collective practices has been replaced by a closer inspection of "the quotidian aspects of the rock group's working life" (2013, 65). He unearths a particularly instructive example in *Dig!* (Ondi Timoner, 2004), but the broad variety of contemporary rockumentaries, he maintains, has turned to "intensive, longitudinal" studies of musicians as they try to manage their own aspirations and the heavy burdens of professionalization (2013, 66). In these documentaries, "independent" musicians are customarily represented as "workers" who are motivated by their desire for social mobility and their daily attempts to manage the many "conflicting demands of autonomous self-actualization" (Stahl 2013, 65). As a consequence, the utopianism of the hippie-era films, always somewhat tarnished by the potential to mystify work-related matters, has been exchanged for detailed investigations of the everyday tension and "crises of rock music making in the early twenty-first century" (Stahl 2013, 66).

By contrast, The Rolling Stones' story is one of incomparable success (they are "the world's greatest rock 'n' roll band"), and their exceptional sense of permanency appears wholly separate from the commonplace actualities of today's struggling rock bands. In fact, The Stones' ongoing survival as a legacy act belies Robbie Robertson's portentous characterizations of "the road" throughout *The Last Waltz*, and Jagger, Richards, Charlie Watts, and Ronnie Wood seem to be beyond the immediate purview of the modern-day rock musician's ordinary worries.[50] Yet *Shine a Light*, I want to suggest, is nonetheless preoccupied with one narrowly perceived feature of the contemporary musician's single-minded efforts at professionalization, and *The Last Waltz* provides a critical model for Scorsese's assessment of this familiar subject matter. Accordingly, the film reintroduces *The Last Waltz*'s twofold emphases and themes: collaboration amongst the core group members (and their invited guest performers) remains a fundamental focus in the director's interpretation of these concerts, yet once again it is complemented by an indirect demarcation of two conflicting kinds of professional conduct. As I've indicated, Robbie Robertson's interviews and anecdotes about The Band's history "on the road" continually redirect one's attention to his own present-day professional deportment and its implied difference from his bandmates' inharmoniousness. *Shine a Light*, however, makes no use of such post-concert interviews, so the film instead combines an outline of prototypical professionalism with its concert segments in the following ways: first, it promptly delineates backstage scenes of the group and their pre-concert management, foregrounding several humorous, spur-of-the-moment telephone conversations and disagreements between Jagger and Scorsese about the Beacon concerts and the film's style (Figure 2.15); and second, it integrates select archival interviews with the band's current members, placing a special emphasis on Richards's and (especially) Jagger's career-long struggles to deflect questions about the band's inescapable destiny as aging professional musicians.

Pre-concert introductory sequences were always meaningful in the hippie-era festival documentaries because they seemed to guarantee the audiences'—and by implication, the films'—extemporary participation in the ensuing concert segments. *Woodstock*, for example, begins by briefly surveying the festival's rural setting while the show's stage is being hurriedly constructed by organizers, but the conviviality and prevailing sense of cooperation during these moments are mere preludes to the event's broader utopianism. Set to Canned Heat's "Going Up The Country," the subsequent views present the film's

Figure 2.15 *Shine a Light* (Martin Scorsese, 2008).

primary participants and confirm the festival's expansive sense of cooperation; arriving in cars and buses, or simply walking to the grounds, Woodstock's swelling audience establishes a counterpart to the stage workers' continuing collaboration during the night. The live concert segments that immediately follow are essentially manifestations of the festival's deeper philosophy. Any similar pre-event passages are either conspicuously attenuated or abolished in Scorsese's *The Last Waltz*, of course, but *Shine a Light* revives several features of the hippie-era concert documentary's foundational moments in order to situate its analysis of The Stones within a framework of thorough decision-making, preparation, and proficiency. Referring spectators directly—and with some humor—to the preliminary, backstage segments in *Monterey Pop*, *Woodstock*, and The Maysles brothers' landmark portrayal of The Rolling Stones, *Gimme Shelter*, *Shine a Light*'s pre-concert sequences strategically redirect their focus to a series of complex organizational elements; as a result, the band's audiences do not figure at all in these images. Composed of several terse telephone conversations, glimpses of Jagger's provisional set lists, small models for the stage's ongoing construction, and the energetic movements of assorted music and film producers, the concert's preamble presents a standard Stones show as the product of rigorous control and prearrangement rather than folk-like assembly. An unmistakable distance between producers and consumers prevails in these instances, so only The Stones and a massive contingent of coordinators, managers, and hangers-on (Bill and Hillary Clinton among them) are presented, and viewers' overwhelming impression is of the event's pressure and professionalism. Whereas Wadleigh's *Woodstock* interprets its concert as the full expression of an emergent youth nation's ideals, *Shine a Light* instead represents The Stones' Beacon Theater performances as the products of an unrivalled commercial juggernaut and the daily effort of professional entertainers. Shot in the midst of the group's lengthy and lucrative "A Bigger Bang" tour (2005–7), the movie's prelude simply extends itself into the always accelerating pace of The Stones' music-making enterprise, and it clearly positions Jagger as the concert event's figurehead.

More importantly, however, *Shine a Light* incorporates select archival interviews with The Stones into its representation of the Beacon Theater concerts, and these establish the film's perspective on the group's long history and contracting future. *The Last Waltz*'s commemoration of The Band's valedictory concert is appropriately unhurried in its methods, relying on relatively lengthy takes of the group's performances to maintain the film's plaintive tenor and clear sense of this event's conclusiveness. Its post-concert interviews are likewise leisurely in their pacing. Although Scorsese sometimes interjects with his familiar rapid-fire expressions, Robertson is generally relaxed throughout these interviews; his demeanor and delivery invariably tend to be deliberate, if not sluggish, and a series of detailed interpretations of The Band's history gradually emerges from the guitarist's confident storytelling. *Shine a Light* is instead propelled by the dynamism of its compositions and the vigorous movements of its principal subjects, Mick Jagger in particular, and though the archival segments are sometimes submerged in Richards's 1970s drug-induced inertia, images of Jagger's restlessness and shrewdness prevail in these periodic journeys through The Stones' past. Indeed, *Shine a Light* manages to release Jagger from the present-day dangers of self-parody (or bored self-imitation), but not by accommodating the singer's preferred portrayal as a renegade or reprobate; rather, the movie represents him as The Stones' prototypical professional (admittedly, another of Jagger's favored public personae), and he embodies this character in both the past and present-day sequences. Jagger's clearly irritated responses to questions about aging suggest an exasperation with journalists for misidentifying the actualities of his job as a musician, while the film's concentration on his energetic performances at the Beacon Theater positions his continuing work as a rebuke to these interviewers. Furthermore, *Shine a Light*'s accumulation of its archival footage persistently re-presents the group's—but especially Jagger's—notorious recalcitrance in the

1960s and early-1970s as a form of stubborn professionalism. In the late-1960s, The Stones knowingly cultivated an anti-utopian aura around their music and concerts, and in a much more significant way than The Band, they were the counterculture's most impassive popular musician-participants. *Gimme Shelter* captures the unanticipated, contradictory limit to The Stones' 1960s attitude, yet the film's penultimate image, a freeze-frame of Jagger's expressionless face, implies disorientation and perhaps an absence of self-understanding. In *Shine a Light*, by contrast, select archival interviews from this same period highlight a very different side of the singer. In each of these scenes, Jagger exemplifies a certain self-awareness, but this involves a recognition of his own status as a working, professional musician. In this way, the movie purposefully positions the young singer's sense of self-direction on a long continuum with the present-day professional on view, both onstage and offstage, and the totality of *Shine a Light*'s images ultimately presents Jagger as the epitome of self-realization.[51]

The film's descriptions of Keith Richards, on the other hand, adhere more closely to a predominant mythology about his indestructibility, and his archival interviews return repeatedly to incredulous questions from reporters about the guitarist's resilience. This particular footage, however, is interwoven with the Beacon Theater concert segments in a noticeably different way. Richards is, along with Charlie Watts, commonly regarded as The Stones' musical foundation, and *Shine a Light* appropriately acknowledges the guitarist's importance to the group; but his second moment in the spotlight as lead vocalist, a slovenly performance of "Connection," discloses how Scorsese's film implicitly sketches two conflicting modes of professional deportment. The performance is repeatedly fragmented by the interpolation of historical interviews with Richards, and these invariably focus on his reputation as a "survivor." Like the "Time Is on My Side" segment in *Let's Spend the Night Together* (Hal Ashby, 1983), *Shine a Light* cuts away from the Beacon Theater rendition of "Connection" to various images from the guitarist's history, but in this case, one suspects that such interruptions were intended to distract spectators from Richards's ragged singing and playing. Regardless, the scene's disconnection from other sequences in the film makes it meaningful: its calm passage between past and present unavoidably links Richards's history to the song's discordancy, yet as a result, it also effectively reconfirms the import of Jagger's more harmonious contemporary demeanor. Like *The Last Waltz*, *Shine a Light* indicates incompatible professional trajectories in its structuring of such scenes, but the film's perspective is clear from the beginning. Indeed, The Stones' earlier rendition of "Faraway Eyes" had inadvertently disclosed a similar dynamic. After the first chorus, Jagger abruptly walks over to Richards's microphone and discourages any further singing from the guitarist (he stumbles over lyrics and his voice is tuneless); the song does eventually feature the bandmates singing together, but their differentiation is palpable. Admittedly, Scorsese and his collaborators make some attempt to give equal screen time to all of The Stones, but *Shine a Light*, like most other films about the band, inevitably takes Jagger as its principal focus, and it foregrounds the singer's personification of control to an uncommon degree (Figure 2.16).

Aligning Jagger/Richards with Robertson/Helm is perhaps too easy, and in the final analysis, not entirely accurate; if Helm and Richards occupy comparably essential positions within their respective groups, Robbie Robertson is not The Band's Mick Jagger. And yet, although *The Last Waltz* and *Shine a Light* both depart from direct cinema orthodoxy in significant ways, they inevitably reiterate the hippie-era concert film's fundamental paradox: the rock concert's shared exhilaration is moderated by the rock star's individuated image of autonomy and control. Jagger and Richards's decades-long feud has established a prototype for intra-band quarreling, but since resuming their work as professional entertainers in 1989 with the "Steel Wheels" tour, they've made this antagonism a core component in their persistently expanding mythology. *Steel Wheels* (1989) followed an especially rancorous phase for the bandmates, yet the album's promotion and associated tour emphasized their

Figure 2.16 *Shine a Light* (Martin Scorsese, 2008).

impartiality and proficiency, and these key attributes have continued to define the band's documentary output ever since.⁵² *Shine a Light*'s method and themes reiterate these characteristics of The Stones' post-1970s cinematic image: it establishes a portrait of the group's professionalism and expertise, while at the same time highlighting Jagger as the exemplary expression of these virtues. The Rolling Stones, like so many other bands of its era, were eventually consumed by the rock concert's hypertrophy in the mid-1970s, but their permanency has unquestionably differentiated them from their contemporaries, and *Shine a Light* accordingly provides a cinematic commemoration of the group's durability. David E. James identifies *Ladies and Gentlemen: The Rolling Stones* (Rollin Binzer, 1974) as a pivotal artifact in the band's post-*Gimme Shelter* cinematic production because it decisively introduces their present-day image of professionalism.⁵³ Significantly, the group's return to documentary filmmaking necessitated the elimination of their audiences, and James outlines this gambit's effects on the subsequent films' representations. The social significance of The Stones' music is expelled, rerouted through the commodity nexus, and the film's "spectacularity […] makes] it a surrogate form of concert—and a repetition and extension of the concert's commodity function" (James 2016, 310). From *Let's Spend the Night Together* to *The Rolling Stones: Live at the Max* (Julien Temple, 1991) and *HAVANA MOON—The Rolling Stones Live in Cuba* (Paul Dugdale, 2016), The Stones' post-1970s documentary production has consistently served as a series of proficiently made supplements to their concerts, basically extending each tour's efficiency and economic purpose.

Scorsese's major concert documentaries are partly bound by this conundrum. *The Last Waltz* is a commemoration of The Band's farewell show *and* a reassessment of the hippie-era concert films' emphasis on the myth of communality, yet its refracted view of The Band's self-enclosed stage essentially forces it to exclude rock music's broader social meanings. As a consequence, it continually narrows its focus to Robbie Robertson's self-interested explanation of the concert's significance. *Shine a Light*, on the other hand, directly embraces The Rolling Stones' Beacon Theater concerts as expressions of cooperative control and professionalism, but the film nonetheless emphasizes Mick Jagger as the personification of such qualities.⁵⁴ Scorsese's ongoing documentary work often finds itself on this same contradictory terrain, especially when it dedicates itself to representations of popular music-making: these films, videos, and television productions adopt an admirably wide-ranging historiographic directive, yet at the same time they typically envision musicians' work in terms of individual autonomy and authenticity. In short, Scorsese's documentaries highlight solitary creators, even as they attempt to position these figures within significantly broader historical contexts. However, if the aristocratic atmosphere of post-Sixties rock music permitted *The Last Waltz* and *Shine a Light* to swiftly bracket the wider social world and instead promote various feats of self-realization, Scorsese's far-reaching studies of the blues, the early-1960s folk revival in America, and George Harrison's time as a member of The Beatles make the exclusion of popular music's social meanings much more difficult to maintain. In these cases, the films' unconditional commitment to individual artists is continually confronted by a vast collection of archival materials, and the filmmakers' need to reassemble these materials within their new documentary frameworks forces different strata of the historical past to more fully permeate the films' stories. This is evident as Scorsese and his collaborators return incessantly to the Sixties and its well-known signposts, but it is especially true when the director turns his attention to his most challenging documentary subject in *No Direction Home: Bob Dylan* (2005).

3

Archival Expeditions: *Feel Like Going Home* and *No Direction Home: Bob Dylan*

Archival Returns: The Ritual of Origins

Chronicles: Volume One (2004), the first in a proposed series of memoirs by Bob Dylan, scarcely resembles the standard rock star autobiography. Not a chronological account of the musician's incomparable life, or a routine tale of professional successes and failures, Dylan's book seeks instead to explain the earliest development of his songwriting and its subsequent adherence to what Sean Wilentz rightly calls a "timeless yet deeply American template" (2010, 297).[1] Indeed, in his excellent *Bob Dylan in America* (2010), Wilentz characterizes *Chronicles* as a non-fiction *bildungsroman*: it depicts the youthful Dylan's first arrival in New York City, his immediate introduction to the principles of folk songcraft and performance, and his discovery of various forms for his imminent work. More intriguingly, however, *Chronicles* also periodically depicts the musician as a fledgling historian, and some of the book's most surprising disclosures come with Dylan's plainspoken descriptions of his continuous immersion in works of history. In an often-quoted passage, one wherein the roots of his longstanding preoccupation with the past are ostensibly unearthed for readers, Dylan remembers his regular excursions to the New York Public Library throughout his scuffling period as a folk singer in the early-1960s. Foraging through the Library's extensive archives, he would re-inhabit different incidents from America's Civil War while simultaneously speculating about their uncanny resemblance to his present-day moment. Wilentz, a professional historian, admits to feeling "mildly thrill[ed]" at learning "that Dylan discovered the cuneiforms of his art in the microfilm room" (2010, 301), yet the songwriter's informal research remained mostly directionless during this period. Uncertain about the broader purpose or significance of his collection of historical minutiae, Dylan confesses to simply stockpiling it for future reference. Accumulated in his mind as fragments, impressions, and memories, this material would be "locked away" and "left alone" until needed: "Figured I could send a truck back for it later" (Dylan 2004, 86).

Chronicles: Volume One, Greil Marcus observes, "is the truck" (2010, 339), although it is perhaps best viewed as only *one* of many such trucks: Dylan's ongoing effort to retrieve and repurpose these stored remnants has provided "the all-encompassing template" for his lifelong work as a songwriter and performer (Dylan 2004, 86).[2] *Chronicles'* investigation of the artist's self-invention and succeeding reinventions is in some ways the culmination to Dylan's continuous retracing of his original archival expeditions, yet throughout the early-2000s he was immersed in a wide-ranging return to America's vernacular music, stories, and historical events. His renewed concentration on folk processes during this period, already evident in his personal selections for *Good As I Been to You* (1992) and *World Gone Wrong* (1993), resulted in the late-career renaissance of *"Love and Theft"* (2001) and *Modern Times* (2006), recordings and music distinguished by their allusiveness and covert assessments of America's histories. But this overriding sense of retrospection also encompassed the steady release of Dylan's multi-volume *The Bootleg Series* (1991–present), an apparently inexhaustible—if occasionally exhausting—accumulation of previously unavailable archival materials (demos, outtakes, alternate takes, and live renditions of familiar songs), and the always resourceful *Theme Time Radio Hour with Your Host Bob Dylan* (2006–9), a satellite program with Dylan-as-host sharing his favorite music, recollections, and an assortment of other ephemera.[3] In each case, the ongoing effort to create new connections between the past and present has clearly underwritten Dylan's diverse work as both a songwriter and performer. When seen in this particular light, the entirety of his present-day production can look like a never-ending tour of archeological sites.[4]

Scorsese's *No Direction Home: Bob Dylan* (2005) was initially conceived by Dylan's longtime manager and principal archivist, Jeff Rosen, in a similar spirit of historical reckoning, but it was also clearly envisioned as an audiovisual memorial to the songwriter's most influential period, 1962–6. As a consequence, it digs methodically through vast archival possessions, and like Dylan's interviews and recollections throughout the film, it reassembles these primary materials to demonstrate how the lived time of a practically mythical "Sixties" was continually interrupted by the musician's unparalleled experiences during this period. Another commissioned assignment for Scorsese,[5] *No Direction*

Home's origins seem to imply a relatively limited degree of involvement for the director, but the film's close affiliation with his present-day commitment to preservation and commemoration is unmistakable. Indeed, its exhaustive archival excavation confirms a significant modification in Scorsese's documentary film practice: the collage-like assemblage of historical resources has increasingly come to define the director's non-fiction productions since *Feel Like Going Home*, his contribution to PBS's *Martin Scorsese Presents: The Blues* (2003), and *No Direction Home* exemplifies this change in approach. Such a refinement in Scorsese's documentary output has undoubtedly been bolstered by the global expansion of a preservationist and archival culture today, yet these fundamental adjustments to his methods also have an internal rationale, namely, the editorial and pedagogical determination to recollect and safeguard the numerous histories of cinema and popular music.[6] *Italianamerican* (1974) and *American Boy: A Profile of Steven Prince* (1978) had also sought to preserve the receding past, and their approaches were definitively formed by the ethnic revival's predominant idiom of reclamation; but these two films highlighted a meaningful interaction between their present-day subjects and the filmmaker/camera in order to render an oral history of migration to America. *The Last Waltz* (1978) was equally dedicated to commemorating the past. In this case, however, Scorsese's self-conscious, critical reappraisal of his direct cinema and concert documentary inheritance ensured an analogous attentiveness to the subject/camera nexus in his film's examination of The Band's distinguished history. The director's contemporary non-fiction films and television productions continue to articulate their relationship with the past in this same idiom of recovery, but like Dylan's spatial transcription of his many archival excursions throughout the early-1960s, these works are primarily vehicles for retrieving assorted documents and resituating them in novel interpretations of otherwise familiar histories.

Scorsese's preoccupation with the history of popular music has strong generational overtones, of course—like so many other baby boomers, his imaginative life has been built on a firm foundation of rock music.[7] Admittedly, the director's cinephilia also takes the baby boomers' Sixties as its primary coordinate, insofar as Andrew Sarris's so-called "auteur theory" (the decade's emblematic—and controversial—development in American film criticism) and a contemporaneous valorization of European "art cinema" establish the benchmarks for his ongoing work in film preservation and presentation;[8] but Scorsese's documentaries on popular music do more than simply salvage and catalogue titles and names, and his generational stake in rock's social meanings is vital to understanding how these films and television productions direct viewers into worlds where musicians and listeners create what Robert Cantwell has in a different context called a "ritual of origins" (2008, 12). Whether the filmmaker and his close collaborators are investigating the Mississippi Delta blues' beginnings in West Africa, Bob Dylan's combative relationship with the 1960s folk revival and his expanding "rock" audience, or George Harrison's meandering professional and personal lives after The Beatles' dissolution, Scorsese's perspective is still fastened to his generation's foundational belief in rock music's unruly, though admittedly obscure potential to re-root its listeners. *The Last Waltz*'s nostalgic recapitulation of the "end of an era," we should recall, had been split between a lingering investment in rock music's unmanageable, utopian possibilities and a more somber reassessment of the latter's dwindling post-Woodstock prospects, while *Italianamerican* and *American Boy: A Profile of Steven Prince*'s oral histories were implicitly separated by this same generational viewpoint. When seen together, however, Scorsese's 1970s documentaries reveal an unexpectedly bleak conclusion for the director's baby boomer cohort. In *Italianamerican* and *American Boy*, a generational divide is finally registered in terms of Scorsese's relation to his immigrant family's story of arrival, adjustment, and modest achievement in the new world. The director listens—and observes—attentively as his mother and father speak about their families, their work, and ordinary accomplishments, yet he is evidently aware of the particular prerogatives of his education and vocation: the filmmaker's present-day success is implicitly situated as the legacy of his immigrant family's humble American striving, and the weight of succeeding his parents is recorded as an unsettled historical obligation. *American Boy*, by contrast, sketches a much more intractable story of deflation and destruction, but once again Scorsese's specific position within this scenario is significant: the entertainment industries, and the world of rock music in particular, offer abundant possibilities and snares, yet the generational imperative ultimately separates this experience from *Italianamerican*'s encouraging descriptions of the past. If *The Last Waltz* combines these perspectives by documenting The Band's nostalgia while at the same time projecting an indeterminate future for the group and their Sixties cohort, it nevertheless reaffirms popular music's significance as a cultural text and authenticates the baby boomer generation's desire to reroute its consciousness through these collectively made sounds.

Scorsese's current music documentaries take a different approach in their rendering of historical accounts. The baby boomer's formative experience of Sixties rock music continues to organize the films' general perspective, but *Feel Like Going Home* and *No Direction Home* both emphasize the folkloric and vernacular "roots" of rock music, what the director repeatedly calls "the music *behind* our music" (Scorsese 2003a, 6; emphasis in original), and the films' "ritual of origins" accordingly involves transporting evidence of a deep blues and folksong ecology to the new frameworks of their respective narratives. *Feel Like Going Home* returns to the Mississippi Delta and Africa for an examination of the blues as modern revolution and ancient folklore, and the film's formal disclosure of the Delta blues' underpinnings is realized through an architectural repositioning of its images and sounds within a broader synoptic design. Envisioned in part as an enthusiast's compendium of archival materials, *Feel Like Going Home* unequivocally accepts the folklorist's mandate and methods in order to unearth and exhibit its novel discoveries to viewers: a living past is ostensibly preserved in the Delta blues, and the film is presented as an audiovisual steward for these important cultural artifacts. *No Direction Home*, Scorsese's most wide-ranging documentary compilation about popular music, resumes the collector's task in its investigation of Bob Dylan's Sixties, but this addition to PBS's long-running *American Masters* series insistently interferes with one's customary understanding of the period by filtering its recognizable signposts through Dylan's unprecedented experiences. In this respect, editing is an elemental device for transporting and recombining resources in *Feel Like Going Home* and *No Direction Home*, and as we'll see, the compilation approach establishes a counterpart to the collection of records. *George Harrison: Living in the Material World* (2011), on the other hand, begins at the pinnacle of Sixties rock and youth culture, and although its story inevitably intersects with America's idiomatic or roots music, this lengthy documentary is dedicated to sifting the collective experience of post-Sixties disorientation through George Harrison's detached and composed consciousness. In other words, the film's archival journey is redirected in order to grasp rock music's historical past *and* potential permanence. Whereas *The Last Waltz* seemed to exclude The Band and their Sixties generation from the future, *Living in the Material World* imparts a broader historical significance to its chronicle of Harrison's calm course through this same turbulent period. Although the film appears to be somewhat misaligned with Scorsese's preceding documentaries about vernacular American music, it nonetheless clarifies a significant feature of their approach: an individualist emphasis continually risks hagiography in these works, yet *Living in the Material World* discloses the films' common purpose in re-rooting their cultural histories in the ground of spiritual biography. As we'll see, *Feel Like Going Home*, *No Direction Home*, and *Living in the Material World* all have to deal in their own ways with the overabundance of mass mediated images, sounds, and representations of the mythical "Sixties," but like Dylan's topographic representation of his many archival returns in *Chronicles*, these non-fiction vehicles reintroduce the past to spectators by reassembling their formerly fragmented historical resources into new totalities.

Long Distance Call: Retrieval and Revival in *Feel Like Going Home*

Although Scorsese's documentary filmmaking practice entered a long period of dormancy after *The Last Waltz*, something of his experience working with The Band clearly remained with him throughout the succeeding years. In addition to his collaborations with Robbie Robertson on the soundtracks to *Raging Bull* (1980), *The King of Comedy* (1983), and *The Color of Money* (1986), Scorsese's film-related activities in the 1980s preserved the defining features of The Band's conflicted historical perspective. Always self-consciously nostalgic, yet at the same time apprehensive about both the present and future, The Band's original music and public presentations merged "a consideration of the old" with what the period's critics consistently called a "disenchantment" with the present: "What The Band has worked out is something that countless other Americans hope for, a sort of watchful, self-protective truce within an encroaching world of noisy commerce."[9] In the years directly preceding Scorsese's *The Last Waltz* and The Band's attendant dissolution, however, the group's previously productive nostalgia seemed to have reached a dead end. Their breakthrough records, *Music from Big Pink* (1968) and *The Band* (1969), were soon followed by the slighter, though still resourceful *Stage Fright* (1970) and the unexpectedly malformed—and impassively received—*Cahoots* (1971), but the group's distinguished ability to balance their world-weariness with a vision of the past's enduring usefulness suddenly appeared seriously diminished. Indeed, *Cahoots'* critical failure prompted The Band to entrench themselves more deeply in their own history. The live double album *Rock of Ages* (1972) was conceived as an expansive summary of the group's significant recent accomplishments, but its status as self-testament would establish an unfortunate template for the future.[10] *Moondog Matinee* (1973), a collection of select cover songs from the group's apprenticeship as The Hawks, similarly commemorated The Band's past achievements, yet a lingering impression of retrenchment overshadowed the forcefulness of Richard Manuel's "Share Your Love" and the expertise of Levon Helm's "Promised Land" and "Mystery Train." *Northern Lights—Southern Cross* (1975) resuscitated *Stage Fright*'s efficiency and greater sense of purpose, but it would be the original lineup's final record of completely new material—the indifferent *Islands* (1977), mainly an "odds and sods" compilation, simply fulfilled a contractual requirement for Capitol Records. *The Last Waltz* (soundtrack and film) managed to surpass the prevailing retrospection of The Band's post-*Cahoots* career, and it definitively realized the emergent commemorative purpose of *Rock of Ages* and *Moondog Matinee*. Its termination of the group's history, however, would also paradoxically foreclose their future. If The Band's best music was sometimes plagued with an uncertainty about the present *and* future, *The Last Waltz* resolved this particular predicament by permanently fixing the group's existence in the past, thereby providing another rationale for the songs' nostalgic tenor as well as a ready justification for Robertson's attempts to retrofit rock's brief history to his developing aspirations as a solo artist.

Scorsese's concurrent first endeavors in film preservation were articulated with a comparable sense of apprehension about the present and future. "Everything we're doing now means nothing," he announced a mere two years after *The Last Waltz*'s initial release, and his subsequent public campaigns to expose the hazards of fading color film stock were undertaken with an educator's dedication: *Raging Bull*'s release in the Fall of 1980 and its appearances at film festivals were followed by a series of lectures/presentations by the director, each describing the quickly deteriorating condition of selected archival prints. The "threat" of prolonged neglect, he argued, was nothing less than the complete eradication of a cultural "heritage" and cinematic history, while an indifference to the significance of this common inheritance would conclusively foreclose film's future.[11] These efforts at film preservation and restoration have continued to the present day, and Scorsese's proper name has now become a vernacular sign for cinephilia, film-related collections, and a deferential attachment to the histories of cinema. Throughout the early-1980s, however, the preservationist program may have also served a more pragmatic purpose for the director. Initiated during a period of intensifying institutional insecurity for holdovers from Hollywood's late-1960s Renaissance, Scorsese's high-profile crusade for film preservation could hypothetically underwrite the value of his historically informed fiction films, and this new and urgent undertaking seemed to supplant—at least temporarily—the historiographic directives of his 1970s documentary production. In other words, a concentration on disintegrating archival holdings narrowed and redirected Scorsese's documentary commitments to the restoration of *film history* during this period, but the insistent emphasis on "dire need" and "crisis" had the potential additional benefit of substantiating his fiction filmmaking as it encountered the new uncertainties of 1980s Hollywood.[12] Regardless, although *The Last Waltz*'s rendition of its historical chronicle had conclusively embalmed The Band's accomplishments in color images, Scorsese's campaigns for film preservation throughout the 1980s disclosed the medium's *vulnerability* and connected it to a somewhat different question about the past's potential *impermanence*. As a consequence, the documentaries' familiar theme of restitution was transferred to a closely related undertaking: the director's approach to the mounting difficulties of film preservation extended the historiographic emphases of *Italianamerican, American Boy: A Profile of Steven Prince*, and *The Last Waltz* into a novel domain, while also implicitly interrogating their despairing vision of generational succession. The documentaries' underlying restorative energy was easily retained in this scenario, but it was increasingly combined with the pedagogical resolve of Scorsese's first lectures and presentations about fading color film stock, and the result was a systematically readjusted attention to assorted archival resources and their importance to understanding both the past *and* future.

Formally established in 1990 to fulfill the mandate of Scorsese's first lectures, The Film Foundation provided an institutional and financial framework for the director's commitment to film preservation and restoration. Indeed, its website reveals a number of pedagogical objectives derived from the "dire need" scenario. Users can navigate easily between pages that describe The Foundation's formation and mission statement, its past achievements and ongoing activities, and its indispensable World Cinema Project; there are also some video testimonials from an assortment of filmmakers about the benefits of film preservation, and acknowledgments of Scorsese's pivotal position as The Foundation's founder and chair; additional links permit one to experience exactly how The Foundation envisions a film appreciation curriculum for students across America.[13] The Film Foundation's principal focus on resuscitating stored—and previously disregarded—archival materials, along with its directly articulated commitment to education, would definitively modify the idiom of retrieval that had defined Scorsese's documentary making throughout the 1970s. As we've seen, *Italianamerican* and *American Boy: A Profile of Steven Prince* were made within the broader cultural context of the 1970s ethnic revival, and they modestly attended to an oral history of immigration and the recovery of such experiences; but as a consequence, these two films used archival materials sparingly. By contrast, the revitalization of Scorsese's documentary practice in 1995 immediately produced a counterpart to The Film Foundation's approach to maintaining and restoring archival objects, and its focus on a pedagogical mission also determined the new films' procedures for compilation. *A Personal Journey with Martin Scorsese Through American Movies* (co-directed with Michael Henry Wilson, 1995) was the original—and perhaps most obvious—manifestation of this shift in approach, but the director's concurrent work as executive producer on PBS's *Eric Clapton: Nothing but the Blues* (1995) provided another important prototype for his subsequent documentaries about popular music. Its accumulation of archival performances by seminal blues artists such as Muddy Waters, Howlin' Wolf, Bukka White, Big Bill Broonzy, and several others was clearly intended to complement Eric Clapton's proselytizing, and the formal disclosure of the blues' living past in a series of contemporary performances by Clapton would establish a flexible model for Scorsese's forthcoming work. In this respect, although *Feel Like Going Home* and *No Direction Home* undoubtedly share a philosophical connection with The Film Foundation's founding mission, they also build upon previous productions like *Eric Clapton: Nothing but the Blues* and *A Personal Journey*.

Initially broadcast by PBS in October 2003, *Martin Scorsese Presents: The Blues* was positioned as the culmination to America's celebratory "Year of the Blues," and its purview was significantly broader than the comparatively promotional *Eric Clapton: Nothing but the Blues*.[14] *The Blues*' commemorative commitments were consistent with The Film Foundation's main foci—even a cursory examination of *The Blues*' supplemental website confirms its parallel emphasis on preservation, instruction, history, and cultural stewardship.[15] But Ken Burns's *Jazz* (2001), an expansive ten-part PBS documentary about the history of jazz in America, provides a more proximate example for *The Blues*' efforts to combine comprehensiveness with its intensive studies of individual players. Like all of Burns's non-fiction work for PBS, *The Blues* integrates diverse archival resources, and like *Jazz*, its interpretation of history often privileges the critical contributions of distinctive personalities. Burns's

Jazz, however, offers a chronological account of its subject, delineating the form's "birth" in New Orleans, its pinnacle in the work of familiar figures like Louis Armstrong and Duke Ellington, and—controversially—its purported decline in the early-1960s. The series' consistency and scope are determined by the guiding perspectives of Burns and his collaborators, Geoffrey C. Ward (writer), Lynn Novick (co-producer), and Wynton Marsalis (senior creative consultant and principal onscreen interview subject). Accordingly, jazz is understood as prototypically "American" music; it originates in the nation's biggest cities, and ultimately develops as a form of "improvisation" which the program recommends as an authentic expression of participatory democracy. *Martin Scorsese Presents: The Blues*, on the other hand, is composed of seven discrete episodes made by different directors, and the result is a collection of individualized, impressionistic visions of the blues and its history.[16] In this regard, *The Blues* attempts, with varying degrees of success in each episode, to circumvent *Jazz*'s more noticeable shortcomings: its dismissal of avant-garde jazz and the attendant omission of several influential post-1960s, that is to say, "contemporary" figures; its prevailing sense of gravity and formality; an overly conservative emphasis on "swing" in its definition of jazz; and the recurrent recourse to sentimental biography as historical interpretation. Simply put, Ken Burns's *Jazz*, purposefully committed to the period preceding jazz's modernist, experimental departures in the early-1960s, is often nostalgic and traditionalist. Despite its evangelizing for the enduring importance of this quintessentially American invention, the program seems to confine jazz wholly to the past. By contrast, *The Blues*' multi-authored composition encourages all seven of its directors to highlight distinctive connections between the blues' past *and* present, and each episode works in its own way to confirm the persistent value of the blues as living history.[17]

Feel Like Going Home, *The Blues*' opening episode and Scorsese's lone contribution as director, is especially preoccupied with reinforcing this relationship between past and present, and like his concurrent work for The Film Foundation, this documentary seeks to establish the long-lasting significance of assorted historical artifacts. *Feel Like Going Home* follows blues musician Corey Harris as he travels first to the Mississippi Delta and then Mali, West Africa, to re-experience the foundations and meaning of the blues. Named after Muddy Waters's "Feel Like Going Home,"[18] the film's title seems to indicate a longing for the familiar ("going home"), thereby implying a form of recuperative nostalgia; but Harris instead offers a sustained, archeological focus on the blues' lengthy history, and he deploys his considerable knowledge to demonstrate this music's enduring significance—"going home" in this case means reassessing a vital past. Indeed, Harris proves to be an especially appropriate selection as *Feel Like Going Home*'s main onscreen representative. His contemporaneous record-making features a thorough, scholarly immersion in the Delta blues idiom, but also a willingness to extend its influence to the present day. *Fish Ain't Bitin'* (1997), *Greens from the Garden* (1999), and *Downhome Sophisticate* (2002) all reveal the breadth of Harris's knowledge and proficiency. These recordings include comprehensive ventures into country or "folk" blues, electric blues, ragtime, reggae, New Orleans rhythm and blues, and numerous other genres, but the music's preponderant direction is determined by Harris's flexible treatment of the Delta blues vernacular. Recalling the work of influential 1960s and 1970s blues revivalists like Taj Mahal (who speaks and performs with Harris in *Feel Like Going Home*) and Ry Cooder, Harris brings a folklorist's knowledge to his performances of traditional songs, yet these tunes are customarily situated alongside his own contemporary blues compositions, the latter always working to deepen the scope and definition of "traditional songs" and establish their present-day connections. The temporal remoteness and "found" quality of "public domain" music are accordingly modified for a new and different purpose. In this important respect, Harris's practically constant presence in *Feel Like Going Home* solves a longstanding documentary challenge: how can non-fiction films fasten their spectators to an onscreen surrogate without denying the integrity of the world on view? That is to say, how can a documentary invest itself completely in this profilmic delegate without appearing to abandon its own obligation to the world and its subjects? For the producers of *Feel Like Going Home*, acquiescing to Harris's central role as guide admits viewers into the Mississippi Delta and its blues music, but it also implicitly acknowledges the high stakes in such documentary surrogacy, particularly as the film journeys through America's deep south, exploring its blues traditions and the region's inescapable record of racism (Figure 3.1). As a result, Harris is more than just another custodian for the Delta blues' immeasurable folklore. His skillful renewal of the blues' well-worn themes and sounds is complemented by his clear suitability for *Feel Like Going Home*'s principal commission: his onscreen work invariably establishes how—and what—the blues signified in own its time, and his scholarly attention can clarify its ongoing modern-day pertinence.

In *Nothing but the Blues*, by contrast, Eric Clapton is characterized as an experienced guardian for blues purism. Interview segments with influential

Figure 3.1 *Feel Like Going Home* (Martin Scorsese, 2003).

blues artists such as B.B. King, Buddy Guy, and Jimmy Rogers substantiate Clapton's standing as a worthy successor to the blues tradition; as a guitarist, he is continually positioned as the very embodiment of post-Sixties blues revivalism, and his distance (geographical, temporal, cultural) from the Delta blues is only attended to briefly. *Nothing but the Blues*' abundant present-day live performances by Clapton are therefore designed to confirm this music's lasting relevance and establish the guitar player's permanent purpose as a champion for the blues legacy. Clapton's undeniably proficient guitar soloing, however, only occasionally distracts from his limitations as a blues vocalist throughout these sequences. The discordance between his guitar playing and singing indicates a certain remoteness from the blues' central material components, and Clapton's otherwise irreproachable assessment of these acknowledged classics risks reducing them to mere "repertoire." Not entirely unlike Ken Burns's *Jazz*, in this respect, the result can appear museum-like, ahistorical: the blues as intellectual ideal rather than historical reality. Similarly, Clapton's interviews return too often to his personal biography, which he connects to the legend of bluesman Robert Johnson. At these moments, his desire to share in the profoundly moral quality in blues music's suffering becomes clear, and he finally implies an untenable equivalency between his past and the blues' much wider social predicaments.[19]

Deep Blues: A Musical Pilgrimage to the Crossroads (Robert Mugge, 1992) is an important predecessor to both *Eric Clapton: Nothing but the Blues* and *Feel Like Going Home*, and it provides several instructive insights into the matter of onscreen surrogacy. Robert Palmer, a musician and distinguished scholar and historian of America's vernacular music, serves as an exceptional guide through north Mississippi, its distinctive landscapes, economy, juke joints, and blues music—the breadth of his musicological and cultural knowledge is obvious throughout the film. Palmer's indispensable text, *Deep Blues* (1981), is the filmmakers' main source of information, and his extensive critical writing about the blues structures the film's perception of Mississippi's music and history.[20] Accordingly, his work lends a specialist quality to the film, but it also tacitly authorizes the filmmakers' titular "pilgrimage" through northern Mississippi and entry into the region's juke joints and African American domestic spaces: Palmer's convivial demeanor with interview subjects alleviates the film's inescapable sense of intrusiveness. Unfortunately, Dave Stewart's intermittent appearances are misguided by comparison, and his accidental interloping eventually disfigures several sequences in *Deep Blues*. Looking like an adventurer or sightseeing white rock star, and far too detached to make a meaningful contribution to the documentary task, Stewart's sequences disclose several potential deficiencies in the film's attempt to produce a documentary experience of the Mississippi blues through this intercessor.[21] Indeed, his palpable disconnection from the world on view inadvertently conjures the lengthy history of white cultural mediators in America's deep south, and more specifically, the music business intermediaries who first made these expeditions to accumulate—and market—the blues in the first half of the twentieth century. Scorsese, on the other hand, forthrightly admits to having started *Feel Like Going Home* from a position of "pure ignorance" (Jarmusch 2017, 194), and as I've indicated, his film's unassuming deference to Harris's onscreen work should be seen as an attempt to avoid the inherent challenges of utilizing a surrogate in these particular circumstances. In a noticeably different way than *Nothing but the Blues* and *Deep Blues*, *Feel Like Going Home*'s principal aim is to sketch a relationship between the blues' past, present, and future, and Harris's wide-ranging immersion in the blues idiom as an *historical form* convincingly underwrites the film's weaving of archival materials and present-day sequences. Simply put, the sincerity of his blues explorations carries *Feel Like Going Home* on its own two-way route between the Mississippi Delta and West Africa.[22]

The film's prologue immediately establishes a framework for Harris's self-described "journey," but it also introduces several narrow parameters for *Feel Like Going Home*'s efforts to amalgamate archival images and sounds with its present-day sequences. Accompanied only by a black screen, Scorsese's voice-over calmly introduces the film with a few devotional words about music and its fundamental, elevated purpose—it is "like a light in the darkness that never goes out," he says. The following fade-in unexpectedly transports spectators deep into America's historical south. In a series of four black-and-white images, we witness an energetic performance of "Oree" by Ed, Lonnie, and G.D. Young, led entirely by fife and drums; set outdoors and in the sunlight, these film fragments rapidly reveal a ritualistic quality to match the tenor of Scorsese's solemn introductory remarks. Indeed, the drums' deliberate marching rhythm and a repetitive fife figure both appear to inspire progressively expressive movements from each of these individuals. They swing and squat at different moments as they stride toward the camera, and just before the segment's conclusion, the fife player suddenly genuflects before both drummers, raises his hands above his head, and slowly removes his hat, definitively confirming the ceremonial component in this group's brief performance.

The succeeding lap dissolve to a traveling color shot of some unidentified, ostensibly timeless territory (mist covered water, a drove of flying birds, tree-lined coast, yet no indication of human presence) appears to designate a momentary modification to the film's immersion in a distinctive southern past; but Harris's voice-over, first heard during the measured dissolve from "Oree" to these images, continues to characterize the blues in familiar genealogical terms—"the blues," he observes, "takes you back to the place where it first came to life" (Figure 3.2).²³ If the represented environment initially seems "timeless,"

Figure 3.2 *Feel Like Going Home* (Martin Scorsese, 2003).

Harris's words nonetheless assure viewers that the film's endeavor remains steadfastly focused on "origins," the beginnings of time *and* the blues' history (Figure 3.3). The subsequent reappearance of black-and-white archival images, in this particular case, footage of anonymous black manual laborers (an "axe gang") as they chop trees, immediately reconfirms *Feel Like Going Home*'s historical emphases, while the sounds of Lightning and Group's "Long John" (its chanted lyrics transcribed in title cards) establish an elaboration of the film's earlier "Oree" segment's methods. Several more extracts from work songs, field hollers, and spirituals promptly follow, and they too are accompanied by closely related archival images of plantation laborers, ditch diggers, and cotton pickers. When Scorsese's voice-over finally returns, he briefly explains how all of these audio recordings were made by John Lomax and his son Alan on their numerous expeditions as self-described "ballad hunters" during the 1930s and 1940s. Indeed, the director characterizes John Lomax as a prototypical preservationist, and supplements his account with representative scenes from the Lomaxes innumerable excursions as song hunters: folksinger Woody Guthrie is seen for a moment in one fragment, while the remaining views quickly outline predominantly rural settings for the Lomaxes field work. Scorsese extols the resulting Library of Congress recordings for having "preserv[ed] the past before it disappeared," and *Feel Like Going Home*'s determination to closely align its own objectives with the Lomaxes lifelong enterprise is unmistakable (Figure 3.4).[24]

Figure 3.3 *Feel Like Going Home* (Martin Scorsese, 2003).

Figure 3.4 *Feel Like Going Home* (Martin Scorsese, 2003).

In less than six minutes, *Feel Like Going Home*'s prologue subtly specifies its approach to reassembling the blues' historical realities. The film's immersion in distinctive layers of time, or rather, its absorption in assorted temporalities, will bring the blues' past and present together in a persistent reciprocal exchange: the passage between different periods (and different places) is the film's principal emphasis, and the overriding preoccupation with the blues' significance is directed to these diverse historical materials. The prologue's concluding moments are especially representative, in this respect. After an excerpt from his live rendition of Blind Willie Johnson's "Dark Was the Night, Cold Was the Ground," Harris's voice-over calmly clarifies how he first learned to play the blues, and was then drawn to the past and his connection with "ancestors" and their common "history." As he recounts his discovery to viewers, black-and-white images show Harris walking in Africa, not America, his guitar at his side or momentarily suspended over his shoulder, and his voice-over explains how his growing expertise in playing the blues disclosed a route to the past, a way to understand his distant roots. The blues, he maintains, promises both its players and listeners nothing less than deliverance: consciousness is possible only if one discerns the past; but every song contributes to this knowledge, and as a result, they all open new paths to the future. John Lee Hooker's unhurried, stomping "Worried Life Blues" closes the prologue on an archetypal note of bluesy apprehensiveness, yet *Feel Like Going Home*'s editing reaffirms the importance of Harris's emphasis upon this music's transport between historical times. Hooker's deliberate country blues is attended by rapidly alternating images of the present and past: Harris driving an automobile in the Mississippi Delta; fleeting archival images, black-and-white traveling shots of practically identical roads; present-day views of Mississippi's landscape; corresponding archival vistas of the same region, and so on. For *Feel Like Going Home*, this successive interweaving of contemporary images with remote historical materials is crucial to fully understanding what Hooker's blues signifies: the film's editing details how the sounds of his voice, guitar playing, and stamping foot resonate with both the Delta's past *and* present. The prologue's combination of various speaking voices (Scorsese and Harris's voice-overs, but other accents can also be heard in the background) had already presented the possibilities of corresponding components, but the pervasive reverberations of singing, chanting, drums, and other instruments in the film, often appearing ahead of images and fastened to unidentified times and spaces, solicit a particular kind of concentration from viewers, compelling them to contemplate and associate different temporal strata. Indeed, the stratification of archival and present-day images is one of *Feel Like Going Home*'s elemental features, and its deliberate deployment during the introduction immediately alerts viewers to the film's purpose in rapidly editing together diverse historical temporalities. A vehicle for examining the possibilities of such journeys through time, *Feel Like Going Home*'s constant cuts from historical views to seemingly unrelated contemporary scenes decisively shape one's experience of the blues as distant folklore and an ongoing concern.

In *Doing Time: Temporality, Hermeneutics, and Contemporary Cinema* (2016), Lee Carruthers characterizes these kinds of "temporal events" (13) as the substance of film viewing. "Time," she observes, is "actively mediated by films" (16); that is to say, the cinema continually creates time-based structures, and as a consequence, spectatorship is conditioned by the effort to assess and interpret a particular film's temporal complications. Carruthers's reading is dedicated exclusively to fiction filmmaking, yet her numerous analyses of "montage system[s]" (127) and their intermingling of times have a broader applicability—they can be usefully extended to include documentary films. The accumulation of archival materials is contingent upon editing, of course, and Scorsese's current films and television productions about popular music have depended upon methods of compilation to disclose their perspectives on the historical past. As we've already seen, *Feel Like Going Home*'s prologue shapes a very specific experience of time, and the film's subsequent sequences deepen this sense of perpetual exchange between the blues' past and present.

Carruthers underscores hermeneutics in her descriptions of film viewing, reminding her readers that making meaning is a core element in the cinematic experience. Scorsese, on the other hand, typically highlights a strategically unformulated conception—"the emotions"—when discussing his documentary filmmaking and its primary foci, and this appears to suggest a direct path to understanding.[25] His terms, however, describe a comparable commitment to interpretation: the director's documentaries about popular music customarily *interpret* their historical resources, but they also ask viewers to derive meaning from the purposeful assemblage of images and sounds. In the final analysis, the continuous process of deciphering these manifold temporalities produces a form of historical comprehension.[26]

According to Robert Cantwell, "vernacular musics" like the blues remain "very rich and powerful bearer[s] of meaning," but the "recovery" of such meaning requires the critical work of hermeneutics—interpretation is what permits one to understand this music's social and historical development (2008, 3–4). "Music," he argues, "is profoundly and unshakably situated, socially, culturally, and historically," and the blues' "affective force, though not strictly semantic or even semiotic, arises out of the very patterning of its own material carriers that sound at once mimetically absorbs and discharges" (2008, 7). *Feel Like Going Home* emphasizes the blues' discordant reverberations, its metronomic rhythms and cadences, and the concreteness of its pitch and modalities because these designate a wider historical reality, and the film's editing guides viewers into this actuality, asking them to make inferences about people, their existence, experiences, and so on. Like editing, music is "an organization of time" (Cantwell 2008, 9), and both editing and music can discern the phenomenality of temporal experience, particularly in its connections to the historical past. In *Feel Like Going Home*'s most representative sequences, one perceives the blues in terms of what it produces (sounds, songs, consciousness), but also as the product of broader historical factors. The film's introduction of Muddy Waters, for example, outlines the full implications of the blues' charged journey from the Mississippi Delta to assorted northern urban/industrial centers in Illinois, Michigan, and Indiana. In a quickly cut sequence of images, spectators are first transported to the Stovall plantation and a verbal account of Waters's historic meetings with Alan Lomax (the "epicenter of a musical revolution," Taj Mahal says), but the film then begins to travel freely between the past and present. One watches—and listens—as Taj Mahal and Corey Harris roam slowly through the present-day Stovall ruins, detailing Waters's original field recordings and his eventual worldwide impact, while a concurrent panoramic view of the farm shifts suddenly to black-and-white and then back to color in a single movement. They play a few bars of Taj Mahal's "Catfish Blues," a close descendant of Waters's "Rollin' Stone," and promptly defer to the film's audiovisual translation of the blues' journeys from the Delta to Chicago.[27] A progression of dissolves and abrupt cuts situates the sounds of Waters's definitive recording of "Rollin' Stone" (1950) alongside assorted images of train treks from Mississippi to Chicago's southside; it then shifts suddenly to his celebrated performance of the same song (with slightly modified lyrics, instrumentation, and arrangement) at the Newport Jazz Festival in 1960 and ends with a brief extract from Waters's memorable appearance in Scorsese's *The Last Waltz*. In this way, *Feel Like Going Home* presents Waters as the personification of the blues' historic relocation to Chicago, yet the film's methodical editing both incorporates and releases the *meaning* of his music's long journey from America's parochial south to an urban modernity.

Indeed, the resourcefully structured Waters sequence specifies a very particular moment in the blues' historical past. The charged migration from Mississippi to Chicago is a foundational event in blues folklore, of course, and *Feel Like Going Home* summarizes this northward movement in a set of propulsive images, directing viewers to comprehend how this music's forms and sounds integrated *and* discharged the significance of such journeys. Harris's voice-over briefly describes the primary impetus for Waters's decisive departure from the Stovall plantation in 1943 (he had received his first recording in the mail and felt emboldened to do so), but the film instantly shifts from present-day images of Harris and Taj Mahal performing "Catfish Blues" on a Stovall porch to two black-and-white photographs of a young Waters (accompanied by the distinctive sounds of his "Rollin' Stone") and the archival images of northbound trains alluded to above (Figure 3.5). In little more than a minute, this segment fully absorbs the speed of train travel and the city's promise of deliverance: assorted anonymous workers are seen departing from Chicago's elevated train platforms, and Waters's electric blues matches these sights of suddenly transformed lives. But the segment's closing views of Waters's triumphant appearance at Newport 1960 and his late-career highlight with The Band at *The Last Waltz* also recognize his growing autonomy, yet another meaning of "Rollin' Stone's" steady forward momentum throughout the sequence. The film's provision of historical time, that is to say, its delivery of a well-defined perspective on the past, is evident in its editing, but these assemblages permit

Figure 3.5 *Feel Like Going Home* (Martin Scorsese, 2003).

listeners/viewers to grasp the blues' story of origins as well as the significance of its touchdown in Chicago. The "ritual of origins," Cantwell writes, is the process wherein musicians and listeners can approach an unfathomable place and time (2008, 12), and the film's forceful impression of the blues' northward course, especially in Waters's pivotal 1943 journey, provides an historical ground for spectators to re-root themselves. In *Feel Like Going Home*'s rendering of this historical material, the blues apprehends the emergent attributes of America's city spaces, fully absorbing them, but also affecting them with its sounds, songs, and performances. As a result, the film's viewers can understand how the blues catalogues its time, while also witnessing how editing incorporates and releases this meaning into a present-day context. In other words, the blues may take an impression of its time and make a mark on its era, but *Feel Like Going Home*'s audiences are permitted to reexperience these historical sounds.

Feel Like Going Home returns momentarily to John Lee Hooker's music in order to develop this account of the blues' electric passage from the Mississippi Delta to northern cities such as Detroit, and it deploys comparable imagery and editing to substantiate its interpretation of this music's wider implication. Beginning with black-and-white television images of Hooker's solo performance of "Never Get Out of These Blues Alive," an especially dirge-like rendition of the song, the film interpolates several archival images of American industry (factories, assembly lines, smokestacks) while Hooker's weary voice and guitar transmit the burden of memory and experiences. Scorsese's voice-over characterizes Hooker's "downhome" blues as "mysterious" and "haunting," yet he also recognizes its possibly "nostalgic" reception by relocated plantation workers. The ensuing segment, however, further develops the meaning of this music's "mystery" by turning to the blues' post-Second World War electrification, its new audience and broader popularity in the 1960s. In Scorsese's account, this emergent (white) audience "knew little, if anything" about the blues' origins in the Mississippi Delta, but the film's short fragment of a televised "I'm Leaving" doesn't diminish the sequence's broader historical purpose. Hooker's legendary disinclination to change chords during his songs produces "I'm Leaving's" protracted, metronomic quality, yet in *Feel Like Going Home*, the sight of a mostly youthful British audience dancing to Hooker's blues can't expel the sound's meaning. "Never Get Out of These Blues Alive," at least in its televisual version, remains permanently connected to a rural folk-blues tradition, but "I'm Leaving" reveals what Cantwell calls an "ideophonic" impression of Hooker's—and others'—experience of urban migration in the 1930s and 1940s (2008, 17). This music's electric cadence, profile, and drive return viewers to the earlier Waters sequence and its plentiful train imagery, but the Hooker segment extends the previous emphasis on industry, work, and urban existence. Hooker's blues, a self-described form of stomping "boogie" (as in his elemental 1948 recording, "Boogie Chillen'"), could be particularly propulsive when accompanied by other instruments (drums, electric guitar and bass, piano, saxophones, etc.), and "I'm Leaving" is meant to exemplify this quality: the song lingers on a lone pattern, as unvarying as the preceding shots of factory assembly lines, and the interaction between music and voice is the sound of frustration and flight. Scorsese calls Hooker's electric blues "old and new at the same time," and the post-Second World War urbanization of this music, that is, the substantial alteration to its traditional rural sound, registers a radically changing existence, an exasperated confrontation with the city and its clearly diminishing possibilities. The mimetic correspondence between the blues and its imagined referents is quickly—but exactly—sketched in *Feel Like Going Home*'s editing and incorporation of archival materials, and its examination of this moment in the blues' past is the film's most completely realized historical assessment.

The immediate transition to Otha Turner's story, his fife playing, and the succeeding scene's prevailing sense of West Africa's polyrhythms, improvisations, and collectively created sounds (particularly in its drumming) brings *Feel Like Going Home* to what Scorsese, following Alan Lomax, calls the blues' "truly ancient origins." This section of the film begins with a quick synopsis of how Turner's fife and drum furnish evidence for the blues' beginnings in Africa, and the director's voice-over describes this music's "survival" as a kind of folklore: these beats, he states, were "carefully preserved and passed down, generation after generation, through slavery, through Jim Crow, right up until the present." Harris's ensuing narration deepens this emphasis, explaining the drums' "interwoven polyrhythms" and percussive attack, yet it also amplifies the implications in Scorsese's voice-over: though slave drums were banned before the Civil War, the percussive rudiments in this music-making were covertly transferred to other instruments. When blues music is urbanized and electrified in post-Second World War America, for example, its "city voice" is projected onto new instruments that tenaciously preserve the melodic and rhythmic qualities of African music; yet the Delta blues had also revealed this same affinity, so when *Feel Like Going Home* cuts back to a televised recording of Son House playing "Death Letter Blues," his slapping pick hand confirms that an identical percussive attack can be transmitted with an acoustic guitar. In musicological terms, *Feel Like Going Home*'s point is sound, of course—these links between African rhythms and the blues are well-documented, and such phenomena as common scales and harmonic structures have been underscored often by historians of music.[28] Robert Palmer's *Deep Blues*, for instance, offers a thorough ethnomusicological analysis of the blues' connection to Africa, citing etymological proof as well as an abundance of anthropological information, and his portrait of the Chicago blues' vast prehistory is situated securely within the material context of slavery (1981, 23–47). But for *Feel Like Going Home*, editing finally reveals how the blues encounters, absorbs, and releases an apparently "ancient" tradition, and its overview of this music's West African inheritance draws a strong parallel between the music's present-day form and its earliest foundations. From the propulsive arrangement of John Lee Hooker's electric "I'm Leaving" to Otha Turner's counter-rhythmic fife and drums and their considerable West African antecedents, Scorsese's documentary subtly discloses a deep blues ecology, tracing it across this wide assortment of expressions (Figure 3.6).

Feel Like Going Home's arrival at its final destination in Mali, West Africa—"where everything began," as Harris puts it—seems somewhat incomplete when compared to previous sections of the film. An idea about the historical past rather than a fully formulated perspective, this lengthy African segment makes almost no use of archival materials, nor is it composed of the preceding

Figure 3.6 *Feel Like Going Home* (Martin Scorsese, 2003).

"urbanized blues" sequences' densely interwoven images of past and present. Instead, the filmmakers depend upon Harris's interviews and exchanges with present-day figures to establish details about the blues' African lineage, and their conversations range across well-known matters such as the use of pentatonic scales, beats, or sounds derived from African resources. In this case, the film's "homeward" trajectory justifies a shift in approach, yet the observations made by Salif Keita, Habib Koité, Ali Farka Toure, and others cannot transcend truisms about the blues' enduring preoccupation with "suffering" (Keita), "melancholy" (Koité), or "roots" (Toure), and nothing here matches the preceding scenes of Waters's migrating "Rollin' Stone," Charley Patton's "High Water Everywhere Part 1," or even Willie King's regeneration of Howlin' Wolf's monotonic growl during a juke joint performance of "Spoonful."[29] The film's concluding universalism is salutary, especially in the post-9/11 context of its production, and its willingness to expand the popular image of blues music is laudable; but as Jonathan J. Cavallero has argued, there is a potential risk in the African sequence's genealogical scenario, namely, the implication of equivalency between the original experience of slavery and subsequent waves of immigration (2015, 225). *Italianamerican*, we should remember, was envisioned alongside the 1970s ethnic revival's new obsession with ancestry, and Harris's homeward voyage might appear to be another version of Scorsese's documentary preoccupation with the quest for "origins." *Feel Like Going Home*, however, wisely avoids the ostensible correspondence between such histories, and if its closing passages lack the specificity of earlier scenes, they nevertheless preserve their sharp focus on African American experience. Indeed, the film's concise, yet detailed description of the Delta blues' many journeys to America's modern cities remains undiminished, and its editing registers the meaning of this music's amplification: the filmmakers' most significant insights are embedded in the compact amalgamation of archival resources with images of the blues' present-day actualities. The blues' history, *Feel Like Going Home* suggests, is a history of processing and recovering—but also extending—this distinctively African American experience, and the film's imaginative retrieval of the blues' post-Second World War moment is inseparable from its overriding effort to outline this music's present and future.

No Direction Home: Collecting and the Interrupted Time of History

If *Feel Like Going Home*'s putative search for "roots" discloses a different ritual of origins, namely, a procedure of editing that both absorbs and discharges the meaning of the Delta blues' historical development, *No Direction Home* complicates the practice of assemblage by turning its attention to Bob Dylan, the Sixties' most self-conscious compiler and collagist of America's vernacular music. Dylan's lifelong immersion in the rock 'n' roll idiom provides a significant countercurrent to *No Direction Home*'s investigation of the early-1960s folk revival, and the film's readiness to interweave its account of the era's folk scene with previously unseen footage of Dylan's tumultuous world tour with The Hawks in 1966 reorders one's routine conception of this well-known moment in the artist's history. *Feel Like Going Home*'s laudatory description of John and Alan Lomax's "ballad hunting" had already signaled a significant interest in the history of American folk music; but this also subtended the film's preoccupation with folk processes and their transformation and transmission of traditional songs, and this would eventually constitute a primary thematic focus in *No Direction Home*. The multiple appearances—and many usages—of "Catfish Blues" in *Feel Like Going Home*, for instance, reveal a fixation on such procedures, and we see different musicians modify and renew a common inheritance: Taj Mahal, Muddy Waters, Corey Harris, and Ali Farka Toure all make subtle adjustments to the song's lyrics and meaning, and the film's mining of a deep blues ecology is directed at discovering these ongoing practices. Scorsese's *Italianamerican* had similarly unearthed the cooperative work of storytelling in its account of history. Indeed, several of its stories are composed of "folkloric" rudiments, that is to say, components acquired from previously told tales, now transformed for the film's present-day production of an oral history of immigration. But in *Feel Like Going Home* and (especially) *No Direction Home*, the interest in folklore expands *Italianamerican's* focus on guileless acts of storytelling. A concentration on the vernacular connects these films, of course, yet *No Direction Home* refines *Feel Like Going Home's* approach to amalgamating its archival resources: Dylan's music borrows from—and transforms—the breadth of America's vernacular music, and the film takes this as a prototype for its own collection of historical records and miscellaneous sounds and images. In other words, *No Direction Home* fully assumes Dylan's collagist approach to reassembling his own musical discoveries and gathered fragments ("folk" songs, "ethnic" music, regional sounds, blues, etc.), and it creates a structure that similarly incorporates and organizes its diverse materials (film and television footage, photographs, posters, music, contemporary interviews) into a new totality.[30]

No Direction Home's production was initiated by Bob Dylan's manager and primary archivist, Jeff Rosen, and Scorsese appears to have been commissioned primarily to gather and consolidate Dylan's extensive archival holdings, finally sifting them into an intelligible whole.[31] Rosen had in fact conducted several of the film's interviews before Scorsese's involvement was secured. The producer's accumulation of resources simply required the additional—yet fundamental—contributions of editing to realize its commemorative aims: the film's compilation of archival possessions provides a groundwork for meaning in *No Direction Home*, a foundation for its potential insight into an otherwise familiar historical moment. Admittedly, like Scorsese's subsequent *George Harrison: Living in the Material World*, *No Direction Home* willingly risks participating in the baby boomers' most valued trade, namely, an apparently inexhaustible—but always lucrative—brand of Sixties nostalgia. The coincidence of generational yearning, an exceedingly sober folk revival, and abundant testimony from the period's foremost participants undoubtedly results in expressions of nostalgia in the film: a few of these subjects are predictably self-aggrandizing or self-congratulatory (Allen Ginsberg, Joan Baez), while others seem to have abandoned themselves completely to their memories of the past (Peter Yarrow, Pete Seeger, John Cohen). *No Direction Home*, however, is much more than a mere *summa* of

Sixties longing, and it adheres closely to Dylan's calculated detachment from the boomers' self-understanding, taking his uneasiness with the folk purists as a pretext for its own disinterested assessment of the period and its significance. In *Chronicles: Volume One*, Dylan distinguishes himself explicitly from the baby boomer cohort, insisting instead on the immediate post-Second World War backdrop to his story. As Sean Wilentz notes, Dylan's touchstones were in fact discovered in the 1940s and 1950s, not the early-1960s, and he "came to New York with a mind shaped and constrained by [the period's] commercial and political culture, from James Dean and *I Love Lucy* to Holiday Inns and red-hot Chevys" (2010, 298). *No Direction Home* closely aligns its project with Dylan's more impassive perception of the Sixties, and it presents itself as an archeological construction, a novel proposition about Dylan's world, his music, and their entangled meanings.[32]

As in *Feel Like Going Home*, *No Direction Home*'s opening passages outline how the provision of time will be a basic task for the film and its principal subject. Effectively an account of Dylan's most influential period as a musician and performer, *No Direction Home* takes detours through the musician's youth in Hibbing, Minnesota, and his college-era stopover in Minneapolis, but its main focus—Dylan's arrival in New York City, his immediate immersion in the folk music revival and its performance venues, his early exchanges with the movement's key players, and his eventual return to rock 'n' roll—is interwoven with extended passages from his turbulent world tour with The Hawks in 1966. These are very well-known stories about Dylan's beginnings, yet *No Direction Home* reassesses the specifics of Dylan's groundbreaking years in unexpected ways, dividing its delivery of material between separate strata of time, and the effect refers repeatedly to Dylan's collagist approach to his own writing. The film's general structuring of temporality is thus reminiscent of *Chronicles*: its leaps between disparate times recall Dylan's penchant for shuffling "time and memory, jumping the line between B.C. and A.D., pulled back even as he plunges forward" (Wilentz 2010, 298). Such rearrangements of time also reverberate strongly with the songwriter's many experiments on *Bringing It All Back Home* (1965), *Highway 61 Revisited* (1965), and *Blonde on Blonde* (1966), the highlights of *No Direction Home*'s analysis of Dylan's Sixties.[33] Indeed, after a brief preliminary sequence dedicated to Dylan's present-day descriptions of his permanent "odyssey" and "homeward" (dis) orientation, *No Direction Home* reveals the first substantial fracture in its temporal construction: the opening snare shot from a live "Like a Rolling

Stone" transports viewers to 1966, and one witnesses Dylan's resolution and composure in the face of his old "folk" audience's infamous resistance to his newest music. This sequence, however, unidentified and without additional editorial comment, is followed by a short discussion about time. An instant cut to still photos of a winter landscape is accompanied solely by Dylan's voice-over. "You can do a lot of things that *seem* to make time stand still," he says, "but of course, you know no one can do that," and three dissolves across these winter photos bring us back to a present-day Dylan as he begins to reminisce about the Hibbing of his youth (Figure 3.7). This relay between the present and past establishes a shape for the film that follows: passages of exposition about the songwriter's life are continually interrupted by the newly excavated 1966 footage, but the dispersal of these images, the pinnacle of Dylan's 1960s work, signals *No Direction Home*'s share in the songwriter's determined metamorphoses. Dylan's recollections about the long-gone Hibbing of his childhood ("obliterated" by "time" and "progress," he claims) accordingly conclude with another dynamic punctuation from "Like a Rolling Stone," now noticeably intensified as the singer, clearly stoned but wholly immersed in the

Figure 3.7 *No Direction Home: Bob Dylan* (Martin Scorsese, 2005).

music, appears both shocked and transfixed by the sounds being made by his band (Figure 3.8).³⁴

In her review of *No Direction Home*, Amy Taubin describes Scorsese's film as a "time-bending documentary" (2005, 31), and its furnishing of a flexible temporality finally registers its full participation in Dylan's exceptional experience of the Sixties. Greil Marcus interprets *No Direction Home*'s recurring cuts to the 1966 tour in similar terms. The film's structure, he notes, "moving chronologically but continually circling around the cauldron of fury in England in 1966, [casts] real, already familiar events into doubt" (2007, 50). Scorsese points to his audiovisual treatment of the Kennedy assassination, or scenes of African American resistance to segregation at a southern luncheonette counter to explain how editing can defamiliarize the past for viewers in this way (Donato 2007, 206), and the film's rearrangement of its archival resources is its main method for plunging the period's most conspicuous signposts into a condition of doubt. In this respect, doubt is the experience of reception: one doesn't doubt the actuality of events per se, but rather, one hesitates at the customary interpretations of Dylan's past. In a review of *Shine a Light* (2008), Paul Arthur

Figure 3.8 *No Direction Home: Bob Dylan* (Martin Scorsese, 2005).

acknowledges the centrality of such editing to Scorsese's documentary work, citing the "cubistic accretion" of particulars in that film's description of The Rolling Stones' live performances, yet he also alludes to a common complaint about *No Direction Home* having been "overcut" by David Tedeschi (Arthur 2008, 48). Editing in this case, however, is the collation or classification of assorted elements, and the abundance of cutting in the film is meant to increase, at least momentarily, one's sense of uncertainty about history. On the one hand, it recalls Dylan's unpredictable juxtaposition of words, images, and characters in his songs' lyrics. On the other hand, however, like the songwriter's countervailing recourse to a permanent framework of folk or blues-based forms, the filmmakers reposition their assemblage within a recognizable narrative design. *No Direction Home* accordingly redistributes rudiments from both Dylan's archival possessions and the public domain: family photos; amateur home movies, one of which captures Dylan's early days in New York City as a silent comedy sketch; existing films, many of them commercially exhibited (*Dont Look Back* [1967]), others somehow abandoned (Pennebaker's planned *You Know Something Is Happening* [1966–7]); posters and other associated ephemera from Dylan's work as a touring musician; and a wealth of stock footage, so much of it compressed into a singular impression of Dylan's professional life and its American context. But *No Direction Home*'s editing reformats viewers' response to the history in question, and the result is a newly legible past. Dylan's long-lasting immersion in a wide range of popular music, his self-conscious transformation of vernacular song forms into the expressions of an emergent rock culture, and his critical interpretations of American modernity are all implicitly re-viewed in the film's arrangement of its archival materials. Indeed, *No Direction Home* returns emphatically to a Bob Dylan who continually reawakens his audiences to the radical potential of popular song. The shuffling of his music within the film's broader chronology gives many of his best songs an uncanny quality (this is particularly true of the electric material from 1965 and the tour of 1966), and this matches Dylan's persistent efforts to reroute his new music through earlier historical moments.

What, then, is the prototypical work of compilation in *No Direction Home*'s universe? The film's preliminary images allude to a certain practice of gathering, a meaningful form of collection that is summoned intermittently throughout the film's two parts. Dylan's recollections about his first experiences with popular music are fastened firmly to the 78s of his childhood. An inadvertently discovered "great big mahogany radio" in his parents' house is the "mystical" conduit to sounds, and Bill Monroe's bluegrass recording of "Drifting Too Far from the Shore," somehow left behind by the radio's previous owner, is the earliest indication that Dylan's lifelong relationship with music and recordings would be shaped by an immediate—and redemptive—feeling of rootlessness. For Dylan, listening to these records was a transformative experience: he started to feel like he "was somebody else," or "that maybe [he] was not even born to the right parents." But these incidents, the film informs us, were "many years earlier," and Dylan's confidence about time's unstoppable forward movement is disregarded as *No Direction Home* lingers over still photographs of winter landscapes before reordering its chronology to reexamine Dylan's beginnings in Hibbing. A few moments later, televised footage of Hank Williams performing "Cold, Cold Heart" is bookended by color shots of another "great big mahogany radio," and the segment follows Dylan's winding expedition along the conjoined paths of radio waves and rotating records. Critics have expressed reservations about the "journey" motif in *No Direction Home* (and Scorsese's other present-day documentaries), and the resemblance between Dylan's explanation of his disorienting "odyssey" and Monroe's "Drifting Too Far from the Shore" may appear a bit too convenient as a preamble to the film. But this peripatetic property is closely associated with *No Direction Home*'s archival project: how can these resources be tracked down, accumulated, and rearranged within the film's otherwise familiar narrative?[35] Collecting, Evan Eisenberg argues, guards one against the absence of absolute principles for selection, and the record collection is in fact a representative reaction to the experience of rootlessness (2005, 18). Dylan's drifting, endless journeys ("don't look back") are set in motion by the spinning 78s and their sounds, he claims, and his retrospection undoubtedly permits a certain amount of myth-making. But the close correspondence between records, "placelessness," technology, and mobility resonates with John Lomax's early twentieth-century "adventures" in ballad gathering, and the artist's self-conscious summoning of this long tradition places his story within the purview of preservation and folkloric collection.[36] Indeed, Dylan's description of himself as a "musical expeditionary" knowingly conjures the fraught history of heroic searches for America's vernacular music, John and Alan Lomax's journeys among them; yet the paradoxical sense of geographic specificity *and* limitlessness implied by the records' sounds (Dylan's constant claim about folk music) is at the core of Dylan's recollections, and this undoubtedly drives him past the Lomaxes efforts to *enclose* music in archival recordings. *No Direction Home* underlines these meaningful relationships between music, the rites of recording, amassing and listening, and the categorizing function of editing because the film similarly presents its sequencing of images as a collection of information about the historical past, but it also serves as an index to Dylan's experiences during the period in question. Taking full advantage of editing's ability to exemplify the conditions of rootlessness and mobility, Scorsese and his collaborators shift freely—and rapidly—between the film's numerous archival resources, thereby inhabiting Dylan's continually changing relationship with his cohort of musicians and songwriters, his audiences, and historical moment.

"It was the sound that got to me," Dylan insists, "it wasn't *who* it was," and throughout *No Direction Home* he characterizes recorded sounds as conduits to the worlds beyond Hibbing. As I've already indicated, so many of the anecdotes in Part 1 essentially underscore the meaning that permeates different recordings—personal record collections, the rituals of listening to music, the reproduction of sounds (on guitars, with voices), learning from records, and in a few notable cases, stealing other people's rare LPs—and these stories are periodically inserted into the film's elementary chronology (Figure 3.9). But within *No Direction Home*'s apparently ancient world, collecting is not—or is

Figure 3.9 *No Direction Home: Bob Dylan* (Martin Scorsese, 2005).

not only—a modern consumerist obligation, nor is it the emblem of aesthetic or media connoisseurship. On the contrary, the focus on records and collections is continually readjusted to reveal a much broader social history. "The history of music," Robert Cantwell maintains, is first and foremost "a history of recovery," (2008, 217), and the collection of records thus echoes this fundamentally remedial work of retrieval. Such collecting constitutes one more form of close listening, and Cantwell leads readers to Harry Smith's *Anthology of American Folk Music* (1952) as the prototypical example of this particular brand of collection: the *Anthology* "transforms what it represents" and resuscitates a distant world for its listeners; it reconditions its audiences to hear a seemingly vanished realm in its organization of recordings (Cantwell 2008, 35). In this respect, if Smith's "anthologizing" designates "a gathering" of miscellaneous materials, it also implies an unanticipated discovery of what previously "could be experienced only in threads and patches." It delivers records in a new "total design, in a structure of fixed elements whose relationships are narratively as well as architecturally organized" (Cantwell 2008, 35). Amassing its commercial seventy-eight records (covering the period 1927–32), Smith's *Anthology* is "among other things a salvage and recovery operation, a set of found objects, or more precisely, junk," but it is at the same time "an intelligent arrangement of elements," a deliberate grouping of phonographic records and the idiosyncratic performances contained therein (Cantwell 2008, 36). In short, Smith's compilation works to connect its disparate constituents. From Dick Justice's "Henry Lee" to Henry Thomas's "Fishing Blues," its eighty-four songs finally disclose a comprehensive configuration and impose "meaningful form onto the 'scatter' of history" (Parks 2017, 74).[37]

In *When We Were Good: The Folk Revival* (1996), Cantwell describes the *Anthology of American Folk Music* as a "memory theater" (189), and Smith's systematic collation of his own possessions, he contends, produces a "thinking machine" (205)—it summons a "peculiar mental discipline," which in turn leads audiences to grasp "a prelapsarian American harmony" (205).[38] Similarly, *No Direction Home*'s many stories do not present record collecting as a repository for "personal" meanings (in the manner of Nick Hornby's *High Fidelity* [1995], for instance), nor do they define collectors like Paul Nelson or Izzy Young as mere representatives for the subcultural ("those records were like hen's teeth," Dylan states while reminiscing about his theft of Nelson's Woody Guthrie LPs). Instead, *No Direction Home*'s attention—like the *Anthology*'s—is devoted to a different aspect of record collecting, namely, its searching reclamation of various vernacular antecedents to modern mass culture. This is a persistent theme throughout Dylan's interviews in *No Direction Home*, especially when he attempts to clarify why "archaic" music reverberated so completely for him as a young person in the late-1950s and early-1960s, and it continues to be a foundation for his songwriting today; but the film's emphasis on the gathering of field recordings and hard-to-find "folk" albums, undoubtedly already an antiquated or specialist practice in 2005, further commemorates some fundamental features of the Dylan legend and his interpretations of modernity. Dylan's songwriting has continually incorporated images of the premodern and used vernacular music as its principal template, yet *No Direction Home*'s highlighting of such matters reveals how Dylan's work confronted the uncertainties and deficiencies of his era (its "present") with these resources from the past. At the onset of the mythic "Sixties" and a new expression of modernity, Dylan's music would witness what he casually describes as history's "obliteration," while at the same time evoking a receding past in the songs' persistent dependence upon models provided by vernacular music. In this way, *No Direction Home* sketches the processes of revision and resolve, not only in Dylan's approach to his own songwriting, but also in the parallel paths taken by popular music throughout the subsequent decade as it metamorphosed into "rock."

As we've seen, Scorsese refers sympathetically in *Feel Like Going Home* to John and Alan Lomax's decades-long preservationist efforts as "ballad hunters," implicitly acknowledging their work as a model for his own documentary about the Delta blues, but *No Direction Home*'s approach to compilation is more consistent with the topography of Dylan's immediate 1960s environment. If the Lomaxes relied on "hunting" or "acquisitive" tactics, Smith's *Anthology* extracts "a larger system of cultural meaning" from records (Moist 2007, 114), and in the integrationist context of its early-1960s reception, its audiovisual gathering could open to a more comprehensive reading of the social and political worlds. In this way, the *Anthology* permitted audiences to hear a broad band of American history in its assortment of sounds. *Feel Like Going Home*'s close association with John and Alan Lomax's reclamation efforts occasionally leads the filmmakers to understate the key role played by cultural arbitrators, John and Alan Lomax among them, in determining the film's particular perception of the Delta blues, Mississippi's local cultures, and individual players such as Lead Belly and Muddy Waters. And while it preserves a welcome sense of self-awareness when following Corey Harris on his journey through America's deep south and West Africa, the film's adherence to the Lomaxes' idyllic vision of "authentic" American folk music is evident in its overinvestment in field recordings. Nevertheless, if *Feel Like Going Home*'s historical perspective is inescapably shaped by predecessors and mediators like the Lomaxes, *No Direction Home* allows for a more complex relationship with its antecedents. Dylan's apparently boundless absorption of roots music establishes a pretext for the film's further excavation of the material covered in *Feel Like Going Home*'s analysis of the blues, but in this case, numerous references to folksong collections, performances in folk settings, and Dylan's eventual rejection of the scene's stringency and seriousness provide the framework for a deeper analysis of how "folk" or "roots" music makes its way through rock culture in the 1960s. In other words, although *Feel Like Going Home* had also looked at the Delta blues as a form of unassimilated vernacular production, implicitly examining its post-Second World War amplification as a precursor to mass (or rock) culture, *No Direction Home*'s 1960s backdrop provides a foundation for Scorsese's additional mining of this same historical material. The film's compilation of its resources thus re-presents Dylan's original amalgamation of folk music and rock 'n' roll at the very moment of the mythical Sixties' arrival, and it catalogues a rapidly developing mass culture's incorporation of earlier, popular, vernacular music-making by reviewing the unparalleled shape given to it by Dylan's recordings—especially *Bringing It All Back Home*, *Highway 61 Revisited*, and *Blonde on Blonde*—and concerts with The Hawks during this period. Bookended by two amphetamine-driven 1966 performances of "Like a Rolling Stone," *No Direction Home*'s narrative seems to advance and withdraw at the same time, and it thereby suggests a story about this seemingly ancient music's disorienting passage through the (modern) 1960s.

It's worth remembering that the *Anthology of American Folk Music*'s cover distinguishes Harry Smith as the collection's sole "editor," and *No Direction Home*'s compilation resonates with the *Anthology*'s collage-like rearrangement of its basic components—not only Smith's shellac 78s, but also the collection's supplementary pamphlet, a strange scrapbook packed with ephemera and assorted reproductions from the period in question.[39] Music historians have looked to the *Anthology* for its accumulation of idiosyncrasies, but the set is also unquestionably elegiac in its emphases: so many of these songs artlessly lament a state of deprivation or defeat, yet one can also imagine how such popular forms were themselves being mourned by the *Anthology* and its audiences in the early-1960s. Smith's *Anthology* is, of course, an invaluable resource for Dylan—and the rest of his coffeehouse cohort—during his initial troubadour or folk-protest phase, even if it is only one of many such folk resources.[40] Throughout his interview in *No Direction Home*, John Cohen remembers how folk music permitted present-day revivalists to be positioned as "pillars of virtue" or "integrity" against the increasing incursions of commercial music, but the early-1960s context produced an unexpectedly incongruous relationship between these performers and their predecessors. For steadfast traditionalists like Cohen and his New Lost City Ramblers, for instance, the folksong's value could finally be found in its considerable distance from urban and suburban life. Always performed with idiomatic accuracy, the revivalists' renditions of southern mountain and bluegrass music were intended to provide access to the unincorporated, premodern America, and in this way, their participation in the "roots music" revival could be understood as a form of cultural activism (Allen 2010, 6). The resulting experience was not without its nostalgic features. Although it may have been promoting its own righteous form of countercultural politics, the folk revival's immersion in traditional song seemed to detach itself from the era's broader turbulence. Dylan, clearly recognizing this disconnect between the folk revival's core proclamations and the changing contemporary world, pressed on with his surrealist turn in 1964 and groundbreaking rock music in 1965–6, and *No Direction Home* provides ample evidence for the attendant disappointment amongst folkie traditionalists. Yet as Greil Marcus (2011, 85–6) and Sean Wilentz (2010, 277; 2012, 5) have both persuasively shown, the type of mysterious music gathered by Smith for the *Anthology* continued to be an essential point of reference for Dylan even after he fled from the parochial folk revival in 1965.[41] If *No Direction Home* appears nostalgic in its own way (for the 1960s and rock music, but also for an unassimilated popular culture), it nonetheless formulates a parallel claim about the songwriter's movements as a "musical expeditionary." The film's insistent interweaving of footage from Dylan's mutinous 1966 tour of England with a chronological account of his arrival and growth as a songwriter in New York City should be understood as a demonstration of his uninterrupted commitment to America's vernacular music, the processual nature of folksong creation, and the flexibility of these templates as he transposed them to a 1960s rock setting.

In this respect, the compilation structure establishes a procedure for grasping what Dylan to this day describes as the permanence of his immersion in folk music and blues as living forms of history. For instance, the film's constant cuts to scenes of tumult from the 1966 tour release a distinctive meaning in the songwriter's "expeditions" through assorted forms of music: images of

Dylan's rise as a troubadour in the early-1960s are recast when set next to the turmoil of his first "gone-electric" world tour, and throughout the film his songs are propelled forward and dragged back simultaneously. In some cases, the connections are easily discerned. "Baby, Let Me Follow You Down," originally recorded by Dylan alone with his guitar and harmonica in 1962, is completely rearranged for its 1966 performance with The Hawks, and the film's editing remakes the former rendition into an embryonic version of the group's new work. In other cases, however, the film's assemblage of images and sounds is more circumspect—editing subtly directs spectators to other strata of significance. For instance, Part 2 of *No Direction Home* begins with fragments from the so-called "Apothecary" scene from Pennebaker's unreleased *You Know Something Is Happening*, a look at the *Blonde on Blonde*-era Dylan, stoned and gaunt, reshuffling words and then throwing them back at the apothecary's signs. After Dylan walks away slowly from Pennebaker's camera at the sequence's conclusion, *No Direction Home* immediately cuts to the singer's exhausted, sarcastic introduction of "Just Like Tom Thumb's Blues" to his British audience. Dylan wearily describes "Tom Thumb's Blues" as one more "protest song," although The Hawks' performance, driven by Garth Hudson's whirling organ sounds and Robbie Robertson's arpeggiated chords, is something other than a simple "folksong." Its momentum pushes away Dylan's perplexed listeners, while at the same time transporting the group through what is rightly regarded as a highlight of their 1966 shows (Figure 3.10).[42] *No Direction Home*, however, cuts through the audience's unreceptiveness and appears to take Dylan at his word: a quick excursion through the disorder of Dylan's daily touring life in this period is promptly followed by the film's return to 1963 ("three years earlier"), its folk music, optimism, conviction, and occasional sanctimony. At such moments, *No Direction Home* shrewdly exposes the mutable enthusiasm of Dylan's initial boosters by continually summoning these images of his implacably hostile English audiences in 1966. Early supporters like Peter Yarrow are suddenly unreliable within this editing structure, and they appear oblivious to the changing nature of Dylan's songwriting, record-making, and performances in the mid-1960s.

This interpretation of Dylan's history is commonplace in accounts of his work during these years. But *No Direction Home*'s editing describes an exceptional determination in Dylan's songwriting, and his varied experiences with America's vernacular music evidently accompany him on the path that divides the revival's traditionalists (and members of the press) from Dylan's

Figure 3.10 *No Direction Home: Bob Dylan* (Martin Scorsese, 2005).

expanding rock or pop audience. As a result, *No Direction Home* continually pulls these two distinct temporal layers together to revise viewers' customary understanding of this important period in Dylan's professional life. Admittedly, such an approach risks simply substantiating the artist's account of his own personal vision, or worse still, the beleaguered, ordeals-of-fame scenario that informs certain parts of the contemporaneous *I'm Not There* (Todd Haynes, 2007). Indeed, *No Direction Home*'s concluding sequence willingly accepts this danger, aligning itself closely with a visionary quality in the songwriter's journey across Europe in 1966. A shrunken Dylan, homesick and disoriented in the film's final archival interview, looks lifeless as he pleads for an escape from the 1966 tour (Figure 3.11), but the notorious Manchester Free Trade Hall rendition of "Like a Rolling Stone" immediately follows, and it confirms the irrevocability of his vocation. The singer's demand for The Hawks to "play fucking loud" is defiant and, with our awareness of his looming motorcycle crash at tour's end, a reminder of the high price paid for his trailblazing in the mid-1960s (Figure 3.12). Nevertheless, *No Direction Home*'s approach to compilation, namely, its integration of diverse temporalities and contrasting trajectories, ultimately manages to evade the plainly romanticized features

Figure 3.11 *No Direction Home: Bob Dylan* (Martin Scorsese, 2005).

Figure 3.12 *No Direction Home: Bob Dylan* (Martin Scorsese, 2005).

of this narrative, and viewers are instead permitted to experience the very different meaning of Dylan's peripatetic relationship with America's vernacular music, particularly as he reshapes it decisively during his "gone-electric" period. This is how the film finally interprets Dylan's permanent import to American popular music. He is *in* his times, but his time always seems to be on the verge of *expiring* in Scorsese's *No Direction Home*; and his full absorption in the wide assortment of blues, folk, and rock 'n' roll music gives Dylan's work the surface appearance of timelessness, while simultaneously providing a resource for his songs' singularity and timeliness in the Sixties.

As a contribution to PBS's long-running *American Masters* series, *No Direction Home*'s commission involves outlining the familiar features of Bob Dylan's history—his first arrival in New York City in January of 1961, the rapid development of his songwriting and his subsequent ascent to stardom as a "folksinger," the supposed apostasy of his return to rock 'n' roll music in 1965, the almost continuous battle with his audience's expectations, and so on. Admittedly, there are only a few surprises in these specifics, and Dylan's *Chronicles* provides a more unpredictable and deeper account of the songwriter's scuffling days in New York City. Nevertheless, the film's substantial interviews with figures such as Dave Van Ronk, Suze Rotolo, and Liam Clancy offer undeniable insights into the well-known Dylan legends, and they establish *No Direction Home*'s affiliation with *Chronicles*' generous assessment of Dylan's New York City contemporaries.[43] In addition to demarcating the steep climb from Dylan's tentative self-titled debut record in 1962 to the landmark *Blonde on Blonde* in 1966, *No Direction Home* summarizes the political and social context of the Sixties, situating Dylan's life and work within the era's tumult. Always the single-minded character at the forefront of changes in popular music, yet apparently unconcerned about his audience's unpreparedness for his shifting directions, Scorsese's Dylan is recognizable yet at the same time eager to refocus our everyday perceptions about him. More importantly, however, the film's excerpts from Jeff Rosen's extensive interviews with Dylan offer incomparable images of the songwriter reminiscing about his history with uncharacteristic candor. Indeed, the sight of Dylan conversing with such openness (within clear limits, of course), and in the same colloquial language/voice as *Chronicles*, is one of *No Direction Home*'s undeniable highlights, and the film's depiction of his searching responses to Rosen's questions confirms its uniqueness among Dylan biographies. Scorsese has similarly emphasized Dylan's present-day interviews as the film's enigmatic core: "In a way those interviews allowed us to open up the film, because there was a truth that Jeff Rosen got at with Dylan" (Donato 2007, 207).⁴⁴ But *No Direction Home*'s most unexpected disclosures come with its excavation of "lost" footage from D.A. Pennebaker's abandoned *You Know Something Is Happening*. Along with its main inference about Dylan's continuous involvement with the wide variety of America's vernacular music, the film's treatment of Pennebaker's discarded material is also part of *No Direction Home*'s understated reassessment of the legacy of American direct cinema. The film's reclamation of this footage clearly parallels the folksong movement's recycling of traditional song, but it also indicates an effort to refocus Pennebaker's observational images. The footage from *You Know Something Is Happening* is composed mainly of concert recordings, and Pennebaker's original plan had been to shift from *Dont Look Back*'s behind-the-scenes backdrop to a more complete concentration on Dylan's onstage work with The Hawks—he justifiably hoped to reposition the anarchic 1966 concerts as the tour's central subject.⁴⁵ Direct cinema's customary reliance upon portraiture and its personal coordinates nonetheless remains fixed in Pennebaker's images of the group's collaborations. When *No Direction Home* resets this same material within the wider framework of its compilation, however, it inevitably reintroduces social history to the observational documentary's standard portrait of well-known personalities and imagines a loosely conceived kind of spiritual biography in its place.

Looking for My Life; or, Living in the Material World

No Direction Home's subject matter—Bob Dylan, the 1960s folk revival, the development of a counterculture and its rock music—inevitably returns Scorsese to American direct cinema, its controversial legacy, and continuing significance. For documentary filmmakers before the 1960s, the assemblage of archival possessions had been a fundamental aspect of interpreting— often in a polemical way—previous versions of events, persons, and in some cases, the broader functioning of the social and political worlds. During the Second World War period, for instance, the radical restructuring of preexistent materials in American documentaries usually fulfilled a clear didactic purpose, and the films' redeployment of archival resources was directed by the war's ideological needs. Frank Capra's state-sponsored *Why We Fight* series (1942–5) makes use of a broad range of existent resources (short newsreels, fiction films, government sanctioned propaganda), and the filmmakers' systematic accumulation and repurposing of their materials are meant to meet several state-mandated objectives. In Capra's *Prelude to War* (1942), a coarsely structured history lesson is easily gleaned from the director's corpus of images and sounds. The reorganization of archival possessions is authorized by the film's certainty about its own urgent necessity, and Capra reshapes his materials as the rationale for America's inescapable involvement in the war. Such methods of compilation would continue to be utilized after the wartime demands for propaganda receded, of course, yet the arrival and predominance of cinéma vérité and direct cinema in the late-1950s and 1960s devalued this practice, at least momentarily, and the development of portable, lightweight film cameras and synchronous sound recording devices further accelerated a considerable shift in documentary priorities. For practitioners and proponents of direct cinema, an elementary ethos of "presence," that is, a philosophy of "spontaneity" and its resolutely "present-tense" accents were connected to individualist coordinates and the creation of "personality" portraits. Furthermore, this categorical commitment to detached observation largely precluded the polemical drive of earlier compilation films. Direct cinema's unequivocal rejection of such modes of documentary making, and its marked antipathy to the political work of New Deal-era filmmakers in particular, typically focused on their blunt attempts to influence spectators—about a matter of government policy, an ideological or philosophical argument, and so on. For a documentarian such as Richard Leacock, direct cinema's innovations could instead be found in its promise to liberate spectators from the authority of interventionist filmmaking, especially as manifested by editing and interviews, and in permitting them to weigh their everyday actualities and act rationally in the public sphere. In other words, rather than having their opinions molded by filmmakers, audiences would be free to watch—and listen to—the documentaries before them, make reasoned assessments about the world, and act accordingly on their reality.[46]

American direct cinema is the most frequent point of reference in Scorsese's intermittent discussions about documentary filmmaking, but his current non-fiction output continues to make extensive use of archives and contemporary interviews, two of direct cinema's primary targets in its effort to move documentary work into an observational register.[47] He unquestionably continues to preserve individualist archetypes in his documentary film and television productions, and his subjects, mostly musicians and filmmakers, implicitly reflect back upon his own vocation in a manner that recalls classic direct cinema. Nevertheless, the director's historical foci recast 1960s portraiture in critical ways. Because Bob Dylan's public portrayal as a 1960s "folksinger" was disseminated so widely—though belatedly and perhaps inaccurately—in *Dont Look Back*, his close association with direct cinema was unmatched by his contemporaries in rock: only The Rolling Stones had a comparably significant involvement with 1960s direct cinema. *No Direction Home*'s investment in these films is considerable, mostly because of Dylan's historic affiliation with Pennebaker, but Scorsese's documentary repeatedly modifies its editing of footage from *Dont Look Back* and *You Know Something Is Happening* by associating these works with contemporaneous—and in some cases, conflicting—modes of film practice. Paul Arthur's analysis of "portraiture" in the conjoined traditions of American avant-garde and documentary filmmaking in the 1960s highlights a shared concern with "immediacy and present-tense observation," describing the latter as a "potent shibboleth in [the era's] art and countercultural activities" (2003, 95). Indeed, the common attributes of portraiture are present in each of these modes of practice: the propensity to situate figures within everyday places; a concentration on faces and expressions; protracted, informally rendered takes; and for practitioners of direct cinema in particular, minimal editorial or authorial intervention. As Arthur notes, this combination of "temporal address with the youthful bearing of many subjects" would in turn highlight "creative spontaneity and the rejection of official history" (2003, 95). In other words, uniqueness would be connected with the energies of the counterculture, and portraiture generated a frame for various kinds of self-actualization. If this philosophy was bound by its conservative—and insular—focus on individuals and self-realization, it was in large part because the era's hippie counterculture was also burdened with such contradictions. Nonetheless, direct cinema's commitment to a detached observation of its subjects' spontaneous activity typically disregarded the historical past, and as a consequence, documentation, archival records, and any temporal discourse directed to the past were eliminated from the films' loosely shared methods. In short, direct cinema's countercultural sense of obligation to the present prohibited it from directing any attention to what Arthur calls "official history" (2003, 95), and though this was undoubtedly a productive and novel critical perspective on America's past, it also precluded more searching questions about history.

In *No Direction Home*, archives are repositories of cultural value, and the film's excavation of its many resources invariably restores the historical to direct cinema's framework of present-ness. As we've already seen, Scorsese's film utilizes abundant footage from Pennebaker's *You Know Something Is Happening*, yet it resituates this material as just one more (admittedly fundamental) archival element within its general architecture. If direct cinema's theoretical emphasis on present-ness forced it to quarantine the archive (and the past), Scorsese's film instead reintroduces history to Pennebaker's images by rearranging their position, that is, by reshuffling their temporality so as to disclose their relationship with other sources. Arthur's study of cinematic portraiture within 1960s documentary and avant-garde filmmaking emphasizes their common processes and purposes, but connections between these movements could also be somewhat more tenuous. Dylan, of course, was a major player in the period's flexible amalgamations of documentary filmmaking, the avant-garde and vernacular culture, and *No Direction Home* refers to these coexisting practices to remind viewers that Dylan's songwriting was rooted in a broader historical context. His silent "Screen Test" for Andy Warhol, for instance, is supplemented with the breakthrough 1965 studio recording of "Like a Rolling Stone," and if the screen test's sitting subject's discomfort is too easily aligned with the song's acid lyrics, one is nonetheless aware of how the film reinvests these images with an historical actuality that would otherwise be beyond their frame (Figure 3.13). The film's redeployment of analogous contemporaneous artifacts such as Jonas Mekas's *Walden* (1968),

Figure 3.13 *No Direction Home: Bob Dylan* (Martin Scorsese, 2005).

or its handling of what would have been formative popular Hollywood films for Dylan's generation (*Rebel Without a Cause* [Nicholas Ray, 1955] and *The Wild One* [Laslo Benedek, 1953]), is best seen in similar terms. These images are returned to history, and they have history restored to them; the film's account of Dylan's origins continually recasts cinematic predecessors as elements in its fine-grained descriptions of the era. But *No Direction Home* adds Dylan's biographical details to everything here, and this finally clears away both the avant-garde's and direct cinema's focus on present-ness and their preoccupation with the new. In other words, *No Direction Home* might maintain direct cinema's individualist foci, yet it constantly reopens its filmic antecedents to the past, that is to say, to the specifics of Dylan's historical moment.

George Harrison: Living in the Material World reiterates *No Direction Home*'s approach to compiling archival resources and present-day interviews. Harrison's story—his formative years in The Beatles, his mounting apprehension at the group's position as Sixties totems, his winding course through a period of disenchantment in the 1970s and 1980s, and his constant religious searching—is closely aligned with Scorsese's other music documentaries. An immediate believer in The Band's *Music from Big Pink* and *The Band*, a lifelong friend of *Nothing but the Blues*' Eric Clapton, and a frequent collaborator with Bob Dylan in the 1970s and 1980s, Harrison's pivotal involvement with 1960s popular music and youth culture drives *Living in the Material World* through the same topography as *The Last Waltz*, *No Direction Home*, *Shine a Light*, and *Rolling Thunder Revue: A Bob Dylan Story by Martin Scorsese* (2019). Indeed, the Harrison narrative allows Scorsese to casually reassess his earlier films' accounts of the Sixties, their relatively grim prognoses for the hippie generation, and their summaries of the period's rock music. *Living in the Material World*'s story initially appears constrained by the well-known Beatles legend (only The Beatles surpass Dylan as an emblem of the mythic "Sixties"), but the film immediately reveals how it intends to sidestep such a predictable account. Beginning with the group's acrimonious official dissolution in 1970, *Living in the Material World* opens with the Sixties' symbolic conclusion, and as a result, the film (very much like *No Direction Home*) imparts a strong sense of jeopardy to its retrospective look at this pivotal decade. The familiar story about Beatlemania's 1964 arrival in America, the group's mid-Sixties innovations in songwriting and recording, and the counterculture's widespread absorption of The Beatles' "all you need is love" ethos seems threatened from the outset, shadowed by the eventual collapse of such ideals at decade's end, and *Living in the Material World*'s attention is directed instead to this tale's reverberations across subsequent decades. In other words, a post-Sixties restlessness is the documentary's true subject: Harrison's composed consciousness offers a spiritual compass for his generation's passage from disenchantment to the calmness described by his wife, Olivia Harrison, at the film's conclusion (Figure 3.14).

In this respect, if *Living in the Material World*'s compilation simply repeats *No Direction Home*'s methodology, adding very little to the former film's outline of this recent music history, its structure nevertheless confirms how the director's documentaries about popular music all rely upon a type of spiritual biography to render historical accounts of the 1960s. Scorsese's non-fiction filmmaking practice entered a prolonged period of inactivity after *The Last Waltz*, yet before completing his commemorative film about The Band in 1978, the director briefly contemplated a permanent move to Italy to produce documentaries about the "lives of the saints" (Kelly 1991, 112). Admittedly, New Hollywood's economic transformations in the late-1970s pushed Scorsese and his cohort into an unexpected position of vulnerability, and his willingness to leave Hollywood is best understood in light of these substantial changes. Nevertheless, the proposed films about Italian saints tellingly share a number of concerns and emphases with the director's present-day documentaries about popular music and cinema. Profiles of revered individuals, these films and television productions begin with their subjects' personal stories, but

Figure 3.14 *George Harrison: Living in the Material World* (Martin Scorsese, 2011).

eventually encompass much more broadly construed histories—institutional and local histories, different traditions, vernacular cultures, and so forth. Peter Guralnick's influence, so strongly felt throughout *Feel Like Going Home*, provides an additional insight into Scorsese's approach to documenting the history of popular music and movies. Guralnick's comprehensive knowledge of America's vernacular music directs Scorsese's examination of the Delta blues and its exemplary figures in *Feel Like Going Home*; but his other writing customarily concentrates on exceptional personalities in American popular music (Elvis Presley, Sam Cooke, Muddy Waters, James Brown), and his descriptions of the critical contexts for music making are deeply rooted in the lives of individual players.[48] *Feel Like Going Home*'s reflection upon Robert Johnson's life is especially representative, in this respect. The film's extended review of the myths and realities of the bluesman's experience sidesteps the dearth of documentation (only two known photos of Johnson exist) to cover accounts by Johnny Shines, Corey Harris, Keb' Mo', Scorsese, and others, and the result is a credible sketch of the 1930s—the musician's peripatetic existence, the abundant everyday dangers of racism in America, and a strong sense of African American resolve. All of this is accompanied by Johnson's unrivaled recordings, and he is represented as an exemplary—if irreducible—character in Scorsese's auteurist universe. He is the embodiment of the predominant blues mythology, of course, yet at the same time he provides the foundation for *Feel Like Going Home*'s interpretation of the Delta blues' history, the Mississippi of the 1930s, and this music's many migrations in subsequent decades.

Robert Cantwell characterizes the Delta blues in terms of its creation of *sound*, or more precisely, the blues musician's deliberate bending of guitar strings, his use of slides, harmonicas, and a solitary voice to make meaningful sounds: "[...] the Delta blues registers the bluesman's physical, intellectual, and moral nature, his strength, perception, precision, and power" (2008, 220). But Cantwell's analyses are focused on individual players because their work is a wellspring for insights about specific historical contexts: these sounds finally "dramatize the unfolding of thought, feeling, and idea in a field of contending human forces" (2008, 220). *Feel Like Going Home*'s examination of prototypical blues musicians offers its own unassuming variation on this approach, but *No Direction Home* and *Living in the Material World* also look at how Bob Dylan and George Harrison's narratives open to the broader field of contending historical forces. To be sure, all of these films, like *The Last Waltz*, *Shine a Light*, and *Rolling Thunder Revue*, devote attention to the inner workings of rock 'n' roll bands, but they ultimately bind their historical accounts to exemplary lives. (In the present-tense context of the concert films, by contrast, exemplarity is an affirmation of autonomy.) For critics, this commitment to individual accomplishment has the same surface appearance—and ideological shortcomings—as so much contemporary commercial filmmaking, but Scorsese's documentaries uncover historical actualities within this biographical frame.[49] Loosely structured as spiritual biographies, his current documentary films and television productions frame their subjects as venerable individuals, as models for living in the material world, yet this is only a pretext for examining the histories that cling to their experiences. *Living in the Material World* surveys Harrison's crises of faith during the 1970s and accepts the popular description of this former Beatle as a mystic. However, its account of the musician's progress through the 1970s and 1980s is surely intended to be representative, an ethical lesson or reminder to viewers about the permanence of the "Sixties" and its ideals. If Scorsese's music documentaries can be criticized for their "hagiography," we should probably take this generic characterization in literal rather than pejorative terms, especially after *Living in the Material World*. This documentary's lengthy exploration of Harrison's exemplary life repeatedly integrates history, and the main subjects of *Feel Like Going Home* and *No Direction Home* are depicted with the same sense of historical consequence.

On the other hand, however, the films' individualist orientation is undoubtedly also derived from Scorsese's unapologetic auteurism, and it definitively establishes the framework for his representations of musicians as well as a wide assortment of films and filmmakers. Indeed, Peter Doyle describes the director's auteurism in terms of its "morality," and this surprisingly resilient critical category, yet another lingering feature from the director's 1960s experience, determines the course taken by most of his present-day non-fiction film and television productions (2007, 71). However, in his cinephile documentaries, this "auteurist morality" establishes a foundation for his return to *Italianamerican*'s primary preoccupation, namely, his family's immigration to America at the turn of the twentieth century. *A Personal Journey with Martin Scorsese Through American Movies*, *Il mio viaggio in Italia* (2001), and *A Letter to Elia* (co-directed with Kent Jones, 2010) all return to well-known masterworks, and they seldom deviate from prevailing auteurist interpretations—Scorsese's cinephile documentaries are not revisionist compendia. Nevertheless, if the choice of films appears to follow conventional criteria, particular images are assembled and utilized for different purposes. In *Il mio viaggio in Italia*, for instance, the filmmaker's compilation stresses a *substantial compatibility* between its celebrated images and the Scorsese family's particular historical experiences—their migrations to America, their lives in the new world, and even a novel type of film and television spectatorship. Similarly, *A Letter to Elia* connects Elia Kazan's movies to Scorsese's personal reminiscences, and it thereby mines another dimension in the immigrant history delineated by *Italianamerican* and *Il mio viaggio in Italia*. As we'll see, in these documentaries, the accumulation and rearrangement of Scorsese's fondly remembered film images direct viewers to new strata of historical meaning. Because *Italianamerican*'s principal storytellers are now deceased, these collections look instead to popular movies to reconstitute the Scorseses' immigrant past, and they do so by matching images with memories, vanishing realities, and—ideally—the experience of history.

4

Personal Pilgrimages: *Il mio viaggio in Italia* and *A Letter to Elia*

Audiovisual Historiography: The Cinephile's Reliquary

More than any other lingering figure from New Hollywood's peak period in the mid-1970s, Martin Scorsese's proper name has become a vernacular sign for cinephilia today. A popular symbol for fervent attachments to the movies, film histories, and the fading memory of "cinema" as the twentieth century's quintessentially modern artform, "Martin Scorsese" travels widely as the contemporary personification of a particular type of film-viewing experience and the pressing need to safeguard it. Indeed, journalists and critics routinely receive Scorsese's fiction films as dispatches from a bygone era of movie mania, and the release of his latest works permits reviewers to once again summon this prelapsarian history of film spectatorship. *Rolling Stone*'s Peter Travers, for example, has continually characterized the director's creations in these terms. *Shutter Island* (2010), he writes, is the "dark magic" of an individual who "makes movies as if his life depends on it." "Cinema is in Scorsese's DNA." And further on, and with the timeworn insistence of cinephilic hyperbole: "No one who lives and breathes movies would dream of missing it" (Travers 2010). Similarly, *Hugo* (2011) evidently materializes from the filmmaker's genetic foundation, and the latter is once again coterminous with the full history of cinema: "Film history is part of Scorsese's DNA" (Travers 2011).[1] *Hugo*, admittedly a perfect vehicle for burnishing Scorsese's biographical legend, also prompted the late Roger Ebert, a lifelong booster and perceptive critic of Scorsese's work, to invoke a familiar auteurist parable in his review of the movie: "There is a parallel with the asthmatic Scorsese, living in Little Italy but not of it, observing life from the windows of his apartment, soaking up the cinema from television and local theaters, adopting great directors as his mentors" (Ebert 2011). In each of these cases, an image of cinephilia adheres to the director and his movies in a very particular way. Screened through a shroud of nostalgia, devoutness, and discernment, Scorsese's fictions are habitually positioned as the embodiment of "cinema," while the director himself is viewed as the incarnation of an historical—and hermetic—ritual of film spectatorship (through "apartment windows," on televisions, in local theaters, etc.). If DNA doesn't necessarily explain such experiences, "Martin Scorsese" has unquestionably become the personification of this venerated cinematic archetype, once defined with a clear sense of mission in the 1950s and 1960s, but now purportedly endangered by profound mutations in movie culture.[2]

The director's unwavering commitment to film history has been rightly celebrated, and his efforts on behalf of film preservation, wandering freely through national cinemas and different historical periods, have only strengthened the familiar characterization of "Scorsese" as the living embodiment of cinema; but this focus on cinephilia has disproportionately framed how his key documentaries about film history are comprehended today. On the one hand, *A Personal Journey with Martin Scorsese Through American Movies* (co-directed with Michael Henry Wilson, 1995), *Il mio viaggio in Italia* (2001), and the Elia Kazan tribute *A Letter to Elia* (co-directed with Kent Jones, 2010) all have a considerable share in safeguarding the history of cinephilia, particularly in its European and American expressions during the 1960s. A virtually mythic story about the cinephile's Parisian ancestry, this pivotal episode in the history of film reception hardly needs to be recounted in detail at this point; yet its fundamental markers are inescapable in these three documentaries. The films' auteurist orientation preserves the classic cinephile's obsession with a cinematic inheritance, a patrimony of films and filmmakers whose authority determines the form of history. Indeed, although checked by Scorsese's categorical abandonment of "objectivity," the documentaries' self-consciously doctrinaire defense of certain directors still reverberates with the countless battles waged by young critics at *Cahiers du Cinéma* in the 1950s and taken up by their numerous disciples in England, America, and elsewhere.[3] Moreover, Scorsese's cinema histories commemorate a particular experience of film spectatorship, traditionally had in movie auditoria, but also in front of televisions, in homes and surrounded by familiars, and this merges intuitively with the unrepentant auteurist coordinates in his subjective summary of film history.[4] *A Personal Journey* fully adheres to this type of connoisseurship. Its indebtedness to Andrew Sarris's 1960s criticism and the latter's classification of film directors, for instance, directly links *A Personal Journey* to a seminal American version of classic cinephilia, and Scorsese's survey of the central Hollywood genres and their sociocultural implications is similarly beholden to Sarris's methods. Yet one can see how *Il mio viaggio in Italia* and *A Letter to Elia* are finally framed by this same cinephilic or critical character, and their focus on familiar directors and films situates them securely within the same auteurist cosmos.

On the other hand, however, the reception of Scorsese's "film histories" has highlighted this cinephilic descent at the expense of their meanings as *documentaries*, and as a result, they have been too quickly summarized as mere echoes of the classic auteurist testaments to cinema.[5] Alberto Pezzotta, for example, is disappointed with *Il mio viaggio in Italia*'s "conventional view of Italian film history" and its clear inclination "to view the history of Italian cinema as a series of masterpieces by auteurs, ignoring the wider context" (2003). He is justifiably dissatisfied with Scorsese's "list of celebrated directors" (overly recognizable to devotees of Italian cinema) and his tendency to disregard "undervalued or forgotten masterpieces" (2003). But assessing *Il mio viaggio in Italia*, *A Personal Journey*, and *A Letter to Elia* solely as tributes to cinephilic knowledge or commitment leaves several important questions about their status as documentaries unanswered. What, for example, do Scorsese's audiovisual histories really seek to *document*? Are they in fact "histories of cinema" in the traditional sense? In other words, if these documentaries are ultimately not revisionist compendia, but rather, memorials to generally acknowledged "classics," how should one characterize their different historiographic aspirations? *Il mio viaggio in Italia* and *A Letter to Elia*, for instance, return viewers to the central concerns of Scorsese's 1970s non-fiction short films, *Italianamerican* (1974) and *American Boy: A Profile of Steven Prince* (1978), and they purposefully reexamine the earlier works' ethnic narratives. Indeed, while the director's 1970s documentaries produce oral histories by attending to the singularity of their storytelling subjects, that is, the comportment and expressive speech of Scorsese's parents and Steven Prince, *Il mio viaggio in Italia* and *A Letter to Elia* reassess the historical past by re-viewing its complexly interwoven links to the director's lifelong cinephilia. In other words, Scorsese's documentaries about Italian cinema and the Greek American film director Elia Kazan permit him to reconsider—and resuscitate—his own family's fading history, but the emphasis has now shifted decisively to venerated movie images because they are key intermediaries in the director's reminiscences. Films, photographs, and other kinds of popular images are often said to enable one's recollecting, of course, but Scorsese's cinema histories are more plainspoken about *why* they choose particular movies to revisit the past.[6] The benchmarks of Italian cinema and Elia Kazan's films generate maps for the director's memories about his family and their migrations to America, while at the same time disclosing a profound—and perhaps newfound—sense of obligation: to the receding past; to his parents, *Italianamerican*'s artless storytellers, who have since passed away along with their world; and most importantly, to the prospect of reopening his family's historical migrations within the context of these present-day collections of film images.

Il mio viaggio in Italia, for example, outlines how Scorsese's selected images function as mobile relics within the film's wider compilation: these celebrated movies and chosen sequences migrated from Italy's sacred topography to a secondary site in New York City's Little Italy, and in the process, they permitted the director's immigrant family members to partake in the original location's value. This recurring rhetoric of transposition and transformation discloses a key to the film's rendering of historical accounts: moving images are enduring and transferable; they can be storehouses for stories and historical experiences, yet they can also be shared in the new context of an audiovisual compendium like *Il mio viaggio in Italia*. As we'll see, Scorsese's recollections about the classic Neorealist films' original passage from Italy to America develop from this same emphasis on relocatability, and they repeatedly highlight a substantial correspondence between moving images and his experience of the world. Having once migrated from Italy to America in the late-1940s and 1950s, these artifacts are repositioned within a novel framework, namely, the audiovisual assemblage on view. *Il mio viaggio in Italia*, like all of Scorsese's cinephile collections, is finally structured by a limited set of precepts: the gathering and arrangement of fondly remembered film images and sounds; a comprehensive use of voice-over commentary by the director, conversational but always informative; and Scorsese's intermittent onscreen appearances as presenter and guide, at once confirming the "personal" nature of his critical-historical work and reminding viewers of their own implication in an analogous cinephilic relation to these (and other) moving images. But *Il mio viaggio in Italia*'s archival sifting is ultimately directed by its belief in resemblance or equivalency, and as we'll see, this is especially true when Scorsese revisits Italian Neorealism. Selected fragments correspond to other images and things, historical experiences and worlds, yet the principle of correspondence allows them to be repositioned—or reincarnated—in the director's cinephile compilation, which in turn gives them a new historical value for present-day spectators.

A Personal Journey with Martin Scorsese Through American Movies initiates Scorsese's production of audiovisual histories of cinema in 1995, but its commission by the British Film Institute (BFI) also coincides with a much broader scholarly reckoning with the medium's history. An inescapable apprehensiveness about the future of "film" (a physical vehicle for capturing and making images) and "cinema" (as cultural institution), provoked in equal parts by celebrations of the medium's centenary *and* the imminent arrival of digital technologies, features in nearly every debate about cinema during this period. Shortly after the production and broadcast of *A Personal Journey*, for example, Susan Sontag famously diagnosed the contemporary "decay of cinema," and the attendant apprehension over film's past and undefined future continually seized upon cinephilia, its purported erosion, and the cinema's inevitable withdrawal from its once prominent position in public life.[7] If such laments had the same surface appearance as so many other "end of the Sixties" formulations by baby boomers, they nevertheless spoke directly to imminent transformations in film culture. Sontag's focus is an apparently endangered cinephilia, but her sense of alarm about the cinema's looming "death" had its close counterpart in a widespread preoccupation with the introduction of digital image-making and its potential consequences. For cinema studies scholars, this manifested in various theoretical reassessments: on the one hand, discussions of cinephilia became common and looked to revivify the 1950s *Cahiers du Cinéma* positions; on the other hand, the fading of film as a "photographic" medium prompted a reconsideration of early film theory and the medium's special attunement to modernity and historicity.[8] Such reflection had the welcome benefit of restoring previously rejected perspectives on the history of cinema, even if it inadvertently participated in the era's pessimism about the medium's future. Although they sometimes also share in these grim premonitions about the cinema's twenty-first-century destiny, Scorsese's documentaries about film histories are led by a noticeably different conception of danger and obligation. The history of his family's migrations is disappearing (from living memory, from the record), and the filmmaker's indebtedness to this past is demonstrated by his accumulation of images and "personal" interpretations of their meaning. As we'll see, *Il mio viaggio in Italia* and *A Letter to Elia* turn to the history of cinema not because the medium is endangered (though they preserve and exhibit their ancient images for this reason as well), but rather, because its moving images are the repository for individual thoughts, memories, and experiences. In other words, for Scorsese and these two documentaries, an extensive archive of popular film images provides the components for summoning an historical past that might otherwise have been abandoned—only these documents can match the director's sense of responsibility, and his gathering of moving images and sounds accordingly reestablishes his connection to the past.[9]

Personal Journeys: Retrieving Cinematographic Remains

According to Michael Witt, today's broadly applied principles of "visual criticism" were first introduced by 1920s modernists. The "reediting experiments conducted on imported American films such as [D.W.] Griffith's *Intolerance* (1916) in the young Lev Kuleshov's Workshop," for example, initiated investigations into film editing's radical capacity for meaning making; and in France, the "First Wave" Impressionists' simultaneous development of cinematographic studies, equally experimental, though lacking the Soviet filmmakers' unequivocal political program, also took to reassembling images for critical purposes (Witt 2013, 105–6). Indeed, although the long history of appropriating or recycling extant film materials can be traced back even further to the earliest years of film exhibition and the editorial repurposing of diverse kinds of footage for short newsreels, Witt rightly highlights the *conceptual* rearrangement of images in these two examples from the 1920s. "Clip-based" assessments and chronological reviews, "didactic cinema histories of cinema," and an overriding "experimentation with film history" were emergent practices, yet audiovisual criticism truly developed within the singular atmosphere of 1920s French cinephilia: "books, lectures, cine-club reprojections and debates" provided numerous opportunities for such experiments, and as a result, these works could be exhibited and contemplated with the gravity of established historiography (Witt 2013, 106).[10] Nevertheless, if the genesis of a cinematic critical approach can be situated within this 1920s setting, its subsequent development intersects with a long tradition of film directors doubling as critics, or in a few notable cases, theorists. The First Wave French Impressionists and Soviet filmmakers like Kuleshov might have initiated this amalgamation of criticism and practice, but directors such as Luis Buñuel, Stan Brakhage, Hollis Frampton, Michelangelo Antonioni, various figures connected with the French New Wave (and its adherents around the world), and many others have continually renewed this close correlation between criticism and production. As Witt's *Jean-Luc Godard: Cinema Historian* convincingly demonstrates,

Jean-Luc Godard's incomparable *Histoire(s) du cinema* (1988–98) is the fullest elaboration of this particular brand of audiovisual historiography, yet the ceaseless "remixing" or reassembling of existing movie images within novel analytical contexts is inescapable in today's new media environments. Encouraged in part by easier access to the archive of film images and user-friendly, relatively cheap digital editing software, the contemporary torrent of videographic essays ranges widely across the internet. It now includes countless prosaic efforts by cinephiles and fans on video sharing platforms such as YouTube and *vimeo*, but it also extends to the more familiar "disciplinary" production of scholars engaged in a "form of multi-media 'writing.'"[11]

Not surprisingly, Scorsese's preliminary work on behalf of film preservation in the 1980s would eventually progress in a comparable way during the 1990s. Although *A Personal Journey* commences his production of cinephile documentaries in 1995, Scorsese's earlier lectures on the hazards of fading color film stock had all been delivered in recognizably cinephilic surroundings. The earliest screenings of *Raging Bull* in 1980–1 were followed by illustrated presentations at film festivals and cinematheques, those longstanding institutional descendants of a French cinephilic tradition, and the very format of a lecture/demonstration recalls the famous cine-club discussions and debates from previous decades. Scorsese's efforts were basically meant to explain a looming crisis for the film medium. The fading or disintegration of color film stock, the attendant loss of a cultural heritage ("cultural suicide," he called it), and his projections for retrieving the artifacts on view—these were the principal foci in his lectures.[12] Scorsese's varied curatorial activities in this period would, however, soon expand his vision of film history, and the growing recognition—or "canonization"—of his fiction filmmaking throughout the 1990s ensured a considerable public profile for the burgeoning work of film preservation.[13] The Film Foundation, established in 1990, created an institutional context for the director's distribution of materials about preservation, yet at the same time presented a more formalized approach to refurbishing or retrieving "lost" films. The Foundation's broadening directives would lead to the World Cinema Project, a wide-ranging assortment of movies from different national cinemas and historical periods, but its main purpose continued to be *preservation* and *restoration*: from Algeria to Argentina, Mexico, Turkey, and the UK, The Film Foundation would remain dedicated to restoring and then exhibiting unknown—or what it calls "neglected"—movies. In this respect, through Scorsese's ongoing stewardship, film preservation has effectively been tailored to the cinephile's inherent need to proselytize on behalf of overlooked films and filmmakers.[14]

A Personal Journey with Martin Scorsese Through American Movies introduced a novel variation on this approach to advancing the appreciation of film's cultural import. Commissioned by the BFI and Channel 4, Scorsese's film was the flagship in a multipart series to memorialize the cinema's centenary in 1995. Executive produced by Colin MacCabe and Bob Last, the "Century of Cinema" proposed documentaries by sixteen "great directors" from around the world who would provide personal accounts of their national cinemas (MacCabe 2003, 299–300). Scorsese's three-part film voyage, the leading—and lengthiest—entry in the BFI program, registers a relatively familiar critical approach to the history of classical Hollywood. Because the project's broader latitude encouraged Scorsese to look at American cinema in personal terms, that is to say, as an "inspiration" for his own filmmaking, the director's study is resolutely auteurist and classificatory. Indeed, in the terms of this expansive account, resourceful directors work within Hollywood's evident strictures in innovative ways, and a wide variety of films can accordingly be categorized as conscious responses to these commercial pressures. Andrew Sarris appears to be the primary model for Scorsese's approach, but the influence of *Cahiers du Cinéma*'s many critics-turned-filmmakers is also unmistakable in *A Personal Journey*. Although the film's all-purpose auteurist configurations—The Director's Dilemma, The Director as Storyteller, Illusionist, Smuggler, Iconoclast—recall Sarris's historiography, Scorsese envisions his personal passage through Hollywood history just as the "Young Turks" at *Cahiers du Cinéma* had throughout the 1950s. He reiterates the well-known highlights of this history (the early discovery of narrative form and film style, the formation of a studio system, the introduction of sound, color, etc.), yet as he indicates from the outset, his principal interest is "not necessarily the culturally correct" films or filmmakers. Instead, his analyses look to Hollywood's peripheral productions—low budget B films, humble genre pictures, and outliers in the industry's mode of production. In this respect, Scorsese belatedly shares in what Emilie Bickerton calls *Cahiers du Cinéma*'s "visionary" undertaking, namely, those critical examinations which discover true "cinema" where others see only ordinary entertainment (2009, xvii). Although the distinguished Hollywood "masters" are given their due in *A Personal Journey*, Scorsese's evident preference for the *film maudit* (and the *auteur maudit*) consistently redirects his researches, and his documentary is ultimately a much less polemical or antagonistic—

though no less compulsive and committed—version of the *politique des auteurs* and its "axiomatic programme."[15]

That said, if *A Personal Journey* incorporates these foci from 1950s and 1960s auteurist criticism, its opening passages briefly sketch another approach to assembling and sharing its *cinematic* account of Hollywood's history, and this would prove to be fundamental to Scorsese's more subjective *Il mio viaggio in Italia* and *A Letter to Elia*. *A Personal Journey*'s unspoken invitation to rummage through its images and retrospectively identify allusions in Scorsese's fiction filmmaking has admittedly been difficult for many spectators to resist. These films have clearly provided a foundation for the director's Hollywood work; yet the temptation to see them solely in terms of their filial position, that is, as the substantiation of "influence," risks diverting attention from *A Personal Journey*'s novel documentary hypothesis. *Force of Evil* (Abraham Polonsky, 1946) and *Raging Bull*, *The Roaring Twenties* (Raoul Walsh, 1939), *Goodfellas* (1990) and *Casino* (1995), Allan Dwan's mobile framing and Anthony Mann's *noir* cityscapes—there is, of course, abundant evidence to confirm Scorsese's references to these and the many other movies discussed in *A Personal Journey*. The film's introductory section, however, guides viewers to a very different emphasis, namely, the work of accumulating images and its specific connections to cinephilia. In short, the *retrieval* of cinematographic remnants is underscored as the key to comprehending how elected moments from the history of cinema can be rearranged in a novel historiographic setting. Scorsese's first appearance in *A Personal Journey* thus concentrates on his motivation for taking this particular course through Hollywood history. Sitting in a medium shot while looking directly into the camera, Scorsese describes his earliest experience with movies. Holding a worn copy of Deems Taylor's *A Pictorial History of the Movies* (1943), the director remembers borrowing this book repeatedly from the New York Public Library as a child and feeling tempted to steal some of its many frame enlargements and other still images (Figure 4.1). Following a quick scan of pictures from *A Pictorial History*, the film returns to Scorsese, now shot in a medium close-up as he delivers his punchline. He did in fact occasionally succumb to this criminal compulsion, he confesses as the camera moves toward him slightly to register his comical "shame," and he stealthily removed and saved several images from Taylor's pictorial summary of Hollywood history. But why? And to what end? *A Pictorial History*, primarily an assortment of pictures with complementary text, is already a methodical collection, a succession of selected images which purports to be a "history of the movies." Yet Scorsese's immediate

Figure 4.1 *A Personal Journey with Martin Scorsese Through American Movies* (Martin Scorsese and Michael Henry Wilson, 1995).

instinct was to take these isolated fragments (but only *some* of these pieces, only elected portions of the whole) and rearrange them according to his own memories or projected experiences of these same films (he had not yet viewed many of them, he admits).

Recalling the essential revelation about François Truffaut's Ferrand in *Day for Night* (François Truffaut, 1973), Scorsese's opening confession quickly sketches an origin narrative. In Truffaut's *Day for Night*, Ferrand is disturbed by a recurring dream, and as the film continues to advance through his nighttime visions, viewers witness the formation of a distinctly cinephilic recollection. The adolescent Ferrand steals several photos from a movie auditorium's lobby, promotional stills from Orson Welles's *Citizen Kane* (1941), and the camera's lingering devotion to these images suggests the filmmaker's deep-seated investment in selecting and stockpiling these particular artifacts. For Truffaut, this scenario inaugurates his complete immersion in cinema, and Scorsese's reminiscence is similarly situated as the commencement of a lifelong film addiction. *A Personal Journey*'s commemorative segment ends with a shot of

Scorsese's index finger pointing to another frame enlargement from Taylor's *Pictorial History*, an image from King Vidor's *Duel in the Sun* (1946), and this introduces the documentary's conjoined foci: recollections about film viewing, invariably from Scorsese's childhood, are combined with winding detours through the history of classical Hollywood filmmaking. But *A Personal Journey*'s audiovisual archival materials continually guide its explorations, and this preliminary sequence indicates how gathering and arrangement, cutting and serialization are the film's principal means for translating these diverse records into history.

The concurrent scholarly recuperation of cinephilia also emphasized this close correspondence between memory, fragments, and the collection of selected moments from various movies. Like the childhood figure in Ferrand's recurrent dream and Scorsese in *A Personal Journey*'s brief introductory sequence, historical cinephiles were explicitly recast in the mid-1990s as prototypical collectors of the arcane. This reconceived cinephilic character was said to habitually accumulate and schematize specific instants from projected films; and these were elected moments which resonated exclusively for the cinephile yet required further verbal articulation, that is to say, a conversion into language to confirm and extend these otherwise obscure experiences. Paul Willemen's contemporaneous reconsideration of assorted critical writings by *Cahiers du Cinéma*'s Young Turks highlights this "notion of collecting" in historical or classic cinephilia. The "moment of cinephilia," he observes, "has to do with the serialization of moments of revelation" (1994, 233). Christian Keathley has similarly underscored the post-Second World War cinephile's fundamental desire to stockpile these cinematic epiphanies, or rather, to store the *recollection* of these singular moments. These are pleasurable experiences, Keathley argues, but they also provide flickers of insight into a film's peripheral or discarded qualities (2006, 20), and the scholarly repossession of cinephilia would ultimately redefine it in terms of this partiality for the movies' typically overlooked features. In each case, however, the *Cahiers du Cinéma* critics are said to have prolonged the potentially revelatory moments in film viewing by reading and (especially) writing about them, and cinephilia in the immediate post-Second World War period would develop from the effort to compile and reiterate such elusive experiences.[16]

As a self-described "final wave" cinephile, Keathley admits to having "spent much more time reading about movies than watching them. To learn about film history, I scoured the library shelves and bookstores for volumes devoted to celebrating those great films that I half-guessed I would never see" (2006, 22). Like Scorsese, he confesses to having finally "swiped" a few of these books from his public library—prolonging the cinephile experience, it seems, entails repossessing a part of its extra-filmic afterlife. But Scorsese's collection is composed solely of audiovisual fragments, and his brief outline of an origin myth leads directly to *A Personal Journey*'s compilation of sequences from American movies and assorted paratexts (interviews with filmmakers and actors, for instance). Explicitly organized as an "imaginary museum," the film's succeeding collection of images quickly abandons its autobiographical frame, however, to look instead at the various actualities of film direction in Hollywood during the classical period. As Robert P. Kolker notes, *A Personal Journey* is in this respect primarily a "practitioner's" vision of Hollywood history (2015, 74), and its substantial insider's acumen about the practices of fiction filmmaking soon surpasses its Sarris and *Cahiers du Cinéma* derived critical evaluations of the films on view. Indeed, Scorsese's route through the culturally "unauthorized" and "overlooked" films is perhaps too predictable for devotees of those fundamental auteurist texts; at times his voice-over narration reverberates too strongly with earlier critical insights (Nicholas Ray is a "smuggler," for example, and *à la* Truffaut, *Johnny Guitar* [Nicholas Ray, 1955] is the evidence).[17] Nevertheless, the familiarity of these movies should direct us to apprehend the different aims of *A Personal Journey* and Scorsese's subsequent cinephile documentaries. Simply put, these works seek to determine how the director's cinephilia and a wider history are interwoven: does the historical past somehow adhere to his recollections of film viewing? *A Personal Journey* establishes a foundation for this type of cinematic research, but *Il mio viaggio in Italia* and *A Letter to Elia* develop it much further. As documentaries, they examine popular moving images for their rootedness in historical realities, yet they construct their respective assemblages from the director's numerous recollections about watching movies. For Scorsese, film viewing, or the memory of film viewing, is a vehicle for understanding particular realities. His family's history of migration, he says, was once reexperienced in the transfer of Italian images to America during the postwar period, but *Il mio viaggio in Italia* revivifies this same history through its cinephilic collection of fragments; while *A Letter to Elia*'s compilation of audiovisual resources alongside Scorsese's voice-over narration releases different truths about the immigrants' lives in the new world. Together these two films provide a reassessment of the ethnic narrative set forth by Scorsese's *Italianamerican* and *American Boy: A Profile of Steven*

Prince, but they do so by extending *A Personal Journey*'s introductory insights beyond the expressions of discernment or practical knowledge. Gathered images, plundered from archival resources or remembered by the filmmaker in a present-day context, now provide the foundation for rendering accounts of a much broader historical past. Moving images intermediate between a past actuality and the director's reminiscences, and their assemblage in these new documentary settings ensures the prolongation of history into the present.

Bringing It All Back Home: *Il mio viaggio in Italia*

If *A Personal Journey with Martin Scorsese Through American Movies* reassembles its film fragments to deliver an assessment of classical Hollywood filmmaking, its commission by the BFI for the cinema's centenary guaranteed its commemorative tenor. Memorials, however, often carry an implication of death and mourning, and Scorsese's celebration of Hollywood inevitably discusses its subject matter as a wholly antiquated phenomenon: classical Hollywood, the studio or "golden" period, is basically obsolete at this point, and this personal course through American movies outlines a history that does not—and cannot—include the historian himself. *A Personal Journey* ends emphatically, of course, just as Scorsese is embarking upon his own expedition as a film director, and a very different future is implied by the film's fleeting references to the director's New Hollywood colleagues. But *A Personal Journey*'s concluding segment settles somewhat unexpectedly on images from Elia Kazan's *America America* (1963), an historical fiction about Kazan's Greek American family's immigration from Anatolia in the early twentieth century. Scorsese calmly connects his personal and comparatively minor passage from Little Italy to New York University (and then Hollywood) with *America America*'s expansive tale of migration, and the sequence introduces a notably new pattern of thinking about American film history and its meaning. In this case, the director intuits a substantial similarity between his experience and the images on view, and the latter in fact direct their spectators through a modern American history—of migrations, of the immigrant's persistent sense of outsiderhood, and so on. As a consequence, the sequence is "personal" in a much more meaningful way than anything that comes before it in *A Personal Journey*: remnants from Kazan's epic film correspond to Scorsese's historical experience, yet they alone can release his particular memories about this period, give them a form and significance.

Within *A Personal Journey*'s broader classification of films, *America America* is the work of an "iconoclast" and a vehicle for "personal expression," but the sequence discloses a distinctive approach to looking at the relationship between history and films. Scorsese's statements here initially seem to simply complete *A Personal Journey*'s foundational origin myth, yet his brief look to *America America* wholly reformulates his explanation of film-related memories. Now movies are said to do more than "color [his] dreams" or "change [his] perceptions" and his "life" as a filmmaker; Kazan's film is a map for knowing the world and the past, though because this insight comes at the end of *A Personal Journey*, the director doesn't allow himself to fully follow this new line of thinking. In *Il mio viaggio in Italia* and *A Letter to Elia*, he takes this primary intuition as a new point of departure.[18]

Originally conceived several years before the BFI's *A Personal Journey* commission, *Il mio viaggio in Italia*'s production did not commence until 1996, and this lengthy documentary would eventually adopt a noticeably modified approach to constructing its narrowly described history of Italian cinema. On the one hand, it plainly preserves *A Personal Journey*'s unapologetic auteurist configuration: the categorization of directors once again provides the frame for Scorsese's survey of a national cinema, though in this case the emphasis on overlooked films is largely eliminated from its narrative. On the other hand, however, the director's previous "imaginary" excursion through the history of classic American cinema had been "personal" only insofar as his choice of movies was often self-consciously idiosyncratic (the capacity for making eccentric selections is an important part of the cinephile's pedigree and self-presentation). As the home of "entertainers," Hollywood was finally dissected from a distance as the workplace for artisans and organized commercial production. *Il mio viaggio in Italia*, by contrast, is structured much more unequivocally as autobiography. The documentary's opening and closing sections reiterate the director's well-known origin story; but the film is focused on unearthing his first experiences as a spectator of Italian cinema, his reminiscences, and the history of his immigrant family's rootedness in these re-collected images. Indeed, while several significant institutional features had been underscored in *A Personal Journey*'s studies of Hollywood (even if they were finally given the Sarris-like status of "productive constraint" in the film's auteurist universe), *Il mio viaggio in Italia* elects instead to supplement its autobiographical introductory segments with detailed descriptions and interpretations of Scorsese's earliest memories of Italian cinema and their embeddedness in his Little Italy actualities. In this important respect, the documentary is only in part an historical review of Italian cinema, and it is best understood as a more fully realized analysis of connections between the young Scorsese's embryonic cinephilia, his family's immigrant history, and his developing comprehension or perception of their shared world.

Peter Doyle situates *Il mio viaggio in Italia* as the key progenitor to Scorsese's present-day documentary filmmaking. *No Direction Home: Bob Dylan* (2005), he observes, strategically incorporates Jeff Rosen's interviews with Bob Dylan into its compilation, yet the "superordinate layer here is not so much Dylan's spoken narrative, but rather Scorsese's more covert hand, his direction, his montage, his *mise-en-scène*" (2007, 68). In a corresponding manner, *George Harrison: Living in the Material World* (2011) continually recontextualizes its extensive archival materials, and in the process, the well-known features of George Harrison's life are reinterpreted in terms of a spiritual biography. The musician's personal history is methodically woven into the film's fabric of images and sounds, and his story is thereby made representative: it stands in for an entire generation's passage from post-Sixties embitterment to serenity. In each of these cases, the meaningful artifact (interviews, films and photographs, sounds) establishes a structural scope for the assemblage of various other archival materials. The filmmaker's interventions as editor—as the one who brings together these objects, yet also implicitly conveys their meaning to viewers—allow him to reconfigure his resources and reshape them into an historical account for spectators. In *Il mio viaggio in Italia*, however, the venerated object is the *substantial* core of the film's approach: its images and sounds are *valued* primarily because they continue to carry a trace of personal and historical experience within them. Doyle highlights Scorsese's "intimate, insistent voice-over" (2007, 68) as the vital element in *Il mio viaggio in Italia*'s collection, but a deeper coordinated relationship between the director's language (and voice), memories, and his elected images and sequences is what finally transports the historical past into the present. In other words, film images are transfigured in this documentary, but not only by Scorsese's always conversant voice-over; instead, his accumulation of images and his subsequent procedure for rearranging them into a new whole produce a survey of cinematic experience and its historical meaning. Moving images had once been stockpiled—as recollections, yet also as material remnants of historical experience—for some undetermined future usage, and the director is now revivifying them in the current context of his cinephile compilation. As a consequence, the images in *Il mio viaggio in Italia* are released from the remote conditions of their initial exhibition (or broadcast) and reception, relocated, and opened to an assortment of new possibilities of exchange with their present-day viewers.

Scorsese's personal voyage through the history of Italian cinema is appropriately named after Roberto Rossellini's groundbreaking *Viaggio in Italia* (1954). Although customarily seen as an obstinately modernist work, Rossellini's film is an elementary, easily grasped resource for the director of *Il mio viaggio in Italia*. It provides his documentary with a relevant and practical title, of course; but it is also simply one more archival object, another piece in his subjective record of Italian film history. In this respect, two of *Viaggio in Italia*'s most important scenes direct viewers to an additional, potentially buried meaning in Scorsese's selection of Rossellini's title for his own documentary. Dudley Andrew refers to these sequences, both devoted to images of excavation or revivification, as analogies for "the historian's encounter with the past" (1998, 177), and Scorsese's approach in *Il mio viagio in Italia* adheres closely to the spirit of retrieval in these key scenes. Katherine Joyce's (Ingrid Bergman) visit to the phosphorous fields at Vesuvius, Andrew observes, concludes in "an immense exhalation from inside this ancient but living and explosive mountain" (1998, 177): a gust of air from the past is gradually drawn into the present by the heat of cigarette smoke and human breath. During a later visit to Pompeii, Katherine and her increasingly estranged husband, Alex (George Sanders), witness the protracted exhumation of a man and woman who had been buried at the very moment of their death several centuries earlier. They—and the movie's spectators—watch as archaeologists carefully work at reestablishing the couple's contours, progressively unearthing new dimensions and substance as they return these primordial, embracing characters to Katherine's apprehensive vision in the present. According to Andrew, *Viaggio in Italia* at this moment alerts us "to the possibilities of exchange between past and present, through the manner by which we look and through our response to being looked at, that is, being measured by a living past" (1998, 2013). Laura Mulvey has characterized the Pompeii sequence in equally pertinent terms. The slowly rediscovered couple, she observes, bears "witness to the reality [of the past's] once-upon-a-time presence" (2006, 107); the reappearance of these two figures testifies directly to the past's durable traces in the present-day world. However, each of these sequences also implicitly reflects upon the processes of recovering—or resuscitating—a material history through cinematic means. That is to say, in these analogies for "the historian's encounter with the past," the cinema reveals its own power to initiate comparable exchanges with buried strata of the historical past. Its distinctive affinity with historiography is partially found in this capacity to unearth and then reassemble a wide variety of images and sounds, and Scorsese's *Il mio viaggio in Italia* presents itself as precisely this kind of repository for his selected images: this documentary provides a new historiographic backdrop for looking at and "being measured by" these well-known movies from the past.

Il mio viaggio in Italia begins with an extended example of such cinematic resuscitation. Following a series of wandering, unhurried images from the concluding segment of Rossellini's *Paisà* (1946), Scorsese shares a few recollections about his original encounters with the postwar Neorealist films, but then shifts quickly to detailed memories about his family's immigration from Italy to America. Essentially introducing himself as his people's final surviving descendant, Scorsese is a conspicuously solitary storyteller throughout *Il mio viaggio in Italia*, and as a result, his reminiscences are supplemented by a wealth of personal family photographs, archival documents (maps, drawings, stock images of the Sicilian countryside, photos of monuments, etc.), and most importantly, moving images from several different resources. In *Italianamerican*, this past had been disclosed by the Scorseses' shared, artless storytelling. Stockpiled in their sense memories, one only witnesses this history's release in the distinctiveness and growing ease of the Scorseses' deportment as they articulate their absorbing tales; one hears and sees it in their colloquial expressions and the general tenor of their exchanges with the film's director and crew. By contrast, *Il mio viaggio in Italia* sifts through its assorted archival resources for novel perspectives on the same history of migration, and this becomes especially apparent in its incorporation of recently discovered home movie footage of Scorsese's immediate family members. One sees the director's grandparents in their crowded New York City dwelling, participating in some animated festivity ("a baptism" he says); we watch Scorsese's father, Charles, almost unrecognizable to anyone who remembers his appearance in *Italianamerican*, surrounded by family and energetically playing a small guitar or mandolin at this same party (Figure 4.2); and we witness several of these figures walking across the early twentieth-century streets of Little Italy, working in their small grocery store, and then finally entering their apartment building (Figure 4.3). Scorsese pointedly allows footage of a 1930s St. Ciro street festival to linger momentarily onscreen before identifying its distant origins: these black-and-white, silent images, recently uncovered and shared

Figure 4.2 *Il mio viaggio in Italia* (Martin Scorsese, 2001).

Figure 4.3 *Il mio viaggio in Italia* (Martin Scorsese, 2001).

Personal Pilgrimages

by his cousin, were taken in New York City, *not* Sicily, he states emphatically. Nevertheless, according to Scorsese, Little Italy's "Elizabeth Street *was* Sicily" in this period; it *was* a relocated material instantiation of Sicilian customs, the region's long history, values, surface appearances, and so forth. Although this historical world has fully retreated into memory, its restoration in these home movies returns it suddenly to the present, and its apparent retrievability produces Scorsese's genuine sense of astonishment at witnessing the figures before him. "I never thought I would see any of these people *move* again," he calmly states. Flickering images from a remote history, these recently unearthed home movies seem to guarantee the past's permanency, but more importantly, they reunite the director with his once living family members as they reappear onscreen during his present-day viewing (Figure 4.4). The uncanny vision of his ancestors clearly moves him, yet their perceptible movement—their reanimation—unexpectedly brings them back to the world as projections from the living past. In other words, they are projected into Scorsese's present-day collection of film images and personal reminiscences. And though this historiographic exercise is generated from an unequivocally stated desire to

Figure 4.4 *Il mio viaggio in Italia* (Martin Scorsese, 2001).

remember his family and their communal relation to cinema, or rather, to reestablish their elemental place in his memories of cinema, these particular images confirm the past's existence for Scorsese. In this respect, they are a type of evidence, and their presence can direct the filmmaker's ensuing attempt to bring various antecedents—familial, cinematic, historical—into the present moment in a similar way. Simply put, images from the history of Italian cinema will also provide *proof* in *Il mio viaggio in Italia*. Something of the past has been preserved in Scorsese's recollections about viewing these films with his family; movies were watched by this particular group of Italian immigrants, yet these elected images now preserve a memory of the Scorseses' shared experiences, who they once were in the "old world," and who they were becoming in America.

The Translation of Place: Watching Movies, From Sicily to Little Italy

This emphasis on the moving image as a type of unadorned evidence intersects with concurrent discussions about "film" as a medium. A reinvigorated attention to the significance of cinema's photographic base, motivated by increasing infiltrations from computer-generated image-making as a potential substitute for celluloid during this period, brought scholars back to the core questions raised by classical film theorists about the medium, its photochemical source, and pertinence to history. Mary Ann Doane, for example, characterizes film's capacity to capture routine contingencies as its principal "lure" for spectators, but this mechanical component is also said to demonstrate the cinema's promise of "historicity" (2002, 225). Indeed, in the effort to restore a connection between the invention of cinema, its photochemical underpinning, modernity, and an associated historiographic character, Doane and many others seized upon "indexicality" as the fulcrum for any understanding of cinema's novelty and theoretical consequence. This photochemical basis for the movies' prospective insights into modern historiography had already been highlighted by classical film theorists like André Bazin and Siegfried Kracauer, but a sharper look at history now guided scholarly accounts of these matters. In a similar equation of film and historicity, for instance, Philip Rosen explains the image's "special credibility" in terms of its mechanical creation of signs (or "indexes"), and these signs can testify directly "to the existence of something" having formerly appeared before a film camera's lens. "In the case of a genuine index," Rosen argues, "the sign's object—that is, its referent—is an existent whose presence is required in the formation of a sign" (2001, 18). In other words, the "genuine index" guarantees the moving image's significance to the rendering of historical accounts: "Since an indexical sign is such by some existential connection between a [...] referent and a signifier, the latter will always provide the subject with irrefutable testimony as to the real existence of the referent" (Rosen 2001, 18). If a particular referent was present "at some moment in the production" of an indexical sign (and we can reasonably deduce how such signs are made by filmmaking technology), then one receives the latter as "evidence" for a prior temporality. In watching a film or looking at a photo, "the indexical trace is a matter of pastness" (Rosen 2001, 20) precisely because the moment of viewing (now) is invariably different from the time of the image's production (then). The resulting experience, Stanley Cavell writes, is at once uncanny and unavoidable:

> Photography maintains the presentness of the world by accepting our absence from it. The reality of a photo is present to me while I am not present to it; and a world I know, and see, but to which I am nevertheless not present (through no fault of my subjectivity), is a world past.
>
> (1979, 23)

In the context of a late-twentieth-century apprehension over film's future, the critical return to such ideas undoubtedly indicated a degree of frustration with the film medium's destiny in the digital era, but it also disclosed a need to prolong the cinema's existence and the life of a certain type of cinematic experience.[19]

Although they aim for thoroughness and have extended running times, Scorsese's cinephile documentaries have a welcome modesty about them, and they do not condescend to viewers with discussions of "film theory" per se, nor do they wholly surrender to the era's predominant "death of cinema" rhetoric. Nevertheless, *Il mio viaggio in Italia*'s preliminary exploration of Scorsese's recently uncovered home movie footage appears to make comparable propositions about the grainy black-and-white images on view.[20] They can instantly substantiate the existence of a preceding period in time and history; and the director, a model movie spectator at this very moment, is evidently moved by the unexpected presence of his deceased family members, by their present-day reappearance as moving figures on the screen before him. However, as a frame for comprehending the subsequent presentation of lengthy sequences from the history of Italian cinema, *Il mio viaggio in Italia*'s introductory passages direct spectators to much finer-grained distinctions in Scorsese's palpable relationship to these images. In short, the director's manner of looking at—and receiving—this flickering footage determines his ensuing arrangement of archival materials in a meaningful way. A closer consideration of this critical sequence discloses alternative maps and principles in *Il mio viaggio in Italia*'s wider re-collection of canonical movie images, and more importantly, it reveals a value or function for these artifacts that exceeds their elementary status as so-called "indexical traces."

As we've seen, the "home movie" sequence is constructed in the unequivocal terms of a close alignment between Sicily and Little Italy. Appearing alone and standing on the rooftop of his childhood apartment building, Scorsese remembers how "Elizabeth Street *was* Sicily" in this period, "and every building was a different village" with its clear strictures against marrying into adjoining "villages" and other "customs carried over from the old world." In this account, the St. Ciro street festival strikingly relocates ancient Sicilian rituals to an early twentieth-century Little Italy, but the director's memories, which "come back to [him] in a flash" as he silently witnesses this footage, indicate the effortless interchangeability of these two remote places. Indeed, on first sight, there really is no substantial difference between Sicily and Elizabeth Street. This, Scorsese concludes as he watches what appears to be a crowded street procession, "is the world of my childhood," a world instinctively transferred from the parched Sicilian landscape to the narrow streets of his Little Italy neighborhood (Figure 4.5). The sequence returns again and again to his categorical interpretations of a substantial correlation between Sicily and Little Italy ("Elizabeth Street *was* Little Italy," "*this* is the world of my childhood," etc.), and these statements should be understood as more than expedient or demotic expressions: they designate a manner of looking at and comprehending what might otherwise appear to be distantly disconnected images and things, and such thinking is extended to both the salvaged home movies *and* the following collection of selected sequences from Italian film history.

The transposition or adaptation of the Sicilian topography to new locations in America is a recurring theme in Scorsese's film-induced reminiscences throughout *Il mio viaggio in Italia*, but it is also a key to understanding how he selects and assembles his assorted fragments, particularly when he discusses the great postwar Neorealist works. Moreover, it helps to explain his focus on the memory of his initial reception of these films as well as his retrospective conceptualization of movie spectatorship in his family's living room. The

Figure 4.5 *Il mio viaggio in Italia* (Martin Scorsese, 2001).

promise and possibilities of migration—the movement of images, but also people, values, localities, things—define Scorsese's recollections about film viewing, and he outlines a set of basic principles for finding correspondences between distinct places, images, and historical times. In this respect, the television set's part in this history is pivotal. *Il mio viaggio in Italia*'s first post-credit shot reveals a replica of the Scorsese family's 1940s/1950s TV; it fills the screen briefly while the director's recognizable speech—offscreen—and pointing index finger, entering quickly from the left side of the frame, begin to describe the TV's make and model (sixteen-inch RCA Victor), but also its fundamental place in his family's lives, his childhood, and their communal experiences with these Italian films. The camera promptly proceeds to tilt up, simultaneously panning to the left and tracking back slightly to reframe the director in a medium shot, now visible within the evidently constricted space of an apartment's living room. Through the dark haze and English dubbing of "some of the worst prints you've ever seen," Scorsese says, he and his family were witnesses to Italy from their crowded living room on Friday evenings in the late-1940s and early-1950s (Figure 4.6). They viewed exceptional filmic

Figure 4.6 *Il mio viaggio in Italia* (Martin Scorsese, 2001).

descriptions of the country's wartime desolation and precarious postwar state. Scorsese confesses to having never asked his grandparents anything about Italy or their own history, nor did they ever volunteer to "teach" him about their birthplace or the experience of immigration. But the transfer of these rudimentary Neorealist images from Italy to his family's apartment, and the associated collective, "emotional" experience of seeing them again permitted him to absorb information about this remote place as well as his immediate relations: "I learned," he tells us, "simply from *watching them* and the movies about their homeland."

This extended chronicle of the director's childhood parallels his earlier account of having pilfered images from the New York Public Library's copy of Deems Taylor's *A Pictorial History of the Movies*. The myth of origins, an important moment in the cinephile's settling of historical accounts, is always generated by an amalgamation of actuality and the inscrutable workings of memory, and as a result, the director's reckoning with the past can appear a bit too convenient, possibly formulated only with the benefit of hindsight. Indeed, Laura E. Ruberto (2015) has attempted to disentangle the facts from Scorsese's potential embellishments of the historical record, justifiably wondering about the plausibility of his descriptions of TV viewing during the period in question. The late-1940s seems to be an unlikely date for Scorsese's earliest televisual reception of Italian Neorealism, Ruberto convincingly argues, and his reminiscences suggest a reflective reshaping of the historical evidence—like any memory, this one is beholden to emotional investments as well as possible oversights and elaborations. *Il mio viaggio in Italia*, however, is making a substantially different point about the *meaning* of one's memory of film viewing and its entanglement with an experience of the historical world. Scorsese's documentary is admittedly vague about when some of the postwar Italian films were broadcast in New York City (the late-1940s? early-1950s?), but the broader interpretation of his—and his family's—spectatorship is not necessarily invalidated; on the contrary, Scorsese refers to a sense of *self-awareness* before these particular Italian films, the *sense* of having seen these films while simultaneously being watched by them, and this emphasis on a very specific memory of the Neorealist classics directs his accounts of film viewing and its consequence. Simply put, his recollection explains a developing state of self-consciousness, and *Il mio viaggio in Italia* seeks to document this experience and the conditions that made it possible.

In another context, Jean-Luc Godard describes "the image" in language that can clarify Scorsese's inchoate claims about his earliest involvement with both cinema and television. "The image," Godard observes, "is the relation with me looking at it [and] dreaming up a relation with someone else" (Sterritt 1998, 190). According to Godard's notoriously intractable formulation, however, this organization of spectatorial exchange is possible only in the unique circumstances of film projection (reflections of light on a movie theater's large screen), not under the conditions of televisual transmission (constant radiations in a household setting), and his broadly disseminated reservations about TV and its elemental differences from cinema should alert us to the novelty of Scorsese's emphasis upon his family's television set throughout his reminiscences. For Godard, particularly in the solitude of his "late" period, "projection" is said to be both a material process (light, films, a reflective screen, the auditorium's large space) *and* a way for viewers to apprehend or constitute a world. In short, it describes "the complex creation of historical knowledge" (Morgan 2013, 212). Television broadcasts, on the other hand, subject audiences to a kind of ideological programming. Michael Witt summarizes the ethical implications of Godard's claims for the cinema's superiority to television in the following way: if "the cinema set itself the project of constructing and reflecting an image worthy of life, an image through which the injuries of life might be 'redeemed' or 'resurrected' (to use the metaphors insisted on by Godard for over a decade), television merely broadcasts *programmes*" (1999, 342–3).[21] For this reason, the movie auditorium was always the final destination—and a sacred location—for the historical cinephile's countless pilgrimages. Godard and his accomplices at *Cahiers du Cinéma* are the archetypal figures for such movements, of course, but many others have offered comparable testaments to their own journeys to movie theaters in the 1950s and the 1960s.[22] Projection, in this respect, guarantees the irreplaceability of a cinematic experience, yet it also widens and releases viewers' perceptions of the historical world.

The young Martin Scorsese traveled in this same current of baby boomer cinephilia during the 1950s and 1960s, of course, but his recollections about his earliest viewings of the Neorealist classics pivot on a substantial inversion of this prototypical configuration of movement and spectatorship. *Il mio viaggio in Italia*'s rendering of its historical account repeatedly resituates remote moving images in the Scorseses' Little Italy home: Italian films arrived as witnesses to a world abandoned by Italian Americans like the Scorseses, and they also confirmed how they—and many other people like them—escaped from a disastrous destiny in war-torn Italy. For this reason, the director remembers these images as critical and illuminating missives from another place: a Neopolitan street urchin ("that could've been me," Scorsese says) descends slowly into the caves of Mergellina, now nothing but barren, terrifying dwellings for the abandoned and suddenly orphaned (*Paisà*); young Sicilian fishermen and their families struggle to survive in an equally unforgiving environment, and they are finally forced to face the grim prospects of their everyday industry (*La terra trema*, [Luchino Visconti, 1948]); and the apprehensive and unemployed, perched precariously on top of Rome's postwar wreckage, search in vain for a solution to their mystifying daily dilemmas (*Ladri di biciclette*, [Vittorio De Sica, 1948]). Scorsese's immigrant grandparents, he recalls, felt a sense of "relief *and* guilt" when seeing these moving images for the first time. In *Il mio viaggio in Italia*'s assessment of the historical past, a very particular type of reception is delineated in its compilation of extended scenes and the director's corresponding voice-over explanations. Something of value is salvaged from Italy's postwar remains and sent reeling to this secondary site in America, but for these spectators, the experience is simultaneously one of reprieve and remorse. Italy is present again in these conditions of reception, although the viewers' absence from the images on view is a cause for regret. As in Scorsese's rescued home movie footage, a well-known topography is subtly redrawn in this transfer of images from Italy to America in the postwar period, and the director's family, gathered together around the television set (and each other), are said to have shared in the Neorealist films' release of moving images in this new location.

The image's status as an indexical sign has a role to play in this reception of Italian cinema, although its visible fidelity to the physical world is surely also a critical factor (that is to say, these images are also "icons"); but in *Il mio viaggio in Italia*, this fragmentary evidence has another value, or another possible use for the film's spectators. In other words, Scorsese's cinephile documentary takes the potential transferability of these images—their transformation in a new location—as a superseding principle in its rearrangement of the sequences in question; and the prospect of realizing such exchanges finally relies upon one's ability to recognize substantial correspondences between things, places, and images. Paul Giles has explained how an "analogical imagination" (1992, 186), a pattern of thinking based on networks of similitude and resemblance, is at the very core of Scorsese's earliest fiction films; but one can also see how it establishes an unassuming method for *Il mio viaggio in Italia*'s compilation. As a structure of thought, the "analogical impetus" envisions "substantial compatibilities" (Giles 1992, 27) in the order of things, and as we've seen, Scorsese's unequivocal descriptions of significant similarities in the Sicily-Little Italy alignment indicate precisely this pattern of evaluation throughout *Il mio viaggio in Italia*. The director's extended reminiscences about his family's initial encounter with Rossellini's *Paisà* return repeatedly to an emphasis on similitude, but this method of assessment also guides other less conspicuous moments in the documentary. A fondly remembered fragment from Vittorio De Sica's *L'oro di Napoli* (1954), for example, promptly transports Scorsese back to his youth in Little Italy and memories about his neighborhood barber, an incurable gambler. In this case, a character's deportment—his comedic eruptions of anger and transparently calculated conduct—immediately summons a brief reminiscence about other neighbors in the Little Italy of Scorsese's youth, but the film compiles its fragments and scenes by seizing on these resemblances (Figure 4.7). If moving images have an historical significance because of their former contact with the world, they are gathered together in this documentary for another reason: they correspond substantially with their eventual relocation in New York City's Little Italy during the postwar years.

Figure 4.7 *Il mio viaggio in Italia* (Martin Scorsese, 2001).

Il mio viaggio in Italia presents itself as another of Scorsese's "personal," cinephilic reckonings with the history of cinema, but the foundation for his selection of assorted fragments and approach to compilation intersects in meaningful ways with contemporary thinking about the medium's place in a today's new media environments. Francesco Casetti, for instance, describes the cinema's capacity for survival in terms of its mobility: fragments or remnants of the medium can be transferred to novel locations, but only according to the principle of "similitude" (2015, 17). Indeed, in the context of a present-day reorganization of the conventional movie-going experience, the cinema's "authenticity" endures in the form of "relics" and the "reincarnation" of traditional movie spectatorship in assorted "simulations" (in the proliferation of so-called home theaters, for example) (Casetti 2015, 9–10). "Film fragments," Casetti notes, "belong to an entity that has now been dispersed, but nevertheless [these remains] are able to make cinema present—they are able to convey its sanctity […] and inform [a present-day actuality] with this sanctity" (2015, 62). Dispersed elements from "the holy body of cinema," hallowed film relics can be relocated while at the same time remaining part of the sacred whole (Casetti 2015, 62). In this manifestly religious framework, one implicitly shared by

Scorsese's *Il mio viaggio in Italia*, film fragments can be installed and viewed—or celebrated—elsewhere because, like the religious artifact of late antiquity, their value can be transferred.[23] *Cinema Paradiso* (Giuseppe Tornatore, 1988) provides Casetti with a representation of these matters, but Scorsese's pattern of thinking in *Il mio viaggio in Italia* venerates the film fragment for the same reasons: the elected image is witness to the entirety of his experience (at least as he remembers it); it can "testify" or "report on the whole to which it belongs" (Casetti 2015, 60). In *Il mio viaggio in Italia*'s collected memories, one learns about spectators being *watched* by the great Neorealist films after the latter have been transferred to a secondary site in New York City's Little Italy. George Kouvaros has described how movies can watch their spectators, and his emphasis on the interweaving of film spectatorship and the frequently fraught experience of migration is especially appropriate in this case. A particular film can confirm one's existence, or it might preserve a memory of the past: "It remains locked to a history that shadows our own, a history that has been covered over in the rush to deal with the exigencies of the present" (Kouvaros 2018, 80). In *A Letter to Elia*'s analyses of Elia Kazan's key movies, one sees how Scorsese's missive to this filmmaker (the "letter" being another vehicle for a "personal journey" through America cinema) is opened to a collective totality, one which includes the vagaries of Hollywood's past, but also the forgotten parts of an immigrant experience and its unresolved aftermath.

Epistles and Apostles: Relocating Autobiography in *A Letter to Elia*

Il mio viaggio in Italia does not—and ultimately cannot—maintain its intensive focus on Italian Neorealism. As the film's second half increasingly turns its attention to European "art cinema," the director's original description of receiving the key Neorealist films as mobile relics is superseded by a more familiar story about the 1960s, aesthetics, and the auteurist discovery of a "personal" cinema. Nevertheless, although Scorsese's discussion of Michelangelo Antonioni's and Federico Fellini's films is more predictable by comparison, *Il mio viaggio in Italia* still manages to evade the pervasive hazard of baby boomer nostalgia. As always, the Sixties provides the principal compass for Scorsese's historical associations, yet *Il mio viaggio in Italia* does not fully capitulate to its era's sometimes patronizing "decay of cinema" despair.[24] Instead, the documentary ends by reaffirming its mission. The ongoing withdrawal of European cinema from America's screens is a cause for alarm, Scorsese claims, and *Il mio viaggio in Italia* is dedicated to extending the life of the assorted movies on view. When it arrives at its final destination, Scorsese's film modestly reiterates the preservationist position that has defined his post-1990s work as a steward for film history. In the same spirit as *Italianamerican*'s oral history, *Il mio viaggio in Italia* attempts to "hand down"—to "young" viewers—what the director explicitly calls "history" in his concluding comments; that is to say, *Il mio viaggio in Italia* seeks to share a cinematic past that is clearly at risk of disappearing from everyone's sight and memory. As we've seen, however, the film's gathering of images and sounds also uncovers the only remaining pathway to a far more remote history: the Scorseses' own vanishing past and the record of their experiences as immigrants in America.

A Letter to Elia, co-directed with longtime collaborator, Kent Jones, marks a departure from cinephilic orthodoxy by embracing the extremely unfashionable Elia Kazan as its principal subject. Presented as a narrated epistle to a formative inspiration, this documentary—another of Scorsese's contributions to PBS's *American Masters* series—examines the director's deeply personal stake in Kazan's 1950s and 1960s Hollywood filmmaking. *A Letter to Elia* is an atypically short documentary for Scorsese. *A Personal Journey* had promptly expanded beyond the parameters of its commission by the BFI, eventually growing into its three-part structure and a running time of 225 minutes.[25] At 246 minutes, *Il mio viaggio in Italia* remains the director's longest non-fiction film, and like his other cinephile works, it allows for wide-ranging selections from the movies being discussed. The recourse to wipes as the preferred technique for shifting from one sequence to the next has the general effect, especially in *Il mio viaggio in Italia*, of recombining disparate film fragments into a new totality, and these histories are ultimately shaped by this effort at re-collecting images. *A Letter to Elia* shares a method with its immediate predecessors, but its comparative concision at sixty minutes introduces a new sharpness of focus: one director's varied production is examined in this case, yet as in *Il mio viaggio in Italia*, Scorsese's interpretations develop from the mainly private realm of reminiscences about his family, childhood, and his permanent cinephilia. In his preceding cinephile assemblage, Scorsese had unearthed home movie footage of his family in New York City's Little Italy, and one could hear the astonishment and ache in his voice-over as he watched these figures "move again" on the screen before him. In *A Letter to Elia*, the director's memories are propelled primarily by Kazan's key fiction films and their relevance to this same history, so Scorsese and Jones limit the range of their filmic materials accordingly: moving images, archival photographs, existent interviews with Kazan, Scorsese's intermittent onscreen appearances as a present-day guide, and voice-overs (by Scorsese himself, but also by Elias Koteas as he reads from Kazan's *Elia Kazan: A Life* [1988]) are the film's fundamental resources. As *A Letter Elia* progresses, its accumulation of details returns to the family story that drives *Il mio viaggio in Italia* (and in a slightly different way, *Italianamerican*), and in this respect, it serves as a culmination to Scorsese's autobiographical documentaries about the closely interwoven histories of film viewing and his immediate family members' lives as Italian immigrants in America.

Once again, however, the director's primary model appears to be *Cahiers du Cinéma*, its 1950s writings in particular. The recent repossession of cinephilia by academic film studies has largely—and understandably—discarded a prominent feature of the Young Turks' *politique des auteurs*, namely, its constant search for a cinematic patrimony of images and filmmakers. In the journal's immediate prehistory, François Truffaut's emblematic adoption by André Bazin would promptly become the stand-in for a much more widespread phenomenon: the critical quest for a cinematic ancestry was directed by the auteurist program, yet the resulting lineage was invariably focused on a cadre of filmmaking fathers. As Emilie Bickerton notes, *Cahiers du Cinéma* was something of an orphanage for wayward juveniles like Truffaut, and it also provided a forum for both celebrating and revolting against assorted cinematic forbearers. In this case, the young critic Truffaut would assume a perspective on his favorite filmmakers, but he would in turn be adopted by these figures and charged with preserving their films for posterity. The filial purpose of so much early *Cahiers* writing would directly influence cinephiles throughout the 1950s and 1960s, and Scorsese's *A Personal Journey*, *Il mio viaggio in Italia*, and *A Letter to Elia* can be seen as belated examples of this attentiveness to a cinematic patrimony—for better or worse, the director summarizes film history as a form of religious ministry, a record of inspirations and authorities who impart belief and guidance to the cinephile. However, if *A Personal Journey* and *Il mio viaggio in Italia* are dedicated to commonly canonized filmmaker-ancestors, *A Letter to Elia* looks instead to the much more difficult example of Elia Kazan, a figure whose standing, at least amongst American cinephiles, has declined steadily since the mid-1950s. Indeed, Andrew Sarris's popular late-1960s auteurist taxonomies had condemned Kazan by coolly placing him in the "Less Than Meets the Eye" category of American directors, while a contemporaneous aesthete-intelligentsia similarly rejected the significance of the director's subjects.[26] Bickerton describes the writing in *Cahiers* as a vehicle for "weaving" one's own history with the stories on screen (2009, 25); but Scorsese's heretical appointment of Elia Kazan as his cinematic "father" digs for a slightly different historical meaning, and it seeks to broaden the individualist course set by the young *Cahiers* critics and their original adherents. For Scorsese, the lengthy history of European immigration to America—and a precise part of the immigrant's experience in the new world—is deliberately activated by his choice of Kazan (and his selection *by* Kazan) as father in *A Letter to Elia*. In other words, the film aims to summarize an important reciprocal dimension in his choice, but it evidently does so within the familiar context of immigration. It clearly intuits a close correspondence between Kazan's experience and the Scorsese family's own migrations, and it aligns its concise biographical portrait of Kazan with Scorsese's ongoing reassessment of the history outlined in *Il mio viaggio in Italia*, *Italianamerican*, and *American Boy: A Profile of Steven Prince*. In the final analysis, the recurrence of these familiar historical themes in *A Letter to Elia* indicates a settling of accounts, a payment of long-deferred debts to the increasingly remote past.

A Letter to Elia releases its personal missive to Kazan in the form of extended excerpts from his work, Scorsese's sometimes elusive accompanying interpretations, and Kazan's observations—or in a few instances, confessions—about his life and films. Like Scorsese's previous cinema histories, the film's first post-title passage is composed of a long fragment from its subject's body of work, in this case a minute-long sequence from Kazan's immigrant epic, *America America*. *A Letter to Elia* unwinds gradually at this moment, and Scorsese's selection here resembles the opening to *Il mio viaggio in Italia*: the dead partisan in *Paisà*, drifting inertly in the Po River, has a revivified counterpart in the Anatolian migrant who is embarking upon his journey to America, a voyage to the new world and "freedom." The film that follows weaves together Scorsese's epistle with elected sequences from Kazan's other films, and once its subject has been introduced, *A Letter to Elia* adheres briefly to the chronology of Kazan's output. Seemingly set for a survey of the director's movies, yet accompanied by a contemporary practitioner's sharply focused assessments, *A Letter to Elia* is essentially primed to deliver another *American Masters* "portrait of the artist." As a consequence, Scorsese swiftly examines embryonic films like *A Tree Grows in Brooklyn* (1945), *Boomerang* (1947), and *Panic in the*

Streets (1950), then moves through Kazan's first theater-to-film success with *A Streetcar Named Desire* (1951) and his momentary experience of Hollywood achievement in *Viva Zapata!* (1952). Kazan's calm course through his work and accolades in this period, Scorsese observes, reveals a "director slowly becoming a filmmaker." But this account of "the filmmaker's" steady ascent through the studio system during the 1940s and 1950s, a recognizable Hollywood story of aspiration and accomplishment, is abruptly interrupted after only nineteen minutes have elapsed in *A Letter to Elia*. Kazan's appearance before the House Un-American Activities Committee (HUAC) in 1952 as a "friendly witness" suddenly obstructs *A Letter to Elia*'s auteurist drive. The film's familiar sketch of an archetypical Hollywood career is halted, as it should be, with this decisive interference by the era's Cold War politics and Red Scare. As a consequence, the film approaches *the* pivotal occurrence in Kazan's professional life with considerable caution, and the hesitation in Scorsese's address to viewers, that is, his obvious reluctance to report on this particular matter, changes what might have otherwise been a routine description of an "American Master" into a much more personal film about his dedication to Kazan's films during these turbulent years, the meaning of his obsessive cinephilia, and the movies' position in his own comprehension of the historical past. In other words, the director's mission in *A Letter to Elia* is conspicuously altered by the incidents of April 1, 1952, and his struggle to reconcile their deeper significance with his other memories. The remainder of the film narrows its focus substantially in order to re-view this inheritance of betrayal and recovery, but only as refracted through the much more personal framework of Scorsese's reckoning with Kazan's work.

"And then something happened." Scorsese's introduction to the most infamous episode in Kazan's life story, and one of the fading Hollywood studios' most notorious capitulations to the American government, initially feels too offhand, too hurried to fully grasp the moment in its gravity and magnitude. In short, his terse and undefined language ("something happened") appears to merely reiterate Kazan's self-exculpatory account of these stained historical events. "Something" did indeed occur, of course, but Scorsese's quick overview of this incident, destined to disappoint anyone in search of a thorough description of the Hollywood blacklist, the HUAC hearings, or Kazan's rationale for succumbing to the government's intimidation, is admittedly rushed. Kazan is permitted to provide the scene's first words (in a voice-over by Koteas), and these are accompanied by a rapid fade-in to a picture of his weathered and enigmatic face (Figure 4.8). The benefit of retrospection, combined with the clear sense of

Figure 4.8 *A Letter to Elia* (Martin Scorsese and Kent Jones, 2011).

pathos and defiance in his words, permeates the image at this moment, but there is a tenuousness about the segment's construction. Scorsese immediately offers additional information about Kazan's explicitly held position in 1952, and he then outlines the aftermath of friendly testimony in terms of its destructiveness and "tragic" consequences. *A Letter to Elia* scans several representative photos from the HUAC investigations, selected citations from Kazan's subsequent self-exculpatory *New York Times* editorial, and finally settles again on a photograph of Kazan's face, now slightly more battered, yet nevertheless unfathomable. Scorsese characterizes the director as a "pariah" during this period, but the assemblage of imagery and Koteas's voice-over narration makes it difficult to discern Kazan's exact response at this moment. Despondency? Defiance? An acceptance of his exile from former friends and associates? In less than two minutes, *A Letter to Elia* describes this essential conflict in Kazan's professional life, yet the sequence's brevity produces its own impenetrability. Its disinclination to linger on the HUAC incident might be seen as a long-deferred amnesty for Kazan and his record as a "friendly witness," or perhaps it indicates Scorsese's unwillingness to permit his portrait to be completely consumed by these events. Nevertheless, as Kazan readily recognized, his HUAC testimony did in fact cast a long shadow over everything that followed. His movies, awards, and his undeniably secure institutional position in Hollywood during the latter half of the 1950s—they would always be stalked by the infamy of his actions on April 1, 1952.

That said, if *A Letter to Elia* refuses to fully parse the particulars of Kazan's testimony, it also clearly seeks to redirect viewers to Scorsese's very different preoccupations, derived in part from Kazan's autobiography, but rooted more deeply in his cinephile documentaries' customary focus on the interchange between movie viewing and historical experience. "But something else happened" after Kazan's 1952 testimony, Scorsese says, and the remainder of *A Letter to Elia* is dedicated to "something else" buried somewhere in this historical episode. Kazan's incisive description of his temperament, a prevailing sense of wariness that he connects to the immigrant's experience in America, is now uncovered in his 1950s films,[27] but Scorsese observes how this same feature of the movies was *watching* him throughout this period. In other words, Scorsese's chronicle wants to account for his viewing of Kazan's films in the mid-1950s, that is, in the years directly following the HUAC testimony, and what he continues to find embedded in such images, in their anger and reticence, their suspicion and impertinence, are remnants of his young self. In the final analysis, this explains *A Letter to Elia*'s principal maneuver, namely, its willingness to accept Kazan's explanation of the grim HUAC incident, but not without also reshaping his story in terms of Scorsese's recollections about seeing the director's succeeding films for the first time. In an obvious sense, of course, these movies anticipate Scorsese's own filmmaking, but *A Letter to Elia* repeatedly grasps at the meaning of Elia Kazan's elected role as cinematic father. By his own account, Scorsese "projected" this character onto Kazan, and the latter's fatherly attributes are easily discerned in *A Letter to Elia*: he is somewhat stern and distant, yet nevertheless in possession of an indispensable gift. "Giving and receiving." "Not film history." This is how Scorsese finally describes the subject matter of *A Letter to Elia*, and in specifying Kazan's cinematic gift to him, he returns to one of his cinephile documentaries' foremost subjects: by compulsively watching movies throughout these years, Scorsese participated in their formation of an historical record; by re-collecting these images for his present-day film, he is once again releasing fragments of the past and acknowledging how his own experiences remain preserved in these reminiscences about the movies in question.

On the Waterfront (1954), a film whose influence on Scorsese has always been apparent, allows for *A Letter to Elia*'s first sustained analysis, and it is followed by an even lengthier study of *East of Eden* (1955). Along with intermittent considerations of *America America*, these analyses offer the substance of *A Letter to Elia*'s reassessment of Elia Kazan's output—both Scorsese and Kazan justifiably consider *Waterfront*, *East of Eden*, and *America America* to be Kazan's major statements as a filmmaker. He "lived through" these movies when they were first released, Scorsese tells viewers, and his uncharacteristically measured speech during this section of the documentary specifies the uncommonly personal dimension in his explanations. Not surprisingly, *On the Waterfront*'s close inspection of a dockyard, its laborers, and their working-class dwellings resonates with Scorsese, but he promptly narrows his attention to the relationship between Marlon Brando's Terry Malloy and his gangster brother, Charlie (Rod Steiger). Kazan's scrutiny of comportment and its psychological implication, a hallmark in his work as both a filmmaker and co-founder of The Actor's Studio, is the focus in Scorsese's interpretations. The inference of working-class want, the characters' eroding sense of self-possession in these circumstances, but also their countervailing resistance to constrictions in their everyday environment— these qualities were all on view in *On the Waterfront*'s images, and Scorsese observes their relation to the Little Italy of his youth (their presence in *Mean Streets* [1973] and *Raging Bull* [1980] is unmistakable). However, *A Letter to Elia* remains immersed in the closely co-existing senses of betrayal and compassion in Terry's final reckoning with his brother. Scorsese combs through *East of Eden* for proof of a comparably intense family drama, and his attention returns repeatedly to significant breaches in the brothers' eroding relationship. At times, Scorsese's deliberations are uncomfortably private, and he refers elusively to an analogous betrayal by his own older brother; but *A Letter to Elia* avoids the more predictable pitfalls of autobiography, attempting instead to understand the meaning of Kazan's "gift" to the aspiring film director. As a consequence, Scorsese's analyses are continually rerouted: if the films seem to be pointing directly at some detail in the young spectator's world, their purview extends to the more expansive experience of immigration as described by both Scorsese and Kazan. In this respect, *East of Eden* might indeed be a representative artifact for baby boomers like Scorsese (it quickly became an emblem for adolescent "angst" in the 1950s, he observes), but the film also outlines an archetypical story of betrayal and benevolence: Adam Trask (Raymond Massey) and Cal (James Dean) are exemplars of distance, bitterness, and in the end, generosity. As a result, although these could be widely shared generational attitudes, within the framework of Scorsese's historiography they are resituated within the more recognizable context of immigration. Adam undoubtedly obstructs or distorts the future for both Cal and his brother Aron (Richard Davalos), yet by the film's end, he has also imparted an opportunity. In Scorsese's accumulation of these images, all of it set against his calmly narrated letter to Kazan, *East of Eden* witnesses a postponed—or perhaps wished-for—reconciliation with a volatile past, and like Scorsese's collected fragments, it testifies to the persistence of history beyond the immediacy of film viewing.

When he reaches *America America* again, Scorsese returns to *A Personal Journey*'s concluding anecdote about his departure from Little Italy and arrival in the foreign worlds of New York University and Hollywood in the 1960s and 1970s. Now, however, the significance of "giving and receiving," *A Letter to Elia*'s description of the directors' fundamental mode of "conversation," is brought into much sharper relief: Kazan motivated Scorsese's original leave-taking; *On the Waterfront*, *East of Eden*, and *America America* provided indispensable maps for his relocation from Little Italy. In this regard, *America America* is the most important of Kazan's filmic remains for Scorsese. It is an epic, insofar as its narrative is essentially defined by the persistent hazards of Stavros Topouzoglou's (Stathis Giallelis) journey from Anatolia/Turkey to the new world in America, the same voyage that establishes the foundation for so much of Scorsese's documentary filmmaking. *America America*, however, is resuscitated in *A Letter to Elia* primarily because it watched and imagined Scorsese's self-described migration in the mid-1960s. Admittedly, when the newly landed Stavros kisses the ground and makes his way through the administrative labyrinth at Ellis Island, his predicament prefigures scenes from Francis Ford Coppola's *The Godfather Part II* (1974) and the wider 1970s ethnic revival. Scorsese recognizes how these particular images of the massive early twentieth-century European migrations to America continue to reverberate, of course, and he compares them explicitly to his family's experience; but as he did in *A Personal Journey*, the director readjusts his attention and focuses on the substantial correspondences between the recently disembarked Stavros and his own migration from Little Italy. These scenes epitomize the mixture of ruthlessness and inexperience, determination and disillusionment at the heart of Stavros's immigrant saga, and they also somehow witness Scorsese's decisive departure for the world of filmmaking. In other words, Kazan's American journey, described in equal parts by his irritable personality and sense of resolve, is on view across these extended fragments from *America America*, yet in Scorsese's account, the film bestows an indispensable gift to its viewer. Stavros's progress encompasses more than a national "epic" or Ellis Island memorial. In *A Letter to Elia*, its position alongside 1960s landmarks such as Jean-Luc Godard's *Breathless* (1960) and Alain Resnais's *Last Year at Marienbad* (1961) discloses how Scorsese associates the images of immigration and self-reliance in Kazan's film with his original admission into the distant world of film directing (Figure 4.9).

In *The Old Greeks*, George Kouvaros stresses a fundamental experience in immigration. Those born in the immediate aftermath of migrations, he observes, are the beneficiaries of a rare gift:

> [...] the freedom bestowed by one generation on the next, from father to son, to achieve success and failure on one's own terms with nothing to measure the various achievements and shortcomings against—no drama of competition or, even worse, expectation.
>
> (2018, 47–8)

In the end, remaining "mindful of where one comes from" is "the only pressing requirement" in this formative giving and receiving (Kouvaros 2018, 47–8). According to Kouvaros, the immigrant's general "reticence" in the new world is precisely what makes the conferral of such a gift possible. Invariably a matter of "family" and "name," this "extraordinary gift of freedom" is vital to survival, yet in the end, it is also a potential burden: autonomy is at once a gift and disorder (Kouvaros 2018, 48). In this important respect, *A Letter to Elia* brings Scorsese's decades-long documentary activity full circle. *America America*'s many images of Stavros in steerage, underscored continually in *A Letter to Elia*'s concluding passages, anticipate the 1970s ethnic revival's elementary iconography, but as we've already seen, Scorsese had resisted using such imagery in *Italianamerican*. His parents' expressive storytelling and memories provided his short film with

Figure 4.9 *A Letter to Elia* (Martin Scorsese and Kent Jones, 2011).

its substantial insights about the experiences of immigration and its present-day resonance. Critics have understandably emphasized Catherine Scorsese's convivial presence in *Italianamerican*,[28] and she does actually seize the film from its director at significant moments; but Charles Scorsese is also a perceptive, if comparatively quiet authority in the film, and one senses his bestowal of the "gift" outlined by Kouvaros (Figure 4.10). In *Il mio viaggio in Italia*, his unexpected appearance in Scorsese's newly discovered home movie footage is the fulcrum in a series of reminiscences about film spectatorship, family, and history. The director has referred to his father's—or rather, his ancestors' Sicilian world's—"medieval" morality (it is a "baron's" morality, he notes), yet the generational distance implied in such a formulation eventually "led" the aspiring filmmaker to Kazan's *On the Waterfront* and *East of Eden* (Jarmusch 2017, 187–8). These two films seem to have disclosed a "link" between what Kouvaros calls "the blunt immediacy of the present" and "the restless persistence of the past" (2018, 26). With the benefit of retrospection, *A Letter to Elia* illuminates this elementary aspect in film viewing, that is, its ongoing effort at constructing connections between the images on screen and a persistent experience of the

Figure 4.10 *Italianamerican* (Martin Scorsese, 1974).

past. The correspondences between Scorsese's cinephilia, inspired in part by *Cahiers du Cinéma*'s interruption of key critical orthodoxies during the 1950s, and the deeper historical reverberations of his family's immigration to America are finally brought together in *A Letter to Elia* (and also *Il mio viaggio in Italia*). The devotional energy in early *Cahiers du Cinéma* criticism is borrowed and modified by Scorsese as he sketches his own cinematic patrimony, but only to corroborate the historical realities of immigration and his reminiscences about his family's experiences in the new world. In the final analysis, *Il mio viaggio in Italia* and *A Letter to Elia* both reach this deeper stratum of the past by compiling elected images and parsing their work as witnesses to history.

Perpetual Migrations: Leaving Little Italy and Compiling Cinephile Histories

Kazan's lifelong identification with the immigrant's sense of outsiderhood, undoubtedly spurred in equal parts by a need for self-justification in the aftermath of his contentious HUAC testimony and an understandable antipathy to the Hollywood establishment, explains Scorsese's devotion to his films. *A Letter to Elia*, however, offers more than a biographical portrait of this formative influence. The documentary records a slightly different journey than Scorsese's 1970s documentaries, of course; nonetheless, although it marks a distance (temporal, formal) from *Italianamerican*, it essentially concludes the same comprehensive project. The experience of migration to America, its continuing reverberations, and various recollections about this past were emphasized throughout *Italianamerican*, and when the director produces *Il mio viaggio in Italia* and *A Letter to Elia*, these themes persist as his primary preoccupations. As we've seen, however, this history exists for Scorsese today solely in the moving images and sounds gathered together in his cinephile documentaries: these compilations are storehouses for—and lingering witnesses to—his family's experiences and memories of migration from Italy to America. But *A Letter to Elia* also completes Scorsese's series of cinephilic testaments to movie spectatorship, the latter's different strata of significance and potential permanence in the face of novel challenges to the cinema's continuing existence. Scorsese's other projected episodes in the history of cinema have not yet materialized, so *Il mio viaggio in Italia* and *A Letter to Elia* stand as his definitive documentary statements on these matters.[29]

Scorsese's methods for sifting through, collecting, and relocating his assorted archival materials are consistent with a wide range of present-day videographic critical work. Casetti tellingly describes these popular practices with two terms: "profanations" and "re-enchantments" (2015, 87). On the one hand, the medium's continuous "ruptures and readjustments" are increasingly evident in pervasive bottom-up, user-driven (and "participatory") exercises such as mash-ups, diverse forms of reassembly, and a recasting of images for both affectionate and ironic purposes across the internet today (Casetti 2015, 88). These are "profanations" because they seek to dislocate or challenge the cinema's customary meanings; in these cases, everyday users push—and potentially destroy—a traditional medium like "cinema" by utilizing new media to reshape it for their own needs and objectives. The earliest utopian accounts of the internet routinely saw the revelation of previously submerged meanings in such practices, although more sober subsequent examinations have expressed doubt about the "democratic" or "participatory" potentials in these economically constrained exercises.[30] On the other hand, however, contemporary works of reassemblage disclose what Casetti has called "strategies of repair," and instead of profaning the medium, these different approaches can "re-consecrate" it and reposition us "within its horizon as effective spectators in order re-enchant us again, thanks to our complicity" (2015, 89–90). Scorsese's cinephile documentaries are best understood as attempts to restore the appeal of films and re-consecrate them in exactly the manner described by Casetti: "They aim at restoring cinema—regenerating it, reinstating its profile—even if they do so by raising spectators from the status of mere believers to that of officiants" (2015, 90). The preservationist origins and impetus for the production of his cinephile documentaries indicate a desire to reacquaint viewers with cinema, but his persona in these films and television productions (he is invariably the exemplification of a "classic" cinephile) has spread to a pervasive type of reparative compilation across various media. Conceived when the cinema was unexpectedly becoming something else in an emergent digital media setting, something subject to multiplying profanations, Scorsese's commemorative *A Personal Journey* and *Il mio viaggio in Italia* seek to reestablish the permanent importance of cinematic experience. *A Letter to Elia* has a slightly different emphasis, yet it too functions as a memorial to Scorsese's perpetual attachment to the cinema and filmmaking, that is, to a particular experience embedded in cinema itself.

Initially conceived with an experience of the "big screen" in mind (Christie and Thompson 2003, 244), *Il mio viaggio in Italia* is paradoxically available today solely as an audiovisual trace: circulating as a DVD or on video-sharing platforms such as YouTube, Scorsese's documentary persists as a series of fragments, more artifacts in the increasing dispersion of these mobile relics. *A Personal Journey* and *A Letter to Elia*'s images are disseminated in a similar way in their contemporary state: destined to disappear because of their ephemeral broadcast schedules, these cinephilic testaments now seem as scarce as the films they revive for their present-day spectators. But *Il mio viaggio in Italia*'s excursus about the television set's important position in Scorsese's developing cinephilia indicates that this phenomenon is not necessarily an inescapable source of despair for the director. Indeed, according to Casetti, the historical, "canonical cinematic experience" (2015, 62) can be reincarnated in several different viewing environments, a household living space among them, and in substituting for such experience, these new settings for spectatorship can reactivate the presence of their cinematic models. An "intrinsic link between copy and prototype" (Casetti 2015, 63) continues to exist: the prototypical film viewing experience endures as a copy whether or not one is aware of its reconfiguration. In *Il mio viaggio in Italia*'s short concluding passage, Scorsese appears onscreen again in a medium shot to reiterate his original incentive for making this cinephile documentary compilation. Now perceived against the markedly different backdrop of New York's contemporary cityscape, rather than the constricted apartment living room of the movie's introduction or the Elizabeth Street rooftop of his childhood dwelling, Scorsese quietly observes how "even today [...] history remains something that is handed down, something that happens between people" (Figure 4.11). In other words, even today, even in this perceptibly new location, the history on view in *Il mio viaggio in Italia* somehow endures. Contemporary audiovisual criticism and film histories on the internet may be expressed in new modes of collaboration, connectivity, and exchange, yet *Il mio viaggio in Italia*'s closing moments seem to acknowledge—and directly invite—the inevitable migrations of cinephile historiographies beyond their traditional territories.

But if *Il mio viaggio in Italia* and *A Letter to Elia* gather and exhibit their film fragments for present-day spectators, Scorsese is a "collector" in a slightly different sense than critics of the documentaries' conventionality have typically allowed: he is what the philosopher Paul Ricoeur has called a "collector of debts" in his writing on historiography (1988, 143). Ricoeur's *Time and Narrative* describes historians as figures who owe a "debt to the past" (1988, 143), and as a consequence, they are invariably insolvent debtors when rendering

Figure 4.11 *Il mio viaggio in Italia* (Martin Scorsese, 2001).

historical accounts. As we've seen, *Il mio viaggio in Italia* and *A Letter to Elia* both present themselves as acknowledgments of Scorsese's extensive borrowing from the history of film, and his many interviews also regularly cast him as the cinematic past's insolvent debtor; yet these compilations persistently recognize an even more profound aspect of the historian's responsibility, namely, his "debt of recognition to the dead" (Ricoeur 1988, 143). In this important respect, *Il mio viaggio in Italia*'s introductory expedition through the director's recently salvaged home movie footage and family photographs is best seen as the manifestation of utopian longing, while *A Letter to Elia*'s delivery of a formative family drama represents an analogous nostalgia for the familiar past. For the narrator of *Il mio viaggio in Italia*, a dislocated and abandoned home (in Italy) is immediately summoned for his family by the transmission of image-relics, but the director's childhood home—the final destination for these images, now lost in time—is thereby recovered from the past. The dead, momentarily unearthed in Scorsese's salvaged home movie footage, continue to move stealthily across his ensuing assemblage of images and memories: his selection and arrangement of images establish an idiom for the director to speak about and acknowledge a debt to his Italian American history. In other words, Scorsese's cinephilic recollecting in *Il mio viaggio in Italia* and *A Letter to Elia* permits him to pay his duty to the dead, and as a result, each film's compilation of remembered fragments is finally directed by this pervasive sense of obligation.

Peter Wollen characterizes cinephilia as "the symptom of a desire to remain within the child's view of the world, always outside, always fascinated by a mysterious parental drama, always seeking to master one's anxiety by compulsive repetition" (2002, 5). If *A Letter to Elia* is occasionally uneasy about its central subject, or if it remains anxious about a certain ruthlessness in Elia Kazan's infamous friendly testimony before HUAC, its collection of images from Kazan's films nevertheless returns obsessively to the "child's view of the world." Its plainspoken assertions are best understood as the cinephile's way of reconciling the remote past and present within the frame of an historical account. *Il mio viaggio in Italia* similarly begins with the extended invocation of a scenario from childhood: the director's early relationship with his family is explained in terms of a communal attachment to the cinema; the world is viewed entirely—and only understood—in the relocation of images from Italy to America. These are Scorsese's memories, his retrospective descriptions of how his developing cinephilia was progressively connected to his whole family's historical situation and their decisive knowledge about immigration. "Cinema" is an experience, Jacques Rancière observes, but it is at the same time "the residue of those presences that accumulates and settles in us as their reality fades and alters over time: that other cinema reconstituted by our memories and our words, which can be distinctly different from what had been projected on screen" (2014, 5). "Shots and effects," he concludes, "vanish in the moment of projection," but they also "need to be extended, to be transformed by the memory and words that make cinema exist as a shared world far beyond the material reality of its projections" (2014, 6). Throughout the cinephile compendia of *Il mio viaggio in Italia* and *A Letter to Elia*, Scorsese acknowledges the cinema's shared world, particularly as it encompasses his family, the very figures who have vanished permanently from his present reality, yet who dwell within these reminiscences about movies and the experience of watching them. The past perseveres in his recollections about having once seen these films; but more importantly, a history remains embedded in the film images themselves, and it can always be summoned once again by the work of documentary compilation.

Conclusion
Martin Scorsese's Documentary Profiles

Martin Scorsese's need to produce documentaries appears undiminished today. The release of Netflix's *Rolling Thunder Revue: A Bob Dylan Story by Martin Scorsese* in 2019 confirmed his ongoing commitment to historically oriented non-fiction filmmaking, and the announcement of several more planned productions guarantees a steady stream of documentaries in the upcoming years. The forthcoming *An Afternoon with SCTV* and a projected movie about New York City's 1970s music scene propose further excursions through the worlds of entertainment, the constant focus of his non-fiction work.[1] At this point, however, Scorsese largely oversees a collaborative documentary undertaking. Since supervising the PBS productions of *Eric Clapton: Nothing but the Blues* (1995) and *Martin Scorsese Presents: The Blues* (2003), the director has consistently relied upon a close cohort of producers, editors, sound designers, and cinematographers to make his documentaries. Margaret Bodde, David Tedeschi, Ellen Kuras, Robert Richardson, and many others have made sustained, substantial contributions to films like *Shine a Light* (2008), *George Harrison: Living in the Material World* (2011), *The 50 Year Argument* (co-directed with David Tedeschi, 2014), and *Rolling Thunder Revue*, and they all continue to establish a foundation for Scorsese's assorted forays into non-fiction. In his countless interviews, of course, the director has typically embraced the original auteurist model of "personal" filmmaking, but his present-day approach to documentary production implicitly recognizes the indispensable collaborative dimension in such work.[2] On the other hand, however, although his direction has integrated a cooperative element, or assumed a more practical commitment to managing these productions, his expanding work as an executive producer continues to gravitate toward his long-established documentary concerns: the fading history of movies and cinephilia (*Life Itself* [Steve James, 2014]); rock music's past in its numerous countercultural expressions (*Long Strange Trip*

[Amir Bar-Lev, 2017], and *Once Were Brothers: Robbie Robertson and The Band* [Daniel Roher, 2019]). In several instances, Scorsese has functioned as a mentor to filmmaker-collaborators such as Kent Jones (*Val Lewton: The Man in the Shadows* [2007], *Hitchcock/Truffaut* [2015]) and colleagues like David Tedeschi, or he has strategically utilized his significant institutional leverage to help certain films get seen; yet even in the more remote role of executive producer, he is still devoted to a vernacular of recovery and commemoration. Not surprisingly, the baby boomers' Sixties—its recollection and ever-present folklore—continues to direct this wider documentary initiative.[3]

That said, *A Letter to Elia* (2010), Scorsese's note to Elia Kazan and his key movies from the 1950s and early-1960s, currently stands as the last of his personal documentary journeys as a film director. Its concision and restricted purview distinguish it from most of his subsequent non-fiction productions, and its conspicuously subjective foci are largely absent from his present-day films. Indeed, the heritage gene, always lurking somewhere in Scorsese's evident preference for preservationist and commemorative work, has become increasingly prominent in his present-day practice. *Public Speaking* directly followed *A Letter to Elia* in 2010, and although it often portrays Scorsese's amusement with its subject's public speech and assorted anecdotes, its tenor suggests a contracted level of investment. The film's fleeting allusion to *Taxi Driver* (1976), for example, inadvertently signals its straining efforts to discover something like the historiographic significance of the director's previous documentary work. Similarly, *George Harrison: Living in the Material World*, though an undeniably impressive compilation of previously unseen archival materials, mostly adheres to the historical pattern set by *No Direction Home: Bob Dylan* (2005), and its reticence about Harrison's abundant recordings after the pinnacle of *All Things Must Pass* (1970) and—perhaps—*Living in the Material World* (1973) indicates some degree of uncertainty about the consequence of this documentary commission. Scorsese unquestionably identifies with Harrison's lifelong spiritual search, yet the documentary's quiet avoidance of the former Beatles' 1970s and 1980s solo work sometimes gives it the rudimentary appearance of "celebrity profile." In a contemporary media environment saturated with various "personality" sketches, the risks of such an approach are obvious: the film's narrow emphasis on a life described solely by its public renown corresponds too closely with today's overload of reality-based media production. Indeed, *Public Speaking*'s Fran Lebowitz is an even more obviously—if self-consciously—unproductive writer, and as a result, the film's lasting impression is of a figure whose distinction is discernible only through stubborn declarations about her "individuality" and "personality." She bemoans the present-day world's countless ills (gas, cell phones, microwave ovens, young people, and so on), but *Public Speaking* eventually discloses her representativeness: "public speaking," regardless of its categorical rejection of contemporary technologies, really sounds like a relatively predictable, monologic use of social media today. Such an individualist ideological alignment appears to be a natural feature of Scorsese's auteurist universe, even if *Public Speaking* consciously expands the variety of his typical documentary portraits. Nevertheless, the overabundance of this brand of portraiture across assorted documentary media makes *Public Speaking* and *Living in the Material World* seem overly familiar. While Lebowitz and Harrison are depicted as personalities, that is, as characters who intermittently resist the core aspects of modernity, they seldom reveal what the previous films' subjects could: the Scorseses' delivery of an oral history in *Italianamerican*, Bob Dylan's deeper excavation of a vernacular American music in *No Direction Home*, or Scorsese's own detailed descriptions of his permanent cinephilia and its links to his family's experience of immigration. By contrast, Lebowitz's renown is indefinable; or rather, her protracted idleness as a writer obliges the film to focus on her ongoing efforts to confirm a public profile. And though his time as a Beatle ensures Harrison's importance as a documentary subject, his growing resistance to celebrity throughout the late-1970s and early-1980s clearly drives *Living in the Material World* into a comparable predicament: the musician's prolonged periods of inactivity can sometimes make this documentary look like another prosaic portrait of fame-induced inertia, a basic product in today's pervasive reality-based media.

This personality-centered approach in Scorsese's current commemorative documentaries coincides with his growing dependence on companies such as Apple, Netflix, and Imagine Docs (Imagine Entertainment's new "Documentary Unit") to support his non-fiction productions.[4] His institutional clout guarantees a degree of independence even in these new settings, of course, but his former working relationships with PBS, the BFI, and others had permitted him to circumvent what is quickly becoming *the* primal fiction for a particular brand of documentary work, namely, that it is delivered from a source other than Hollywood's conglomerates. Scorsese had previously situated his documentaries within established sites of exhibition—premiere presentations at film festivals (Toronto, Telluride, or New York), public broadcasting, and in many cases, subsequent releases as home videos and DVDs. These common methods of circulation guaranteed the films' close proximity to comparable documentaries, yet they also specified a form of autonomy within their varied production settings—the differences between Scorsese's *The Blues* and Ken Burns's *Jazz* (2001) are not insignificant, in this respect, even though they travel in analogous ways. Any production is constrained by the allocation of resources, its ensuing distribution, and the vagaries of its reception; but one should distinguish such restrictions in qualitative terms, and the artifacts themselves retain traces from their diverse circumstances of production. Scorsese's contributions to PBS's long-running *American Masters* series, for instance, were certainly structured in part by the requirements of their "masters" remit. Nevertheless, although the director's auteurist cosmos can easily assimilate the *American Masters* focus on individual achievement, his historiographic aspiration is preserved in the films' distinctive assemblage of archival images and sounds. PBS's perceived differentiation from Hollywood could partially insulate productions like *The Blues*, *No Direction Home*, and *A Letter to Elia* from their immediate—and unavoidable—associations with Scorsese's concurrent big budget fiction movies (*Gangs of New York* [2002], *The Aviator* [2004], *The Departed* [2006], *Shutter Island* [2010], and *Hugo* [2011]). Or rather, while his documentary filmmaking undeniably benefits from his significant symbolic capital, its distribution by PBS had nonetheless secured a recognizable framework for interpretation: this non-fiction output could be received within the wider framework of public broadcasting, its documentary position ostensibly assured. Netflix's *Rolling Thunder Revue*, on the other hand, plays in a new and as yet undefined context, and this latest instalment in Scorsese's rockumentary output has accumulated noticeably different meanings in its online setting. PBS is generally viewed as the overly staid antecedent to today's developing types of distribution on streaming services and other online platforms, but its purview consistently gave Scorsese a pragmatic documentary itinerary: from *Italianamerican* to *A Letter to Elia*, his work could be both personal and historical, yet its circulation would buttress its apparent differences from his contemporaneous fiction movies.[5]

    Scorsese's currently planned documentaries appear tethered more tightly than ever to the economic actualities of his fiction filmmaking, but their methods of distribution portend potential changes to his non-fiction output. The director's developing partnership with Netflix could prove to be decisive, in this respect. The release of *The Irishman* by Netflix in November 2019, just six months after *Rolling Thunder Revue*'s appearance on the same streaming service, understandably overtook the director's "Bob Dylan Story" as the year's most noteworthy Scorsese-related public event, but it also brought certain elements of this documentary's status into sharper relief. On the one hand, the films' synchronism is an inescapable practical circumstance of much contemporary media production: the release of these films on Netflix ensures their coexistence on the service's platform, and this promise of a perpetual side-by-side obtainability is an in-built feature of these new brands of circulation. On the other hand, it also indicates several potential differences in the ongoing reception of Scorsese's documentary works—in short, the films' meanings are altered in these novel frameworks. *Rolling Thunder Revue* and *The Irishman*, for example, are far-reaching looks at certain facets of America's history, yet their concurrence on Netflix appears to rouse the old shibboleth of academic film studies: "A Bob Dylan story by Martin Scorsese" is, presumably like every documentary, finally best defined as a work of "fiction," while *The Irishman* might be said to implicitly *document* an inexorable moral desolation in present-day American political and public life. This is an oversimplification, of course, but the director's documentaries now coexist with his fiction films in unexpected ways, and one will have to discern potentially different kinds of comprehension and reception in the future. This appears especially pertinent for documentary films and videos. These emergent arrangements with streaming services constitute welcome and innovative opportunities, even for established filmmakers like Scorsese, yet they can always also introduce unanticipated constraints on production and reception.[6]

Rolling Thunder Revue returns Scorsese to his investigations of Bob Dylan's music and its cultural meaning, but the film's emphasis is the mid-1970s, Dylan's recommitment to touring, and his ongoing reemergence as a public figure after a protracted period of seclusion (sketched in *No Direction Home*'s closing account of his 1966 motorcycle accident and its aftermath). *Rolling Thunder Revue* takes Dylan's 1975 concerts at smaller halls in America's northeastern states as a deferred follow-up to the events examined in *No Direction Home*. It reviews Dylan's rediscovery of the early-1960s folk revival and his attempt to resurrect several of its primary participants as a new nomadic troupe of musicians (Figure 5.1). The film's principal attraction, however, is its trove of concert footage—Dylan's backing group is no match for The Band (briefly reunited with the singer for a tour in 1974), but a Bob Dylan revival is highlighted in Scorsese's generous use of these archival resources and select fragments from *Renaldo and Clara* (Bob Dylan, 1978). *Rolling Thunder Revue*'s mockumentary or "self-reflexive"

Figure 5.1 *Rolling Thunder Revue: A Bob Dylan Story by Martin Scorsese* (Martin Scorsese, 2019).

components admittedly appear slightly outmoded in 2019, but they're all aligned comfortably with the contemporary preoccupation with mutable personae and their potential pertinence to documentary. Indeed, against the Netflix backdrop, *Rolling Thunder Revue*'s close proximity to cognate productions such as *Springsteen on Broadway* (Thom Zimny, 2018) perhaps makes its emphases ordinary: the story of Dylan's "self-invention" is an archetype in documentary portraits across various media today. *Springsteen on Broadway*'s director, Thom Zimny, has in fact emerged as something of a sub-Scorsese in the surplus creation of films about legacy musicians. *Elvis Presley: The Searcher* (2018) borrows its structure and purpose from *No Direction Home* as well as *Living in the Material World*, while *The Gift: The Journey of Johnny Cash* (2019), released directly to YouTube as a contribution to "YouTube Originals," is similarly dependent upon Scorsese and his collaborators' method of organizing previously unseen archival materials. As Warren Zanes has observed, the 2005 broadcast of *No Direction Home* prompted a boom in rockumentary production, and the music industry's associated "legacy culture" has only gathered more momentum in the intervening years (2015, 291). *The Searcher* and *The Gift* are both products of—and possessions for—this heritage culture, as is *Springsteen on Broadway*, and the latter's apparent rummaging through *The Last Waltz* (1978) for various camera setups and movements is an added reminder of Scorsese's substantial influence on this variety of documentary making—commemorative examinations of legacy musicians are now indispensable to Netflix, YouTube, and other developing sites for the production and distribution of non-fiction works.[7]

In many ways, *Rolling Thunder Revue* shares the foci of Scorsese's other rockumentary and concert films. *Feel Like Going Home* and *No Direction Home*'s emphasis on the repurposing of antecedents (the American folksong tradition, but also a practice of reprocessing documentary images) is reiterated in Dylan's radical reimagining of his early songs for the 1975 tour. Changes in key distinguish some songs from their familiar recorded versions; altered chord progressions modify tunes substantially ("Simple Twist of Fate"), while differences in time signature (a revamped "A Hard Rain's A-Gonna Fall") and arrangements (Guam's folk-rock version of "The Lonesome Death of Hattie Carroll," the up-tempo shuffle of "It Takes a Lot to Laugh, It Takes a Train to Cry") shift many of these songs in unexpected ways. Along with Dylan's always forceful vocalizing, these variations effectively re-present his earlier songs as something old *and* new, but they are paradoxically reset in a new *and* old historical situation. Indeed, *Rolling Thunder Revue*'s brief outline of America's Bicentennial observances positions the 1975 tour within a broader context of national celebration and spiritual weariness. Significant geopolitical and economic failures were inescapable facts in 1975, and the film's opening images capture an America attempting to revive various historical ancestors while at the same time struggling to erase its present-day actuality: *Rolling Thunder Revue* underscores a carnival-like atmosphere in its prelude, but it also discloses how the period's retrospection was burdened with fantasies and doubts about America's current condition. The "Rolling Thunder Revue" was itself envisioned as a carnival act or "medicine show," and its political-aesthetic undertaking involved a revision of historical precursors, whether it be Dylan's early songs or other American symbols. At its most rudimentary level, Scorsese's *Rolling Thunder Revue* also retrieves/recycles its extended concert segments from preexisting resources, Dylan's seldom screened *Renaldo and Clara* foremost among them, and it aims to transform these images and sounds into an account of the past *and* present. This "Bob Dylan Story by Martin Scorsese" presents itself as a "Re-vue" in the film's opening credits sequence, and its subsequent reexamination—or re-vision—of these pivotal passages in Dylan's history selects fragments from the 1975 tour's journey primarily for their present-day reverberation. In other words, although this is an uncharacteristically irreverent documentary for Scorsese (the film is a self-described "conjuring"), *Rolling Thunder Revue*'s repossession of ancient images and sounds clearly recalls the methods of his other post-1990s archival compendia.[8]

Of the film's major emphases, however, Dylan's perpetual self-invention is immediately foregrounded as the center of "Rolling Thunder Revue's" political-aesthetic endeavor. Indeed, the tour's itinerary is summarized as the effect of Dylan's continuous shapeshifting, and Scorsese's *Rolling Thunder Revue* uses this as a pretext to modify its own documentary project. The interpolation of miscellaneous fictitious characters is, in this respect, an expansion of the film's focus on Dylan's ceaseless metamorphoses in 1975. Scorsese's broad stratagem includes several interviews with an imaginary tour promoter, assorted fans/hangers-on, a politician, and a snobbish filmmaker who seems to be creating *Renaldo and Clara* as he shadows the company's journey. These people were never actually part of the tour, of course, and the film does very little to signal their fictional status to spectators; but conjured images and sounds are linked with *Rolling Thunder Revue*'s archival fragments, and the result is a blurring of the record and an elaboration of *the* Dylan axiom: "Life isn't about finding yourself, or finding anything. Life is about creating yourself and creating things." Any additional explanation of the film's associated mockumentary approach, however, isn't very easy to detect. If the film's critical aim is to extend the "Rolling Thunder Revue's" preliminary gambit—the gathering of players, programs, and performances—into the present and its surfeit of analogous simulations of reality, then its reckoning with this particular history sacrifices a core part of its *pastness*. Simply put, the tour's broader project is too quickly condensed in this opening sleight of hand, and as a consequence, *Rolling Thunder Revue* largely forgoes the opportunity to reexamine these incidents in the wider context of Dylan's work and its meaning in the mid-1970s. As Michael Denning notes, "Dylan's fundamental long form, the frame for his songs, is not the album, but the concert and the concert tour" (2009, 31), and among the principal themes of this "long form" is Dylan's integration with an ensemble of compatible players. According to Denning,

> Rolling Thunder was one of Dylan's most powerful attempts not only to recreate the political-artistic community by force of will, but to counterpoint the monody of deprivation of his solo ballads (an enunciating mime in whiteface) with the euphoria of the Revue's carnivalesque singalongs.
>
> (2009, 39)

In Scorsese's *Rolling Thunder Revue*, by contrast, Dylan is the traveling company's indisputable leader *and* its most mutinous member, and this "Bob Dylan Story" unavoidably reinforces the singer's position in the dialectic described by Denning (Figure 5.2). In other words, *Rolling Thunder Revue* elaborates the rock concert's "euphoria," yet continually moderates it with an individuated portrayal of Dylan's autonomy, and the film's mockumentary rudiments paradoxically increase this sense of Dylan's self-sufficiency. In some ways, the implicit deliberation on autonomy reiterates a central conundrum in both *The Last Waltz* and *Shine a Light*, but in 2019, this type of documentary focus on self-invention and self-reliance (pseudofiction and fact) has accumulated a much wider currency as the emblem of sincerity. As Bruce Springsteen puts it in one of *Springsteen on Broadway*'s many anecdotes about self-creation and myth-making: "I made it all up" (Figure 5.3).

The close correspondence between films like *Springsteen on Broadway* and *Rolling Thunder Revue* on Netflix points to a contraction of possibilities for directors like Scorsese when they turn their attention to non-fiction work. *Springsteen on Broadway* is an unexceptional concert movie, and its directive is to document Springsteen's ostensible demystification of his public persona.

Figure 5.2 *Rolling Thunder Revue: A Bob Dylan Story by Martin Scorsese* (Martin Scorsese, 2019).

Figure 5.3 *Springsteen on Broadway* (Thom Zimny, 2018).

However, although the movie attempts to deflate the aura of authenticity that still adheres to its central subject, it in fact burnishes Springsteen's formative mythos: in the final analysis, "self-invention" is little more than another description for self-reliance and individuated achievement. Springsteen's sermons about the rock band's utopian possibilities, for example, are contradicted by the scene of this solitary figure scrubbing an acoustic guitar or piano and relating his qualified stories of accomplishment. Indeed, the rock band and rock concert, both specifically post-Sixties social—and economic—entities, are defined in utopian terms by Springsteen, yet the film itself offers little evidence to support his use of such language. Instead, the principal point of view expels the audience and its experience from the film's frames, and while *Springsteen on Broadway* stretches to revise its subject's legend, it ultimately reiterates a fable of self-creation.[9] If *Rolling Thunder Revue* appears to conform to a parallel pattern, it is partly because of Dylan's historical centrality to the elaboration of this vision of rock stardom; but it may also be the consequence of constrictions in these new backdrops for documentaries and their reception. In the contemporary moment, a vague philosophy of "self-invention" is held at an unusually high premium, and it has provided a foundation—or perhaps a condition—for the production of various successful brands of documentary, the legacy rockumentary foremost among them. This, of course, is an archetypal American conception of self-generated autonomy and achievement, but the wider reverberations of such an individualist, neoliberal ideological positioning are unfortunate and difficult to ignore in the present moment.[10]

Rolling Thunder Revue and *The Irishman* were themselves unexpectedly overtaken by Scorsese's November 2019 statements about the Marvel Comics movie franchise. The director's entanglement in this online phenomenon quickly fastened onto his apparent aesthetic assessment of such films, his defense of an historical cinephilia (i.e., its 1960s manifestation), and the plainly preservationist dimension in his position. As always, the cinema's ongoing transformation in the digital era was at the root of this debate, and to his critics, Scorsese's position appeared to defend traditional kinds of exhibition and reception, one fixed to the existence of movie theaters. Lost in the resulting social media fallout, however, was the director's implicit recognition of momentous changes to how films are distributed in today's new media environment. His trolling intervention on this matter acknowledges how the concentration of economic power in present-day media has noticeably thinned the options for producers and spectators; the subsequent arguments, however, remained ominously oblivious to these economic realities, and perhaps confirm the desolation in Scorsese's assessment.[11] He is evidently aware of the opportunities and dangers in these evolving configurations, and he appears resigned to imminent transformations in the production, distribution, and reception of his films. His candid diagnoses, however, refer solely to the new situation faced by fiction filmmakers, and his silence about *Rolling Thunder Revue*, his concurrent documentary, is telling. *The Irishman*'s production was financed by Netflix, and the director is understandably encouraged by the novel opportunities offered by such arrangements, yet he is nevertheless more cautious when making predictions about their long-term prospects. As a consequence, he rightly describes online streaming as a "revolution" and welcomes its attendant possibilities for narrative and stylistic "experiments," while at the same time worrying over whether or not his movies will be watched on iPhones.[12] *Rolling Thunder Revue*'s experiment in relaying its "Bob Dylan Story" is undoubtedly received by spectators in an analogous way, yet the director seems to see this as an inescapable fate for documentary filmmaking in the future. As he has frankly admitted in promotional interviews for *The Irishman*, his days as a director are now coming to an end, and these shifting institutional frameworks will effectively determine how his final movies are produced and viewed. Yet even within these evolving sites for film production and reception, Scorsese's documentaries will continue to render their historical accounts, regardless of how these works eventually reach their destinations.

Notes

Introduction

1. Monaco freely acknowledges the "moralistic" (1979, 154) tenor of his account of Scorsese's apparent accommodations to Hollywood's demands, yet his evaluation of the director's work equivocates precisely because of this evident oscillation between documentary and fiction. Like his fellow "movie brats," Scorsese worked primarily as a commercial filmmaker throughout the 1970s, but his contemporaneous documentaries permitted him to maintain the appearance of defection from Hollywood's more mainstream tendencies; and by the late-1970s, of course, the impression of rebellion or defection had already become a disintegrating fiction about the movie brats and their existence in Hollywood. In this respect, Scorsese's resurrected documentary work has been similarly useful in the 2000s, that is to say, during the most commercially driven period of his career.

2. See Ian Christie and David Thompson for Scorsese's characterization of his documentaries as "smaller projects" (2003, 113). Early auteurist studies refer to Scorsese's *Italianamerican*, but the film is viewed primarily as a substantiation of the director's Italian American background. See, for instance, Michael Pye and Linda Myles (1979, 193), Les Kyser (1992, 1–3), and Lawrence S. Friedman (1997, 20–2). Mary Pat Kelly's *Martin Scorsese: The First Decade* weaves its brief look at the film into a more wide-ranging discussion of Italian American history (1980, 103–19). Richard A. Blake uses *Italianamerican* in a very similar way (2005, 153–62). Robert Casillo's expansive *Gangster Priest: The Italian American Cinema of Martin Scorsese* offers the most comprehensive analysis of *Italianamerican* and its relation to Scorsese's ethnic identity (2006, 3–55). Later editions of Robert Kolker's *A Cinema of Loneliness* dedicate more space to Scorsese's documentary work, although the main focus is *A Personal Journey with Martin Scorsese Through American Movies* (1995) and its confirmation of auteurism (2011, 188–94). More recent studies by Leighton Grist (2013, 21–38; 306–9) and Marc Raymond (2013, 79–86; 127–64) provide extended analyses of Scorsese's documentary output. Paul Lopes's *Art Rebels: Race, Class, and Gender in the Art of Miles Davis and Martin Scorsese* (2019) is largely concerned with Scorsese's "biographical legend," yet the director's documentaries somehow do not figure in the book's analyses of this "public story." Nevertheless, Lopes does briefly situate *Italianamerican* at the

beginning of Scorsese's lifelong efforts to document aspects of America's various "hyphenated" white ethnic histories (2019, 157).

3   In addition to the Robert Phillip Kolker passage cited above (1988, 166), see Adrian Martin on the "relatively conventional" (2007, 53) *No Direction Home: Bob Dylan* (2005). Marc Raymond discusses many of Scorsese's documentaries in *Hollywood's New Yorker: The Making of Martin Scorsese* (2013), mainly as the director's means for consolidating his "cultural capital," but he likewise describes the films and television productions somewhat pejoratively as "conventional" works. See his discussion of *No Direction Home*, for example (2013, 191). The perceived ordinariness of Scorsese's documentary making is coterminous with the tendency to see it as a digression from his Hollywood work. The disciplinary purview of film studies was founded on an opposition between modernist experimentation and popular (commercial) orthodoxy, but this framework hasn't always fit comfortably when transposed to the field of documentary film and television production.

4   Once again, see Robert Kolker's indispensable *A Cinema of Loneliness* for the emblematic instance of this application of modernist aesthetics to Scorsese's Hollywood movies (2011, 185–261). Leighton Grist provides a wide-ranging elaboration of this same framework in his excellent two-volume study of Scorsese's filmmaking (2000, 2013). In each case, the documentaries and fiction films are said to exist in a reciprocal relationship, and this tangled reciprocity unavoidably makes Scorsese's documentary work meaningful only when it merges with his fiction films. On the "blurred boundary" between fiction and non-fiction, see Bill Nichols (1994).

5   See, for example, Adrian Martin (2014) on the "documentary temptation" for select directors who work primarily as fiction filmmakers. According to Martin, Scorsese's documentaries "occur within special parentheses," that is to say, as a kind of "moonlighting" from his Hollywood job (2014, 8–9). When digitally restored versions of *Italianamerican* and *American Boy: A Profile of Steven Prince* were at last released by The Criterion Collection in May 2020, they were positioned alongside three of Scorsese's early student short films and collectively described as "a fascinating window onto his artistic development." In other words, they were once again framed as a type of apprenticeship for Hollywood filmmaking.

6   Scorsese has also directed or co-directed several shorter non-fiction films and videos during this same period. "The Neighborhood" was featured in *The Concert for New York City* (2001), and the urgency of its post-9/11 directive is evident in the film's brevity and directness. *Lady by the Sea: The Statue of Liberty* (co-directed with Kent Jones, 2004) is also a product of this same urgent historical moment: it commemorates The Statue of Liberty's post-9/11 reopening while at the same time providing a brief lesson about its historical import. If Scorsese needs "smaller projects to keep [himself] moving" today (Christie and Thompson 2003, 113),

however, he typically produces television commercials for Coca Cola, Apple, and American Express (among others) as well as advertisements like the comic short film, "The Key to Reserva" (2007). In many ways, these slighter works have their roots in the 1980s. The early-1980s were a time of increased institutional instability for the director, but also the period of his prolonged inactivity as a documentarian, and he turned instead to television programs, music videos, and commercials as his "smaller projects" during these years. *Mirror, Mirror* (1986), an episode for Steven Spielberg's *Amazing Stories*, music videos for Michael Jackson's "Bad" (1987) and Robbie Robertson's "Somewhere Down the Crazy River" (1987), commercials for Armani as well as a short film portrait of Giorgio Armani, *Made in Milan* (1990), were all explicitly framed by Scorsese as extensions of his need to alternate between fiction and non-fiction filmmaking in the 1970s.

7   In his lengthy supplemental interview for The Criterion Collection's *Scorsese Shorts* (2020), Scorsese reiterates this characterization of *Italianamerican* and *American Boy: A Profile of Steven Prince*, and he describes more recent productions such as *Public Speaking*, *Living in the Material World*, and *Rolling Thunder Revue* in a very similar way. The latter are no longer independently made short films, of course, yet they nevertheless continue to be defined as a type of preparation for the director's concurrent Hollywood filmmaking.

8   See, for example, Eric Ames's comprehensive *Ferocious Reality: Documentary According to Werner Herzog* (2012). See also Helen Hughes's "Documentary and the Survival of the Film Auteur: Agnès Varda, Werner Herzog, and Spike Lee" (2016). Varda's documentary filmmaking has been thoroughly studied, but as Ames convincingly demonstrates, the analysis of Herzog's abundant documentary output has only really begun in recent years. Spike Lee's inclusion in Hughes's short survey of this particular brand of documentary auteur filmmaking is slightly unusual, in this respect. Scorsese's lengthy personal and professional affiliation with Spike Lee appears to extend to the comparable peripherality of their non-fiction films, videos, and television productions in critical discussions of their filmmaking, yet Lee's work as a documentarian has nonetheless been the subject of at least one book-length study, Delphine Letort's *The Spike Lee Brand: A Study of Documentary Filmmaking* (2015).

9   The historical focus in Scorsese's post-*Goodfellas* (1990) work has been noted by several scholars. See, for instance, Michael Henry Wilson (2011, 305–11), Patrick McGee (2012, 69–144), Marc Raymond (2013, 127–64), and Mike Meneghetti (2017).

10 In Ian Christie and David Thompson's Revised Edition of *Scorsese on Scorsese*, the director describes "starting work" in 1999–2000 on a proposed "Part Two" of *Il mio viaggio in Italia* (2003, 247). Similarly, Christie and Thompson refer to a

"second part of *My Voyage to Italy*" "getting started" at the time of *Gangs of New York*'s release in December 2002 (2003, 268). This documentary, however, has yet to appear. Elsewhere, Christie and Thompson briefly mention the director's projected studies of "British and Russian cinema" alongside a reference to his "documentary profile of Bob Dylan," but only *No Direction Home: Bob Dylan* has since materialized (2003, 271). One can only speculate about these histories of British and Russian cinemas, of course, and there are any number of explanations for why their production has been postponed or abandoned (financing, logistics, scheduling, and so on); but the personal *A Letter to Elia* now appears to have concluded Scorsese's cinephile surveys of film history. His contributions to histories of cinema since 2010 have been much more diffuse—his ongoing association with The Film Foundation and its preservationist mission, his numerous appearances as an interview subject, his work as an executive producer and mentor. His own documentaries, on the other hand, have narrowed their focus to a slightly different kind of cultural portraiture: the studies of film auteurs have been supplanted by profiles of writers and (especially) popular musicians, almost all of them still viewed from the familiar baby boomer perspective. In these cases, Scorsese's presence as a conversational, colloquial narrator has been sidelined, although the resulting films invariably retain the earlier works' sense of cultural stewardship.

11 The Conclusion's survey of Scorsese's documentary output since 2010 situates his work within the broader present-day context of rockumentary production, especially as it has migrated to new sites for the creation and distribution of such films and videos. In many ways, Scorsese's *No Direction Home* was instrumental in initiating the ongoing boom in rockumentary production (and those documentary profiles devoted to legacy/baby boomer musicians, in particular), but his output is now positioned in close proximity to the surfeit of such films and videos on various streaming platforms. His documentary filmmaking since 2010 is therefore best understood in this wider—and substantially altered—context for reality-based media production, and the Conclusion briefly examines this developing framework.

Chapter 1

1 *Italianamerican* was "financed by a Bicentennial Award from the National Endowment for the Humanities" (Michael Henry Wilson 2011, 112). See Matthew Frye Jacobson (2006, 53–4) and Paul Lopes (2017, 570) on *Italianamerican*'s relation to the period's wider "white ethnic revival." Robert Casillo (2006, 36) and Les Keyser both characterize the film as "the bedrock of Scorsese's art" (Keyser

1992, 3). On the two different versions of *Italianamerican*, see Michael Henry Wilson: the version "distributed in the United States by Audio Brandon was shortened to twenty-eight minutes [for television]. The story of the trip to Italy, among other things, was cut out" (2011, 88).

2 See Les Keyser on Scorsese's projected "six-part series on American immigrants" (1992, 99). See also William Rothman on the important coincidence of American documentary filmmaking and various Bicentennial observances in 1975–6 (2000, 428).

3 Jacobson's dismissiveness seems directed in large part at Scorsese's ever-present auteurist legend. Paul Lopes (2017, 2019) adopts the terms of Jacobson's critique in his equally dismissive account of Scorsese's efforts at recovering an ethnic "heritage." Lopes situates the director's "biographical legend" and a certain popular auteurist reception of his work within the context of contemporary America's "Hyphen-Nationalism" (2017, 563). Scorsese, Lopes contends, has traveled from "Italian American to White-Ethnic American" over the course of his lengthy career (2017, 562). Lopes, however, fails to completely consider the more complex rationale for Scorsese's conspicuously non-hyphenated *Italianamerican*. See Robert Casillo on Scorsese's film and the meaning of its title's explicit disregard for such hyphenation (2006, 39–40).

4 See also Mary Pat Kelly on Scorsese's initial disinclination to accept the *Italianamerican* assignment unless he was permitted more autonomy in determining the film's final form (1991, 17). Scorsese reiterates many of these same points in a lengthy 2006 interview with Jim Jarmusch (Jarmusch 2017, 186).

5 A very early—and substantially shorter—version of this chapter first appeared as "Anamnesis in Acts: Documentary Performance as Intercession in *Italianamerican* and *American Boy*" (Meneghetti 2015).

6 This is a consistent theme in interviews with Scorsese. On *Casino*'s (1995) documentary implications: "Well, there are a lot of tracks and zooms; as well as pans and zip-pans. There are also more static angles, cut together very quickly, because of all the information being crammed in the frame. If you did too much moving you wouldn't be able to see what we're trying to show. So that became the style—a kind of documentary" (Brunette 1999, 231). See Leighton Grist on the entanglement of non-fiction and fiction throughout Scorsese's work (2000, 16–17; 2013, 21–2). Adrian Martin describes Scorsese's documentary filmmaking as a type of laboratory for experiments—and refinements—in his customary "fictive style" (2014, 9).

7 Scorsese's elusive claims about *Italianamerican*'s "key event" were made shortly after the completion of *No Direction Home: Bob Dylan* (2005), and he notes how his "fascination" with Dylan's present-day interviews immediately

reminded him of his earlier absorption in his parents' storytelling throughout *Italianamerican* (Donato 2007, 207). Dylan's typically enigmatic comportment as an interview subject in *No Direction Home*, along with the deliberately inscrutable quality of his contemporaneous recordings and writings ("*Love and Theft*" [2001], *Modern Times* [2006], and his memoir, *Chronicles: Volume One* [2004]), surely contributed to Scorsese's searching assertions about the key event in documentary, that is, "the human being" and "human face." Dylan's self-conscious, self-referring foray into fiction filmmaking during this same period, *Masked and Anonymous* (Larry Charles, 2003), only increases the overriding sense of ontological mysteriousness here.

8 As I've already indicated, Scorsese's use of this phrase usually designates a straightforward and vernacular meaning: the emotions are subjective and psychological; they are simply the expressions of a subject and therefore disclose another stratum of truthful descriptions about the past, and so forth. In *Italianamerican*, for example, Scorsese's parents "stick to the emotions," and this unexpectedly reveals their tale to have been a "love story" (Kelly 1991, 18). This is a decidedly ordinary formulation ("love is an emotion"), not necessarily a philosophical one, but it nonetheless indicates the humanist emphases in the director's explanation of *Italianamerican*'s approach. It also distinguishes his idiomatic use of these terms from present-day theoretical work on such matters. Scorsese's methods in *Italianamerican* are invariably drawn from proximate 1970s resources, American documentary filmmaking and the ethnic revival foremost among them, not "theory." By contrast, a vast field devoted to theorizing the "emotions" or "affect" has emerged in recent years, and its claims are significantly more abstract than Scorsese's pragmatic pronouncements. See Belinda Smaill (2010) for a theoretically inflected study of emotion and contemporary documentary. See also Rei Tarada (2001) for a summary of the emotions' prominent place in certain strands of post-structuralist theory and more recent inflections of Continental philosophy. *Italianamerican* has a great deal to tell us about history and historiography on film, and its novel insights about these matters undoubtedly have philosophical value; but "the emotions" in Scorsese's usage finally implies the film's humanist approach, and this is best understood in its immediate historical context.

9 Bill Nichols has repeatedly outlined this history (2001, 607–10). See Michael Renov for a similarly narrow emphasis on various particularisms, subjectivities, and the primacy of "voice" in what he describes as a "post-vérité" turn to "first-person films" (2008, 39). Laura Rascaroli provides an excellent summary of these matters, especially as they relate to the so-called "essay film" (2008, 25–6). And in a slightly different context, Timothy Corrigan helpfully identifies the "drama of subjectivity" as a central feature of many post-Second World War essay films (2010, 223),

although elsewhere he also sees subjectivity being "tested" and challenged in such works (2011, 30–5).
10 See William Rothman (1997, 112–24).
11 Many current popular documentaries have renewed the observational approach. See Danny Birchall, for example, on the persistence of direct cinema's methods in the digital era: "Forms considered surpassed in the linear 'evolution' of documentary such as propaganda documentaries and uncomplicated 'truthful' vérité have re-emerged, or reminded us of their continued presence as modes of documentary making" (2008, 283).
12 *Italianamerican* does not figure in historical surveys of 1970s American documentary. William Rothman mentions it briefly in the context of 1970s "family portrait films" (2000, 446), but Scorsese's work is rarely situated as a representative cultural artifact, nor is it seen as a novel contribution to documentary's changing self-understanding during this decade.
13 I am using the phrase "person-sized spaces" in the sense given to it by Matt Stahl. The objective of direct cinema, he writes, "rushing out to examine the experiences and lives of individuals who were often at crossroads or in crises, was to create person-sized 'spaces' in otherwise inaccessible social situations into which audiences could imaginatively insert themselves" (2013, 71).
14 Several of the essays in Robert Perks and Alistair Thomson's *The Oral History Reader* (1998) directly address the widespread turn to oral history during the 1970s, its theoretical implications, methodological conundrums, and so on. In addition to Portelli's essay in *The Oral History Reader*, see Paul Thompson (21–8), Ronald J. Grele (38–52), and the Popular Memory Group (75–86) for varied assessments of oral history's contributions to historiography during the period in question.
15 Leighton Grist characterizes these self-reflexive opening passages in terms of the period's predominant cine-modernism (2013, 23–4). Marc Raymond discusses them in very similar terms (2013, 80–1).
16 Like Scorsese (Donato 2007, 203), Lawrence S. Friedman considers it an "awkward moment or two" (1997, 21).
17 The literature on these matters is vast, but because of his proximate writings about cinema, Barthes's short book about photography has had a disproportionate influence on contemporary film studies. See Christian Keathley (2006, 33–4) and Philip Rosen (2001, 171–8) for just two examples of this influence.
18 William Rothman provides an especially suggestive description of direct cinema's relation to fiction: "what is fictional about a classical movie resides in its fiction that it is only fiction; what is fictional about a cinéma-vérité film resides in its fiction that it is not fictional at all" (1997, 111). Direct cinema's disavowal of fiction, of course, involves eliminating any trace of its subjects' self-consciousness before the camera and filmmakers.

19 See Matthew Frye Jacobson (2006, 72–129).
20 Jonathan J. Cavallero thus identifies a more "nostalgic treatment" of ethnicity in the director's non-fiction films (2011, 73).
21 Scorsese has encouraged critics to see his documentaries in this way: they are "counterpart[s]" to his fiction films, he says (Christie and Thompson 2003, 113). For Marc Raymond, the 1970s documentaries "authenticate the fiction" (2013, 79).
22 Prince makes a brief appearance as himself in Linklater's *Waking Life* (2001), but he has clearly been cast as the gun-toting figure from *American Boy* (he refers explicitly to the "Ethyl and Regular" anecdote) and *Taxi Driver* (his role as Easy Andy). Tarantino famously restaged Prince's "overdose/adrenaline needle" tale in *Pulp Fiction* (1994).
23 "Oral history" is Scorsese's own description of *American Boy: A Profile of Steven Prince*: "I'd like to preserve on celluloid an oral history of America by getting the people I know to talk" (Michael Henry Wilson 2011, 88). See also Michael Pye and Linda Myles for Scorsese's description of these filmed oral histories: "I believe in these 16mm films. […] They should be like chronicles of the period. They should be very rough, like oral history, magazine profiles, character studies" (1979, 193).
24 For instance, an *IndieWire* piece about Tarantino's homage to *American Boy* inaccurately describes Scorsese's documentary as a "lost film," "never-released," and available only in the form of "bootlegs" (Dry 2017). The Criterion Collection's May 2020 release of a digitally restored version of *American Boy* has now nullified this longstanding fiction about the film's commercial availability.
25 Pasquale Verdicchio describes this type of immigration narrative as "creation myth" (1999, 204). If *Italianamerican* essentially establishes a "generative beginning" for this expansive story about immigration, it is eventually succeeded by *American Boy*'s movement "toward [the] present in a manner that is often incongruous and illogical" (Verdicchio 1999, 204).
26 According to Scorsese, in *American Boy* he simply "observe[s] the way [Prince] talks and his behavior toward the camera" (Michael Henry Wilson 2011, 90).
27 See Peter Biskind's *Easy Riders, Raging Bulls* for assorted anecdotes about Scorsese's widely acknowledged drug use during this period (1998, 386–7).
28 Kehr's short essay appears on the outer sleeve of *Three by Scorsese* (1990), a laserdisc that collects the director's short student film "The Big Shave" (1967), *Italianamerican*, and *American Boy*.
29 *American Boy* was shot in 1976, "two weeks after The Band's final concert in San Francisco, the one featured in *The Last Waltz*" (Michael Henry Wilson 2011, 88). In other words, like *Italianamerican*, *American Boy* was produced in the immediate context of America's Bicentennial observances, but the film offers a strikingly recalcitrant form of national celebration. See Matthew Frye Jacobson on

ethnic particularism as the new form of American assimilation: "ethnicity *is* the assimilated norm," he argues (2006, 75).

30 I am merely—and loosely—referring to the Catholic doctrine of intercession or invocation: the saints are invoked and said to intercede on behalf of the earthly. See Peter Brown's excellent discussion of these matters (1981, 57–63).

31 Scorsese's 1970s films, the documentaries included, are typically discussed in terms of "cine-modernism," but they also contain a forceful antimodern accent that has not yet been fully parsed. See Robert Kolker (2011, 185–261) and Leighton Grist (2000, 1–9; 2013, 1–20) for comprehensive accounts of Scorsese's cine-modernism. Grist's discussion of The Band's music and *The Last Waltz* hints briefly at this strain of antimodern sentiment (2013, 27–8), but much remains to be said about this matter.

32 Significantly, Scorsese did not conduct or shoot these interviews with Bob Dylan. They were undertaken by Dylan's longtime archivist and manager, Jeff Rosen. According to Scorsese, when he "was looking at the interview, [he] realized that if anybody *other* than Jeff had done it, it probably wouldn't have worked" (Donato 2007, 206; emphasis in original). "In a way those interviews allowed us to open up the film, because there was a truth that Jeff Rosen got at with Dylan. *A* truth, as opposed to *the* truth" (Donato 2007, 207; emphasis in original).

33 On Dylan's self-understanding as a key intermediary for the mythic Sixties, see his wide-ranging interview with Jonathan Lethem: "Did I ever want to acquire the Sixties? No. But I own the Sixties—who's going to argue with me" (2006, 477)? Dylan's "Murder Most Foul," a seventeen-minute single released on March 27, 2020, is essentially a vast compendium of the baby boomers' Sixties, and it perhaps confirms the songwriter's "ownership" of this period: beginning with the cataclysmic assassination of John F. Kennedy, the song surveys the subsequent years in terms of moral and spiritual decline, while also measuring the passage of historical time with allusions to various forms of popular music.

34 On Scorsese's decades long involvement with the "music documentary," see Michael Brendan Baker (2015b).

35 Rock critic Robert Christgau on The Band's *Rock of Ages* (1972): this is "the testament of artists who are looking backwards because the future presents itself as a vacuum." See Christgau, https://robertchristgau.com/. As we'll see, Scorsese's *The Last Waltz* shares this perspective, but something of his working experience with The Band would remain with the director in each of his subsequent documentary film and television productions. The prevailing retrospection of Scorsese's documentaries tries to reconcile the past and present, the individual with history; the future, however, is invariably a source of apprehension.

Chapter 2

1. Scorsese emphasizes the initial "archival" mandate in his interview with Richard Schickel (2011, 132). Similar recollections are also featured in the director's extensive voice-over commentary for the twenty-fifth anniversary DVD edition of *The Last Waltz* (2002). Robbie Robertson originally contemplated recording the event with multiple video cameras, but Scorsese appears to have been committed from the outset to creating a filmed document of The Band's farewell concert. The collaborators eventually agreed to shoot the entire documentary in 35-mm and with multiple cameras. "End of an era" and "elegy" have been common critical descriptions of *The Last Waltz*, but Scorsese immediately saw the concert and projected film in these terms (Schickel 2011, 131). See Leighton Grist on the film's "modernist nostalgia" (2013, 27) and "modernist mythopoeia" (2013, 34–6). The Band's past, he claims, is finally "mourned" by the film (2013, 37). In his memoir, Robbie Robertson also acknowledges this characterization of *The Last Waltz* (2016, 493).

2. Each of these numbers was shot on an MGM soundstage several weeks after the original Thanksgiving Day show. See Michael Henry Wilson (2011, 79). "The Weight" and "Evangeline" had been performed and recorded at the November 25 concert, but according to Levon Helm, The Band's performance of the former was "less than magical" (2013, 270). In his expansive liner notes to *The Band: A Musical Journey* (2005), Rob Bowman quotes Robbie Robertson's description of the November 25 performance of "Evangeline" in similar terms. The filmmakers thus hoped to use a set of studio-bound performances to improve or transform the songs in question: The Staples accompanied The Band on a re-recorded version of "The Weight," thereby emphasizing the song's close affiliations with gospel and soul music (and The Staples's own 1968 cover version); while Emmylou Harris joined them on "Evangeline," a simple country waltz. "Theme from The Last Waltz" was composed by Robertson expressly—and hastily—for both the concert and film (Robertson 2016, 475). According to the concert's musical director, John Simon, the majority of the music in *The Last Waltz* was re-recorded and/or altered during the film's lengthy postproduction process (Helm 2013, 275).

3. The legacy of the collectively made *Street Scenes 1970* (1970) also remains unusually contentious, but for different reasons. See Marc Raymond's substantial account of the film's production and exhibition history, particularly as they relate to Scorsese's authorship (2013, 31–45).

4. Robbie Robertson and Garth Hudson are the last surviving members of The Band's original lineup. Hudson, The Band's keyboardist and most accomplished musician, has said very little about *The Last Waltz* and its aftermath, but Robertson has

devoted most of his post-Band existence to securing the film's (and his own) legacy. *The Last Waltz*'s twenty-fifth anniversary was duly celebrated with a theatrical re-release in 2002 (soon followed by a new DVD with the obligatory extras features, voice-over commentaries, and so on), and Robertson has overseen the remastering, repackaging, and expansion of the film's original soundtrack. The comprehensive box set, *The Band: A Musical History* (2005), is the emblematic product of Robertson's lifelong effort to shape the group's legacy in his own terms, and the collection culminates—inevitably—with several tracks from *The Last Waltz*. However, it conspicuously ignores The Band's brief reemergence as a recording act in the 1990s (Helm, Hudson, and Danko were the group's only remaining original members). The disappointing *Once Were Brothers: Robbie Robertson and The Band* (Daniel Roher, 2019), based in large part on Robertson's *Testimony* (2016), further perpetuates this abridged version of the group's history.

5 *The Last Waltz*'s "twenty-fifth anniversary" was celebrated in 2002, perhaps splitting the difference between the Thanksgiving Day commemorative concert, which took place in 1976, and the official release of Scorsese's film in 1978.

6 The opening chapters of Helm's *This Wheel's on Fire* quickly establish a recurring emphasis on labor, beginning in the Arkansas of his childhood and his family's farm (2013, 13; 27–31), and continuing through his account of *The Last Waltz* and its immediate aftermath (274–8). In the book's expansive tales about 1940s Arkansas, Greil Marcus observes, one can "see [Helm's] grin and feel his ache" (2015, 235), but one also sees and feels Helm's bitterness as he recalls his days with The Band. For Helm, his work within The Band evidently existed on a continuum with his early experiences as a laborer on the family farm, and his disappointment with the group's eventual disintegration stems directly from this conception.

7 J.P. Telotte provides an excellent interpretation of *The Last Waltz*'s focus on this passage from expression to exhaustion (1979, 12–13).

8 Michael Brendan Baker describes this period's rockumentary output as a "golden age" and situates *The Last Waltz* at the end of its "second wave" (2015b, 246).

9 See Reebee Garofalo on the music business' rapid transformation during this period (1999, 336–9). See also Simon Frith (2007, 65–7).

10 See music critic Dave Marsh's assessments of Robertson's self-importance: "For all of Robbie Robertson's brooding self-importance—and if there have been more brooding figures in rock, for self-importance he has no equal—he's simply nothing like a household word" (1989, 400). See also Marsh's rather harsh dismissal of Robertson's work with Scorsese in *The Last Waltz*: "His [Robertson's] street wisdom quickly decayed into hucksterism; the interviews in *The Last Waltz*, where Robertson interrupts Rick Danko and Richard Manuel at almost every turn, are gross self-promotion, indulged with aplomb if little subtlety" (1985, 125). See

Henry Adam Svec for a reconsideration of Robertson's self-promotion in *The Last Waltz* (2012, 436–40).

11 Once again, see Reebee Garofalo on the music industry's mounting crises in the late-1970s and 1980s (1999, 342–7). See also Steve Knopper (2009) on these various continuing—and intensifying—crises.

12 *The Last Waltz*, of course, was staged and recorded only a few months after America's Bicentennial observances had ended, and this is yet another of the film's loose connections to its immediate predecessor, *Italianamerican*. Bob Dylan's "Rolling Thunder Revue," completed shortly before The Band's farewell concert, was also loosely linked to the nation's Bicentennial commemorative events. Dylan's attentiveness to early American history exerted a strong influence on members of The Band, Robbie Robertson in particular, and songs like "The Night They Drove Old Dixie Down," "The Weight," and "Up on Cripple Creek" must have resonated differently throughout the summer of 1976 as the original incarnation of The Band toured together for the last time. See Sean Wilentz's excellent account of Dylan's "Rolling Thunder Revue" and *Renaldo and Clara*'s (1978) Bicentennial implication (2010, 167–8). The opening passages of Scorsese's *Rolling Thunder Revue: A Bob Dylan Story by Martin Scorsese* (2019) briefly review the Bicentennial context for Dylan's tour of America's northeastern states in 1975.

13 Recordings of these shows circulated for years as bootlegs, but they have since been officially released by Bob Dylan as part of an extensive "bootleg" archival series. See *Vol. 4: Bob Dylan Live 1966, The "Royal Albert Hall" Concert* (1998). There are several very good accounts of The Band's formative years. See Hoskyns (2006, 29–86), Bowman (2005), and Marcus (2010, 324–33).

14 Attempts to explain the rock 'n' roll band's volatility, fragility, and complexity were common among Marcus's cohort of 1960s rock critics, particularly after The Beatles' disintegration in 1970. See Jon Landau's bewildered review of Paul McCartney's *Ram*, for instance (1971). For a more recent consideration of the rock group as distinctive social entity, see Warren Zanes's *Petty: The Biography* (2015).

15 The Band's relationship to nationality and nation has been framed differently by critics. Composed primarily of Canadians, the group's music is nonetheless typically situated in an American context. See Hoskyns's *Across the Great Divide: The Band and America* (2006), for instance. Greil Marcus characterizes The Band's songs as archetypically "American" music, and he interprets the group's work according to the familiar "pilgrim's" tale and its Christian—that is to say, Protestant—ethos (2015, 35–59). In other words, Marcus's American perspective draws heavily from the "Protestant poets who presided over the nineteenth-century synthesis of a redemptive cosmic drama with an ideology of self-reliance" (Cantwell 1996, 27). See Bart Testa and Jim Shedden's "In the Great Midwestern Hardware

Store" for a perceptive reassessment of the group's music in terms of its nationality. They situate The Band as "North American" because of their music's abundant "regional allusions" and deliberate detachment from any precise "historical sources and references" (2002, 188–92). Like Bob Dylan's contemporaneous work, The Band's songs are often best situated in the past archaic. On this critical aspect of Dylan's music, see Michael Denning (2009, 29–30).

16   *Time* magazine devoted its cover to The Band on January 12, 1970. This image and accompanying profile piece seize upon the group's self-described eccentricity as a key to their distinction from contemporaneous rock musicians. In their respective memoirs, Helm and Robertson also insist upon The Band's difference from the era's hippies (Helm 2013, 173; Robertson 2016, 349–52). The *Time* profile was written by Jay Cocks, Scorsese's longtime friend and collaborator.

17   D.A. Pennebaker followed Bob Dylan during the latter part of his 1965–6 tour with The Hawks; the aim was to create a second documentary about Dylan. See Hoskyns for an account of this abandoned project (2006, 116–20). Dennis Hopper's evocative use of "The Weight" in *Easy Rider* (1969) was the lone example of The Band's music interacting with contemporary currents in popular American cinema. "The Weight" has since become a convenient shorthand for "The Sixties" and/or "baby boomers," finding its way into numerous mainstream Hollywood films. Davis Guggenheim's *It Might Get Loud* (2008) concludes with Jimmy Page, Jack White, and The Edge delivering a ragged acoustic version of the song.

18   According to Levon Helm, The Band's Woodstock performance was omitted from Wadleigh's film because of a dispute over fees for The Band's appearance (2013, 200). Dimly lit images of The Band's Woodstock set can now be seen on various video sharing platforms: an excellent "Tears of Rage" featuring Richard Manuel; an overly hurried, seemingly nervous rendition of "The Weight." The DVD extras included on *The Band: A Musical History* (2005) reveal a technically accomplished, yet stiff group of performers. As Greil Marcus observes, The Band could burrow deeply into an orderly proficiency onstage, but too often their expertise came at the expense of excitement or meaningful exchanges with their audiences. See especially Marcus's obituary for Rick Danko, "The Man on the Left" (2010, 239–41).

19   *Festival Express* was eventually released in 2003 (directed by Bob Smeaton and Frank Cvitanovich). Except for Rick Danko's brief—and comically drunken—performance of "Ain't No Cane on the Brazos," The Band are conspicuously absent from other scenes set on the festival train. See Hoskyns on The Band's mixed experiences on *Festival Express* (2006, 245–7).

20   The Band did, however, make a few appearances on television during this period. See Helm on The Band's varied experiences on TV (2013, 204).

21   See David E. James on *Blackboard Jungle* (Richard Brooks, 1955) and its affirmation of the cinema's ethical superiority to rock 'n' roll (2016, 23–32).

22 There were several important precedents for the hippie-era concert documentary, of course. See David E. James's excellent summary of the developing documentary/popular music alignment throughout the early-1960s (2016, 183–99).

23 This is a prominent feature of Pennebaker's *Shake! Otis at Monterey* (1986), a short film composed of Redding's performance at the festival as well as footage not used in the original theatrical release of *Monterey Pop*. Booker T. and The M.G.s work with a greater sense of shared purpose and cohesion than most of the West Coast rock groups at Monterey Pop. Al Jackson Jr. is an especially good example of the band members' easy adaptability to Redding's extemporaneous additions throughout his short set.

24 Richard Schickel briefly discusses Scorsese's work as an editor on *Woodstock*, noting that he was eventually fired by the film's producers (2011, 81–2).

25 Scorsese's subsequent work as associate producer and editor (uncredited) on *Medicine Ball Caravan* (François Reichenbach, 1971) and "montage supervisor" for *Elvis on Tour* (Robert Abel and Pierre Adidge, 1972) sometimes combines images and sounds for similar effects, but it's ultimately difficult to determine the extent of Scorsese's contributions. In their analysis of *Medicine Ball Caravan*, David Sanjek and Benjamin Halligan make no mention of Scorsese's involvement with the film (2013, 100–12). Greil Marcus refers briefly to *Elvis on Tour* in the excellent "Presliad" chapter of *Mystery Train*, describing it somewhat disapprovingly as a film "with gestures toward History" (2015, 160), but once again, it remains difficult to attribute anything in the documentary definitively to Scorsese.

26 David E. James summarizes these contradictions in the film's mode of production and politics (2016, 243–5).

27 I have gathered most of this information about The Band's initial critical reception from the invaluable website, http://theband.hiof.no/, an exhaustive collection of various materials about the group's history, individual members' solo careers, and all other Band-related ephemera. The *Time* profile (January 12, 1970) and hundreds of other reviews and stories from the period are conveniently archived here.

28 Many of the West Coast psychedelic rock bands began as commercial folk acts, but The Band did not. Robert Cantwell, for instance, refers briefly to Jefferson Airplane's and the Grateful Dead's origins as "bluegrass, blues, and folk musicians" (1996, 310). See Hoskyns's account of The Hawks' very different formative years as a scuffling rock 'n' roll band (2006, 29–86). *Time*'s designation, "country rock," anticipates a major trend in early-1970s popular American music, but as Hoskyns rightly notes, The Band's approach was mostly unrelated to Los Angeles' "Nudie-suited cowboys" (2006, 2). That said, The Band's formalist inclinations often led them to the past and an attendant preoccupation with mythos, nostalgia, and/or the melancholic. These were the primary themes in much American country-rock,

of course, yet The Band weren't necessarily afflicted with the latter's predominant sense of stasis.

29 J.P. Telotte provides an insightful interpretation of this aspect of the film (1979, 12). See also Leighton Grist (2013, 37). Keith Beattie's analysis of the film's revisionism is similarly focused on its excision of the Winterland audience (2005, 30–1). Scorsese addresses this matter in Michael Henry Wilson (2011, 82).

30 Brian Ward's *Just My Soul Responding: Rhythm and Blues, Black Consciousness and Race Relations* distinguishes black forms of rhythm and blues in a very useful way (1998, 7–10).

31 Eric Clapton's "Further on up the Road" concludes this blues segment, but his expansive soloing upsets the preceding ensemble playing slightly. Unlike Dylan and Hawkins, Clapton momentarily leads The Band to an uncertain kind of interplay: Robertson's impromptu soloing is uncharacteristically sloppy, and this somewhat clattering rendition of an otherwise familiar song rushes to its conclusion alongside Clapton's extended guitar solo.

32 The Butterfield Blues Band's performance of "Love March" was nevertheless included on the original *Woodstock* soundtrack (1970).

33 See Stephen Mamber, however, on the conventionality of direct cinema's various "crisis" scenarios (1974, 115–40). See also William Rothman's excellent discussion of direct cinema's indebtedness to the themes of so-called "classical" Hollywood films (1997, 117–24). By contrast, many other critics have linked the concert film's emergence to the thoroughgoing erosion of classical Hollywood's various genres throughout the 1960s, in this particular case, the musical. See David E. James (2016, 11–22). See also Keith Beattie (2011, 23–4) and J.P. Telotte (1979, 9–10).

34 See also Jonathan Kahana's discussion of direct cinema's perennial focus on individuals (2008, 293–7).

35 See Leacock's collected essays at http://www.afana.org/leacockessays.htm. See especially "A Search for the Feeling of Being There" (1997) and its preoccupation with this apparently "neutral" presence. Matt Stahl provides a very good account of direct cinema's implicit concern with encouraging rational judgments about the public sphere and an attendant participation in "democratic political processes" (2013, 69).

36 Leacock makes this claim in Les Blank and Gina Leibrecht's *How to Smell a Rose: A Visit with Ricky Leacock in Normandy* (2015).

37 Once again, see Les Blank and Gina Leibrecht's *How to Smell a Rose* for Leacock's narrative/autobiographical account of his growing disillusionment with the Left throughout the 1950s and 1960s. "Marxist hangover" is Leacock's description of Jean-Luc Godard's late-1960s work in "A Search for the Feeling of Being There" (1997). See Leacock's programmatic "For an Uncontrolled Cinema" (2016, 491–2).

See also Kahana's invaluable discussion of *Primary* and the Cold War context (1999, 100). See Michael Curtin (1995) for a critical account of 1960s television documentaries and the Cold War.

38 See Jeanne Hall's lengthy critical analysis of *Primary* (1991, 24–50). See also Hall's discussion of Pennebaker's *Dont Look Back* and its self-justifying critique of the traditional media's coverage of Bob Dylan throughout the mid-1960s (2014, 237–52).

39 As Robert Cantwell pointedly observes, "folkie" revivalists of the early-1960s "were not moved primarily by an ideologically inspired resistance, but by a generally shared belief in a world better furnished with the means of postwar society's promise of personal fulfillment" (1996, 119). If Dylan could function as the folk revival's most important totem, it was because he appeared to authenticate this emphasis on self-realization. The folkies, of course, were subsequently scandalized by Dylan's return to rock music in 1965, but their response simply refused to acknowledge how he continued to project this same quality into the era's rock music and youth counterculture.

40 The Monterey Pop festival was presented as a non-profit event, and as David E. James observes, it was "designed to validate rock 'n' roll as a fully mature form, equivalent in status to the jazz and folk of previous festivals" (2016, 212). In short, this non-profit festival sought the "credibility" of a "genuine folk event" (James 2016, 223). The Woodstock Music and Art Fair would eventually also become a "free festival" for its audience, but it was originally conceived as a private business venture. Discussion of such economic realities is completely absent from Pennebaker's *Monterey Pop*, and after the film's brief introductory images of John Phillips and his fellow organizers, the festival is rendered as a spontaneous manifestation of the counterculture's "vision" and "freedom." By contrast, Wadleigh's *Woodstock* refers repeatedly to the organizer's financial investment and inevitable losses, but only to confirm the festival's expanding autonomy and utopianism as fences are broken and the audience grows to an unprecedented size.

41 Except for Garth Hudson, who didn't sing on The Band's recordings, Robertson was the group's weakest singer by some measure. He sang lead only on *Music from Big Pink*'s indecipherable "To Kingdom Come," *Islands*' "Knockin' Lost John," and *The Last Waltz*'s "Out of the Blue," and it's difficult to hear his vocal contributions to The Band's abundant live recordings. In *This Wheel's on Fire*, Helm, perhaps a little uncharitably, disparages Robertson's poor singing voice and insists that the guitarist's microphone was in fact turned off during *The Last Waltz*'s concert performances. The guitarist's subsequent recordings as a solo performer tend to corroborate Helm's assertions: Robertson's post-Band songs, always elaborately produced, are invariably sung in a whisper or rasp. The otherwise excellent *Classic*

Albums: The Band (Bob Smeaton, 1997) allows Robertson to explain his singing in the following way: his newborn babies typically required quiet, and he therefore composed *The Band*'s songs with this voice. Unfortunately, his subsequent spoken/whispered performance of "The Night They Drove Old Dixie Down" on piano flattens the song's melody, making it almost unrecognizable. In his memoir, Helm repeatedly accuses Robertson of taking undue songwriting credit (and money, of course) for The Band's first two records, and this remains a contentious part of the group's legacy (2013, 209–11). The relative dearth of Helm's post-Band songwriting credits perhaps belies his claims to some degree, but one could certainly make a case for the centrality of Richard Manuel's songwriting on *Music from Big Pink*.

42 Scorsese admits as much to Richard Schickel, describing a "real tension" in his interviews with The Band (2011, 134). The interviews were all conducted in the midst of the group's post-concert disintegration. See also Helm's account of his "country" rudeness during interviews with Scorsese (2013, 271).

43 Robertson briefly reiterates his understanding of Elvis's significance in *Elvis Presley: The Searcher* (Thom Zimny, 2018).

44 As he did in *American Boy: A Profile of Steven Prince*, Scorsese asked his documentary subject to "repeat [his final line] several times," though in this case the director excised his intervention from the finished film. See Michael Henry Wilson (2011, 79).

45 For Axel Honneth, "the claims to individual self-realization which have rapidly multiplied, beginning with the historically unique concatenation of entirely different processes of individualization in the Western societies of thirty or forty years ago, have so definitely become a feature of the institutionalized expectations inherent in social reproduction that the particular goals of such claims are lost and they are transmuted into a support of the system's legitimacy" (2004, 467). See also David Harvey for a similar assessment of these matters (2005, 41).

46 According to Bill Nichols, for example, the "newer, post-1970s 'wave' of documentary film, like the modernist avant-garde before it, revises our understanding of the subject; it displaces the individual from the stable position of correspondent with the state" (2001, 609). Michael Renov offers a very similar formulation (2008, 39). In both cases, the individualist emphases in direct cinema are simply intensified according to the dictates of neoliberalism. Scholars typically point to a discord between "theoretical" statements made by practitioners of direct cinema and the documentaries themselves. As a result, various proclamations about "observational neutrality," minimal editorial intervention, and so on, are said to be specious, yet the films often reveal a readiness to forgo such principles. See Keith Beattie (2005, 21–31; 2011, 11–21) and Stella Bruzzi (2006, 73–80) on these matters, for example.

47 This emphasis on labor is pronounced in Scorsese's 1970s documentaries. An extended passage in *Italianamerican* is devoted to the Scorseses' account of work—their own jobs in New York City's garment district, but also the wide variety of their parents' humble employment (on construction sites, at the bottom of ships, in markets and stores, as seamstresses, and so on). *American Boy: A Profile of Steven Prince* is similarly preoccupied with its subject's anecdotes about work across the entertainment industries. If the movement from *Italianamerican*'s communal storytelling to *American Boy*'s solitary narration discloses the high costs of ethnic assimilation in America, we should also notice how the Scorseses' discussion of menial labor is eventually replaced by Prince's comically wasted take on the Hollywood hustle, thereby highlighting a self-directed—and paradoxically self-defeating—quality in Prince's creative work. *The Last Waltz* manages to combine these two conceptions in its fraught reckoning with The Band's history.

48 Joe McElhaney's analysis of *Gimme Shelter* describes The Rolling Stones' "physical distance" from their audiences (2009, 82). See Robert Christgau's assorted writings about The Stones for an excellent account of the band's calculated distance, its development, and shifting significance. See especially "The Rolling Stones: Can't Get No Satisfaction," "The Rolling Stones," and "Winning Ugly," all collected at Christgau's website, https://robertchristgau.com/.

49 *Shine a Light* also revives *The Last Waltz*'s working methods. The film's multiple cameras were operated by many of the industry's most distinguished cinematographers, including Robert Richardson (a frequent Scorsese collaborator), Ellen Kuras, John Toll, and *Gimme Shelter*'s director, Albert Maysles.

50 Jean-Luc Godard's *One Plus One* (1968) had already depicted The Stones' exceptional status as workers within the music industry. As David E. James notes, in Godard's film, the group's "unrestricted access to studio time, their expensive instruments and extensive equipment, and a small army of engineers, assistants, studio musicians, and hangers-on indicate their privilege as labor aristocracy and by implication their product's financial value for the culture industry" (2016, 268). In a contemporary context, they've retained this sense of aristocratic control, and this undoubtedly places them beyond the modern-day rock musician's everyday concerns.

51 One could rightly see the film as overly generous, in this respect: Jagger's career-long "distance" has become a form of cynicism at this point, and his "professional" deportment can be understood simply as self-interest or economic opportunism. But The Stones' *A Bigger Bang* (2005) was received positively by many critics, and *Shine a Light* provides some evidence for Jagger's reinvigorated commitment to the group's music.

52 The album/tour's promotional television documentary, *25x5: The Continuing Adventures of The Rolling Stones* (Nigel Finch, 1990), basically reconfigures the

band's entire history in these terms and thereby inaugurates their ongoing work as a "legacy act."

53 *Ladies and Gentlemen* is a "pure" concert documentary; that is to say, the film is set wholly on The Stones' stage, and the audience is mostly abolished from its images. Drawn from the tour for *Exile on Main St.* (1972), *Ladies and Gentlemen* captures The Stones at their creative peak. Robert Frank's infamous *Cocksucker Blues* (1972) documents the same tour, but its sordid backstage scenes (junkiedom, groupies, and so on) impelled the band to limit its distribution. The different fates of these two documentaries indicate the group's decisive assertion of control over their cinematic image after the experience of *Gimme Shelter* and its representation of the events at Altamont.

54 Scorsese and Jagger would work together again as executive producers on the HBO television series, *Vinyl* (2016), a fictionalized rendering of the 1970s music business in New York City. The show was a critical and commercial disappointment, however, and its representations of "control" and "proficiency" frequently border on humorless self-parody. It is in many ways Scorsese's least compelling effort at historical fiction.

Chapter 3

1 In the present-day moment of online streaming and diminishing income for musicians, the rock star memoir has become a staple product, particularly for "legacy" performers and baby boomers. See Bob Dylan's occasional collaborator Eric Clapton (2007) for a more conventional example of the rock star autobiography. In this case, Clapton's retrospection initiates a familiar return to childhood origins; this is followed by a very candid account of professional successes and failures, personal trials (drug and alcohol addiction, divorces), and concludes with an image of the guitarist's late-life contentment. *Chronicles: Volume One*, by contrast, tells readers almost nothing about Dylan's childhood, his parents, upbringing, marriages, children, and so on, and the book remains focused on his expansive cohort of musician friends and fellow songwriters. In its plainspokenness, *Chronicles* is the clearest antecedent to Neil Young's *Waging Heavy Peace: A Hippie Dream* (2012) and Bruce Springsteen's *Born to Run* (2016), although it is adamantly non-hippie in its emphases and never resorts to Springsteen's strategic sentimentality. Richard Hell's excellent *I Dreamed I Was a Very Clean Tramp: An Autobiography* (2013) frequently matches Dylan's generosity when it is reminiscing about collaborators or rivals, yet its expansive account of Hell's childhood, adolescence, and substantial drug problems ultimately distinguishes it from *Chronicles'* deliberate elusiveness on such matters.

2. See Greil Marcus's "Dylan as Historian" for an authoritative analysis of the songwriter's retrieval of diverse historical materials (2010, 155–61). Marcus's *The Old, Weird America: The World of Bob Dylan's Basement Tapes* (2011) is similarly insightful about one of Dylan's most important expeditions through American vernacular music. Benjamin Feline provides a useful overview of the songwriter's lifelong commitment to "folk processes" (2000, 204–32). "Dylan's most enduring product," Feline writes, "is the example he offered of how to negotiate the relationship between past and present" (2000, 232). Dylan's description of "folk music" in *Chronicles: Volume One* is consistent with his spatial transcription of the New York Public Library's archive and speaks directly to his immersion in the creation of such music: "Folk Music was a reality of a more brilliant dimension. It exceeded all human understanding, and if it called out to you, you could disappear and be sucked into" its "mythical realm" (2004, 236).

3. *The Bootleg Series* currently stands at fourteen volumes, although more releases have been promised. See Chris Willman's (2019) and Jon Blistein's (2019) anticipation of Scorsese's Netflix documentary about Dylan's "Rolling Thunder Revue," *Rolling Thunder Revue: A Bob Dylan Story by Martin Scorsese*, as well as its projected soundtrack. (An accompanying entry in *The Bootleg Series* would eventually be released as a mammoth fourteen-CD box set.) This ongoing archival dig appears to have several different rationales. On the one hand, Dylan's management is evidently attempting to widen and reinforce the songwriter's substantial legacy by relocating previously unreleased and unseen materials to these new present-day frameworks (CDs, films and videos, online streaming services, and so on). On the other hand, however, this has been equally driven by significant business considerations: a concern with protecting the aging songwriter's various expiring copyrights has also produced a parallel set of releases, CDs without *The Bootleg Series*' apparent "archival" mandate. See Allan Kozinn (2013) on Sony's cheaply made, limited European CD releases of Dylan's early outtakes and live recordings for the sole purpose of "copyright extension." See John Sakamoto (2014) on the music industry's broader adoption of the "copyright-driven collection" for Sixties legacy acts such as Dylan, The Beatles, and The Beach Boys.

The introduction of CDs provided a considerable boon for the archival retrospective, but the success of Dylan's 5LP *Biograph* (1985) encouraged a certain historiographic orientation in collections devoted to various performers from the rock era. Neil Young's 3LP *Decade* (1977), personally overseen by Young himself, was an important precursor to *Biograph*, but Dylan's collection, released at the start of a conspicuously fallow period for the songwriter, was instrumental in establishing the retrospective tenor of so many of his present-day releases. See Reebee Garofalo on the increasing value of "back catalogue" and "artist retrospectives" during the CD era (1999, 344). See also Steven F. Pond on "retrospective reissues" and their historically oriented liner notes (2003, 17). *Martin Scorsese Presents: The Blues* (2003), *No Direction Home: Bob Dylan* (2005), and *George Harrison: Living in the Material World* (2011) all share a certain historicist perspective with these CD collections, and the films' multi-platform, cross-merchandising strategies indicate how they are finally underwritten by economic features of the present-day recording industry.

4   One could, with some reservations, add Dylan's more recent surveys of a Sinatra-style "American songbook"—*Shadows in the Night* (2015), *Fallen Angels* (2016), and *Triplicate* (2017)—to this wider context of "archeological" excavation.

5   See Scorsese's interview with Raffaele Donato for a brief account of *No Direction Home*'s genesis (Donato 2007, 205–7).

6   The global reach of this present-day emphasis on "archiving" and preservation has produced a vast body of scholarship. Scorsese's early-2000s turn to the documentary compilation of historical resources coincides very closely with a new emphasis on the changing meanings and politics of "the archive." See Stuart Hall's succinct overview of archiving's major themes and questions during this period (2001, 89–92).

7   See Anthony D. Cavaluzzi (2015) and Giuliana Muscio (2015) on Scorsese's use of rock music in his fiction films. Scorsese describes his first experiences with rock 'n' roll in reverential terms: "I discovered rock 'n' roll in 1956—real rock 'n' roll, Little Richard, Fats Domino, Chuck Berry, Elvis, Sreamin' Jay Hawkins. For me, it was a real revolution" (Pye and Myles 1979, 190).

8   See Andrew Sarris's explanation and reaffirmation of his controversial "auteur theory" in *The American Cinema* (1996, 25–37; 269–78). Sarris's many entries on European directors confirm the significant coincidence of auteurism and a valorization of so-called "art cinema" throughout this period. See Thomas Elsaesser's "Two Decades in Another Country: Hollywood and the Cinephiles" on the transnational exchanges that produced such critical positions (2005a, 233–50). See also Jonathan Rosenbaum's nostalgic reminiscences about 1960s film culture and Sarris's legacy (2010, 331–6). Robert P. Kolker briefly discusses Sarris's tacit influence on Scorsese's *A Personal Journey with Martin Scorsese Through American Movies* (2015, 73–4).

9   See Jay Cocks's profile of The Band in *Time* magazine (January 12, 1970), the template for contemporaneous characterizations of the group's self-conscious nostalgia. The *Time* magazine article and countless other reviews and profiles of The Band from this period can be found at http://theband.hiof.no/.

10 See Robbie Robertson's *Testimony* for this characterization of *Rock of Ages* as a summation of The Band's accomplishments (2016, 388–95).

11 See Ian Christie and David Thompson on Scorsese's first "illustrated lectures on the problem of color fading" (2003, 84–7). The "clock is ticking" formulation remains a prominent feature of Scorsese's present-day film preservation. See, for instance, his

Encyclopedia Britannica entry, "Film Preservation: A Dire Need" (May 25, 2018). See also Scorsese's lengthy interview with frequent collaborator, the critic and filmmaker, Kent Jones (October 27, 2015). Scorsese and Jones dedicate a significant portion of their conversation to The Film Foundation, its origins and ongoing activities, and the perpetual "dire need" of film preservation.

12 See Marc Raymond's extended summary of this pivotal moment in Scorsese's career (2013, 94–8).

13 See The Film Foundation at http://www.film-foundation.org/.

14 The 107th Congress of the United States declared 2003 an official "Year of the Blues." A commemorative "kick-off" concert was held at Radio City Music Hall on February 7, 2003. This in turn produced a concert film (*Lightning in a Bottle* [Antoine Fuqua, 2004]) and soundtrack (*A Salute to the Blues: Lightning in a Bottle* [2004]). Scorsese's introductory notes to the *Lightning in a Bottle* soundtrack position *Martin Scorsese Presents: The Blues* as the culmination to the year's celebratory events. *Eric Clapton: Nothing but the Blues* followed the release of Clapton's *From the Cradle* (1994), his long-deferred collection of blues recordings, and the documentary emphasizes complete live performances of several of its songs. In this respect, the film is both promotion and a commemoration of *From the Cradle*'s return to Clapton's putative "roots" in American blues.

15 See *Martin Scorsese Presents: The Blues* at http://www.pbs.org/theblues/. Many of the website's media links are no longer active (legacy players have been retired), but its main interface remains in place, and users can navigate to brief descriptions of individual episodes, an extensive discography, short biographies of the series' featured musicians, and a map for a proposed "blues road trip." More interestingly, the site provides a "Blues Classroom" for teachers. Collected essays, lesson plans, an expansive viewing guide for teachers and students, a useful glossary of terms and concepts, bibliographies and discographies, and short explanations of blues fundamentals such as the twelve-bar form can all be found here.

16 In addition to Scorsese's *Feel Like Going Home*, the series includes the following contributions: *The Soul of a Man* (Wim Wenders), *The Road to Memphis* (Richard Pearce and Robert Kenner), *Warming by the Devil's Fire* (Charles Burnett), *Godfathers and Sons* (Marc Levin), *Red, White & Blues* (Mike Figgis), and *Piano Blues* (Clint Eastwood). As many critics have observed, Charles Burnett is the lone African American among these filmmakers.

17 Ken Burns's *Jazz* has been written about extensively. See Theodore Gracyk (2002) on the program's inexplicable, factional refusal to completely document jazz's history beyond 1960. See also Lee B. Brown (2002) for a similar focus on Burns's avoidance of avant-garde jazz and the series' attendant shortcomings as history. Scott DeVeaux (2001) outlines the historiographic consequences of Burns's

emphasis on the swing era, its purported popularity, and so forth. See Steven F. Pond (2003) on *Jazz*'s varied reception. *Martin Scorsese Presents: The Blues* was conceived, like *Jazz*, as a cultural event. In addition to its broadcast on PBS in October 2003, *The Blues* was (again, like *Jazz*) accompanied by a website and book, and supplemented with twenty-five CDs of closely related music: a *Best of The Blues* single-CD compilation, a five CD box set, individual soundtracks to all seven episodes, and twelve single-CD "artist collections." The box set, a broad overview of music related to *The Blues*, clearly aims to outline this music's present-day pertinence. Selections include music by seminal figures such as Robert Johnson, Muddy Waters, and Howlin' Wolf, but also 1960s revivalists like Eric Clapton, Taj Mahal, and The Butterfield Blues Band. Los Lobos, Corey Harris, and several other contemporary artists bring this music into the present. For Scorsese, this is "the music *behind* our music" (2003a, 6; emphasis in original), so the 1960s provides a foundation for the box set's general perspective: Bob Dylan's "Highway 61 Revisited" is therefore set comfortably between Mississippi Fred McDowell's "You Gotta Move" and Junior Wells's "Hoodoo Man Blues." Elijah Wald describes 1960s rock music's understanding of the blues as "precursor" or "prehistory" as an unwitting reinstatement of the color line (2009, 230–47).

18 Muddy Waters's "Feel Like Going Home" appeared on *Folk Singer* in 1964 as an acoustic rendition of his earlier "I Feel Like Going Home" (1948), which was itself a reworking of the much earlier "Country Blues." "Country Blues" is among the famous field recordings made by Alan Lomax in 1941–2 and used extensively in Scorsese's *Feel Like Going Home*. Waters recorded yet another version of the durable "I Feel Like Going Home" for his final album, the Johnny Winter produced *King Bee* (1981). "I Feel Like Going Home" (1948) plays briefly during the film's closing credits. See Robert Palmer's account of Alan Lomax's visits to record Muddy Waters on the Stovall plantation during this period (1981, 2–7). See also Benjamin Filene's short discussion of Lomax's first meetings with Waters (2000, 76–8). Steve Waksman provides an overview of Waters's field recordings, helpfully positioning them on a continuum with his subsequent electric blues at Chicago's Chess Records (1999, 113–47). Peter Guralnick's excellent *Feel Like Going Home* (2012), a collection of artist profiles named after the same Waters song, is probably the immediate source for the film's title. As its principal writer and consultant, Gurlanick's influence on Scorsese's film is considerable.

19 See George Lipsitz for a critical assessment of Clapton's lifelong identification with Robert Johnson's story and music (2006, 118–39). See also Ulrich Adelt on Clapton's blues purism and his admittedly romanticized vision of Johnson's work and life (2010, 57–77). Clapton's profound investment in the blues is sometimes ambivalent, shifting between reverence, insecurity, and as Adelt shows, an

unwitting internalization of the color line. Indeed, in Scorsese's *George Harrison: Living in the Material World*, Clapton eagerly describes himself as a "blues missionary," and the mixture of good intentions and inadvertent paternalism is unmistakable. Mike Figgis's contribution to *The Blues* series, *Red, White & Blues*, is devoted to the 1960s British blues revival, and Clapton is a frequent interview subject throughout the documentary. The guitarist cannot explain exactly *why* he and so many other white Englishmen were fascinated by American blues during this period, but to be fair, no one else in Figgis's film provides an answer to this critical question either.

20 For just two examples of Palmer's expert accounts of the blues, see his liner notes to Muddy Waters's *The Chess Box* (1989) and Elmore James's *The Sky Is Crying: The History of Elmore James* (1993). See also the extensive notes to Bo Diddley's *The Chess Box* (1990) for evidence of Palmer's ability to situate this music in multiple musicological and cultural contexts, past and present.

21 Dave Stewart, formerly of The Eurythmics and The Spiritual Cowboys, makes his appearances early in the film, although most of Palmer's subsequent voice-over narration is directed to Stewart as a series of updates about the production's daily progress. Stewart's involvement was surely instrumental in securing the film's financing, and his brother John is also credited as executive producer on the project. Nevertheless, his general aloofness undermines *Deep Blues* at several moments.

22 In essence, *Nothing but the Blues*, *Deep Blues*, and *Feel Like Going Home* are all entangled with the perennial conundrums of ethnographic or anthropological filmmaking. See, for example, Edgar Morin's account of his work with Jean Rouch on the seminal *Chronique d'un été* (1960) and his various descriptions of the participatory approach (2016, 461–72). See also David MacDougall (2016, 565–70).

23 The apparently timeless and anonymous quality of these images is made more meaningful when the film arrives at its West African destination. Viewers can easily discern a strong resemblance between the two locations.

24 Scorsese characterizes John Lomax's work with Lead Belly (Huddie Ledbetter) as a foundational moment for the preservation of vernacular culture, but the Lomax/Lead Belly arrangement was not without its exploitative elements. See Benjamin Filene (2000, 47–75) and Robert Cantwell (1996, 69–79) on Lomax's "ballad hunting" and his work with Lead Belly. See also Karl Hagstrom Miller on Lomax's conception of "folklore" within the Jim Crow context (2010, 85–120). As Filene and Hagstrom Miller both demonstrate, the preservationist efforts of cultural brokers like the Lomaxes frequently determined how "folk music" would be defined and received. See Jeff Allred for an account of Lomax's often fraught working relationship with Lead Belly in the 1930s (2002, 99–102). For an insider's

perspective on what "song hunting" entailed, see Ronald Cohen's collections of Alan Lomax's letters (2011) and other voluminous writings (2003). See also Alan Lomax's own *The Land Where the Blues Began* (1993).

25 On Scorsese's use of the very loosely formulated "the emotions" to explain his primary documentary approach and foci, see Chapter 1. See David Hesmondhalgh for a short overview of music's philosophical relation to emotions (2013, 11–17). For Scorsese, of course, "sticking to the emotions" is invariably a matter of making meaning.

26 The compilation documentary has only recently been subjected to sustained scholarly attention. Bill Nichols provides a summary of the "formal, ethical, and aesthetic complexities of the compilation film" (2014, 146). The first comprehensive discussion of such documentaries is Jay Leyda's *Films Beget Films: A Study of the Compilation Film* (1964). See also William C. Wees (1993) for a slightly different emphasis on found and/or recycled footage. See Jaimie Baron's reconceptualization of the "appropriation film" as an experience of reception (2014). The "archive effect," Baron writes, is produced by two "constitutive experiences" (11). First, the spectator's perception of a "temporal disparity" (17) between different images gives archival materials their evidentiary power, but also reinforces their claim to be providing representations of the past. In *Night and Fog* (Alain Resnais, 1955), for instance, the perceived disparity between a "then" and "now" permits one to comprehend the film's black-and-white Holocaust photographs as both archival and historical. Second, one's recognition of a "previous intention ascribed to and (seemingly) inscribed within the archival document" results in an experience of "intentional disparity" (23). According to Baron, the spectator's ability to discern disparate intentions behind archival documents and their "present" recontextualization is crucial to creating the archive effect and historical understanding. Although Scorsese's documentaries about popular music make substantial use of archival materials, they are also filled with present-day interviews and thus are not "compilation films" in the strictest sense. Nevertheless, their organization of newly excavated archival materials reveals meaningful temporal and intentional disparities, and one's comprehension of the films *as* historical accounts is contingent upon the interpretation of such matters.

27 The film attributes this version of "Catfish Blues" to Taj Mahal (Henry St. Claire Fredericks). However, when Corey Harris takes up the song with Ali Farka Toure in Africa during the film's concluding segments, it is identified as "traditional," although Harris appears to incorporate lyrics from Muddy Waters's later, slightly revised version of "Rollin' Stone."

28 See Gerhard Kubik's *Africa and the Blues* (1999). In *The Blues*' accompanying book, Scorsese recalls seeing Bo Diddley in concert as a teenager, and the musician

apparently paused repeatedly to explain the African origins of various drum beats (2003b, 62–3).

29 The filmmakers meet with figures in West Africa who should be recognizable to longtime listeners of American blues. Ali Farka Toure, for instance, has recorded with both Ry Cooder and Taj Mahal.

30 See Rona Cran for a summary of the countless characterizations of Dylan's songwriting as a form of "collage" (2014, 187–211).

31 See Scorsese's description of *No Direction Home*'s genesis (Donato 2007, 206) as well as some of the attendant strictures placed upon him by Dylan's management (Jarmusch 2017, 191–4). Scorsese's involvement was also clearly meant to increase the sense of *No Direction Home*'s import: initial screenings of the film at film festivals, like its subsequent broadcast on PBS, registered as significant cultural events in part because of Scorsese's presence. See Greil Marcus (2007) for an account of the film's first appearance at the Telluride Film Festival, for instance.

32 In a wide-ranging interview with Jonathan Lethem, Dylan claims to "own the Sixties," but in his crucial qualification, he also insists that he never wanted "to acquire" the Sixties (2006, 477).

33 They also resonate with Dylan's later experiments with temporality in "Tangled Up in Blue" (1975). See Rona Cran on the "collage" construction of this and other *Blood on the Tracks* songs (2014, 202–4). See also Michael Denning on Dylan's experiments with time (2009, 29–30).

34 The performance is identified at this point as "Newcastle, England May 21, 1966." Greil Marcus describes D.A. Pennebaker's footage of Dylan's live take on "Like a Rolling Stone" as "unspeakably intense, suffused-with-danger [...], with Dylan a dervish possessed by a god you do not want to meet" (2007, 50).

35 Adrian Martin calls the journey motif in *No Direction Home* "sentimental" and "hackneyed" (2007, 55). Scorsese's emphasis on "voyages," "personal journeys," and "home" in his present-day documentaries undoubtedly has a nostalgic or "sentimental" quality, but in *No Direction Home*, it is more consistent with Dylan's work than some critics are willing to allow. By contrast, in *All That Is Solid Melts into Air: The Experience of Modernity* (1982), Marshall Berman refers briefly to *Bringing It All Back Home* (1965) in terms that seem to describe Scorsese's Bob Dylan: "This brilliant album, perhaps Dylan's best, is full of the surreal radicalism of the late '60s. At the same time, its title and the titles of some of its songs—'Subterranean Homesick Blues,' 'It's Alright, Ma, I'm Only Bleeding'—express an intense bond with the past, parents, home, that was almost entirely missing in the culture of the 1960s, but centrally present a decade later" (332).

36 John Lomax's autobiography (1947) characterizes his ballad hunting as a series of "adventures." See Jeff Allred on how Lomax exchanges the "labor of compilation" for the "romantic notion of 'adventure'" in his autobiography (2002, 94).

37 Scorsese's interest in record collection seems substantial. See, for instance, Greil Marcus's account of a *Last Waltz*-era meeting with the director and their discussion about rare 78s, Ray Charles's "Hallelujah, I Love Her So," Alan Freed, *American Hot Wax* (Floyd Mutrux, 1978), and other music-related matters (2010, 80). Scorsese, like any serious collector, insists upon his "love" for the more obscure flip side to Charles's "Hallelujah," "What Would I Do without You." See also Scorsese's conversation with Bruce Springsteen at a 2019 Netflix-sponsored event. When asked about the use of music in his fiction films, the director claims to "still have" all of his "78s and 45s" (Willman 2019). Scorsese's recollections almost always return to his formative experience with vinyl records, 78s and singles in particular.

38 This "prelapsarian American harmony" refers to the close integration of commercial blues and country music in the *Anthology*. Indeed, Smith's arrangement of his audio and visual materials deliberately obscures the race of these performers. See Cantwell (2008, 39; 1996, 193–4; 207). PBS's *American Epic: The First Time America Heard Itself* (Bernard MacMahon, 2017) explicitly revisits the sounds and themes of the *Anthology of American Folk Music*. The soundtrack provides an excellent—and much better sounding—complement to Smith's collection, but the documentary's survey of early commercial recordings is essentially structured in terms of traditional categories such as class and race (Anglo American/mountain ballads and African American/Delta blues).

39 I am referring to Folkways' 1997 CD reissue of the *Anthology*. Elements of the original "handbook" have also been reproduced in this reissue of the *Anthology*, although the experience of rummaging through Smith's reproductions has clearly been diminished—or at least altered—in this new context of reception: present-day critical commentary has been added as an introduction to the booklet; short observations from various present-day musicians about the set's enduring influence appear throughout its pages, and so on. See Cantwell on the original *Anthology*'s accompanying catalogue (1996, 194–7).

40 The importance of Smith's *Anthology* to the 1960s folk revival is a matter of some contention among music scholars. See Katherine Skinner's (2006) persuasive argument against overstating the *Anthology*'s importance to the urban folk revival. See also Ray Allen (2010) on the New Lost City Ramblers and their exposure to a wide range of vernacular music during the 1950s and 1960s. As Allen rightly notes, the Lomax collections would have reached urban listeners like John Cohen before the *Anthology*'s arrival in 1952 (2010, 28). Dylan has—unsurprisingly—been inconsistent when discussing the *Anthology*'s influence on his own work. In a lengthy interview with Mikal Gilmore, for example, he deliberately diminishes the central position assigned to Smith's *Anthology* by Greil Marcus in *The Old Weird America* (2011), his seminal study of Dylan's *The Basement Tapes*. See Gilmore (2006, 450–2).

41 Clinton Heylin makes a similar point throughout *Revolution in the Air: The Songs of Bob Dylan Vol. 1: 1957–73* (2010). He alerts readers to familiar examples like "Sad-Eyed Lady of the Lowlands" (358–61), but his discussion of "Highway 61 Revisited" compares its opening lines to the "popular ballad convention" (312) of having characters tell their story to listeners. See also Benjamin Filene on Dylan's "Highway 61 Revisited" and the singer's reliance upon—and parody of—classic blues emphases and phrasing throughout (2000, 227–8).

42 See Clinton Heylin on the significance of the 1966 tour's rendition of "Just Like Tom Thumb's Blues" (2010, 316–17). The Liverpool performance was eventually released as a B-side to the "I Want You" single in 1966.

43 Sean Wilentz refers to Dylan's many expressions of "gratitude" (2010, 294–5) throughout *Chronicles*. Scorsese's *No Direction Home* manages to preserve this same sense of generosity, not only in Dylan's reminiscences, but also in its treatment of various interview subjects.

44 As Peter Doyle notes, "Dylan's voice and his twitchy physical presence are cinematically powerful. You want to look" (2007, 69).

45 See Frank Verano on Pennebaker's original plans for his second collaboration with Bob Dylan (2015, 254–5). See also Keith Beattie (2011, 50–1). Michael Denning frames "each of Dylan's films" as "replies" (2009, 31) to Pennebaker's *Dont Look Back*, and *No Direction Home*'s repurposing of footage from the aborted *You Know Something is Happening* is in part a continuation of this project. One might say something similar about Scorsese's *Rolling Thunder Revue* (2019) and its substantial recycling of Dylan's *Renaldo and Clara* (1978). In all of these cases, of course, the wider legacy of American direct cinema is always in question.

46 See Paul Arthur on this characterization of direct cinema (1993, 119–26; 2003, 99). On the many affiliations between these philosophical emphases and the development of rockumentaries in the 1960s, see David E. James (2016, 186–9).

47 In his wide-ranging interview with Raffaele Donato, Scorsese refers repeatedly to American direct cinema and acknowledges its formative influence on his thinking about documentary. See Donato (2007, 201–4).

48 See especially *Last Train to Memphis: The Rise of Elvis Presley* (1994) and *Dream Boogie: The Triumph of Sam Cooke* (2005). *Feel Like Going Home: Portraits in Blues and Rock 'n' Roll* (2012) provides a template for his approach (and the title of Scorsese's *Feel Like Going Home*), but Gurlanick's studies of Elvis Presley and Sam Cooke are more completely developed examples of how he weaves together the stories of exemplary figures and a wider historical context. The same should be said of the excellent *Sweet Soul Music: Rhythm and Blues and the Southern Dream of Freedom* (1986).

49 Marc Raymond, for example, sees Scorsese aligning himself with Dylan's individualist "rejection of politics in favor of art" in *No Direction Home* (2013, 193).

Chapter 4

1. Travers's enthusiasm for Scorsese's work also extends to his current documentary output. His review of *Rolling Thunder Revue: A Bob Dylan Story by Martin Scorsese* (2019), for example, concludes with a comparable moment of cinephilic overstatement: "Rockumentary-wise, you've never seen or heard anything like it" (Travers 2019). *Rolling Stone*'s predictably laudatory reviews of work by baby boomer staples like Bob Dylan or Bruce Springsteen indicate its continuing generational affinities, and Travers's reception of Scorsese's films appears to fit an easily discerned editorial pattern. Nevertheless, the director's films are currently received in these same terms beyond the pages of *Rolling Stone*.
2. This is how the history of cinephilia has been outlined in several studies. See Paul Willemen (1994), Thomas Elsaesser (2005b), and Christian Keathley (2006) for historical surveys of cinephilia. On changes to cinephilia after the advent of digital media and the internet, see Marijke de Valck and Malte Hagener's *Cinephilia: Movies, Love and Memory* (2005).
3. See Emilie Bickerton's *A Short History of Cahiers du Cinéma* for an excellent overview of *Cahiers du Cinéma*'s peak period of influence throughout the 1950s and early-1960s (2009, 15–48).
4. As many scholars of cinephilia have noted, this phenomenon cannot be wholly restricted to its French/Parisian manifestation. Nevertheless, a mythology has been attached to the various French expressions of cinephilia, particularly as they emerged from the pages of *Cahiers du Cinéma* during the 1950s and 1960s. See Thomas Elsaesser (2005b) on the Parisian orientation of 1960s cinephilia.
5. See Robert P. Kolker on *A Personal Journey*'s adherence to Andrew Sarris's 1960s film criticism (2015, 73–4). See also Marc Raymond for a very similar account of Scorsese's Sarris-like efforts as a "film critic" in these cinephile documentaries (and elsewhere) (2013, 140–1). According to Raymond, however, Scorsese's film criticism is part of a much broader effort to situate his "authority" (142) and ensure his "cultural prestige" (163) as a defender of film history.
6. Several passages in George Kouvaros's *The Old Greeks* (2018) describe how films and photos can facilitate remembering. See his discussion of *A Place in the Sun* (George Stevens, 1951), for instance (63–86).
7. See Susan Sontag's "Decay of Cinema" (1996), republished as "A Century of Cinema" (2001).
8. For examples of the scholarly recuperation of cinephilia, see Christian Keathley (2006) and Thomas Elsaesser (2005b). See also special issues of *Framework* (Buchsbaum and Gorfinkel, 2009) and *Cinema Journal* (de Valck 2010) for overviews of this renewed interest in cinephilia, its meaning, and future prospects. Much of this revivified cinephilia has returned to overly familiar topoi, however, and

one sometimes senses a simple retrenchment in the field—without a critical project to justify its existence, academic cinephilia is now primarily an historiographic undertaking. For attempts to parse the theoretical implications of digital image-making during this period, see Philip Rosen (2001), Mary Ann Doane (2002), Laura Mulvey (2006), and David Rodowick (2007). These ruminations typically focus on the photo's status as "index" and the ostensibly different storage capabilities of "the digital." See especially Rodowick on the uncertain destiny of indexicality in the digital age (2007, 36–7). For persuasive objections to such formulations, see Tom Gunning (2004, 2007) and Daniel Morgan (2006) and their phenomenological approach to understanding these matters. I say more about this below.

9   Although his cinephile documentaries clearly have different preoccupations, Scorsese is nevertheless unavoidably immersed in the period's apprehension over the film medium's future. See his "Preface" to Paolo Cherchi Usai's *The Death of Cinema: History, Cultural Memory and the Digital Dark Age* (2001), for instance. As always, Scorsese adopts the preservationist's position, insisting upon the urgency of the problem, but nonetheless arguing for the importance of protecting and preserving a cinematic heritage.

10 See Emilie Bickerton for a succinct summary of this moment in French film history (2009, 2–3). See also Antoine De Baecque on this new historiographic aspiration amongst French cinephiles during the 1920s (2008, 6).

11 I am referring to *[in]Transition*, "the first peer-reviewed academic journal of videographic film and moving image studies." This scholarly "disciplining" of videographic studies has been accompanied by copious theoretical and critical reflection. See, for instance, Michael Witt (2017), Christian Keathley (2011, 2012, 2014), Catherine Grant (2014), and Cristina Álvarez López and Adrian Martin (2014) for just a few examples. Witt provides an especially good summary of various changes to audiovisual criticism since the adoption of digital editing procedures in the early-2000s. Much of this work has argued emphatically (and exclusively) for the "experimental" or "poetic" possibilities in audiovisual criticism, so Scorsese's cinephile documentaries can appear somewhat prosaic—or to use Keathley's pejorative term for this kind of work, "explanatory" (2011, 179)—by comparison. Nevertheless, the director's approach in *A Personal Journey*, *Il mio viaggio in Italia*, and *A Letter to Elia* intersects in many ways with this pervasive academic discourse.

12 See Marc Raymond for Scorsese's characterization of deteriorating film stock as "cultural suicide" (2013, 132).

13 See Marc Raymond on the "canonization" of Scorsese's fiction films (2013, 152). At times, Raymond too easily characterizes Scorsese's 1990s "cultural work" as mere "self-promotion," although he rightly sees the director's involvement with various cultural institutions during this period as crucial to further enhancing his "prestige"

or "reputation" (2013, 129). After a brief period of institutional insecurity in the mid-1980s, Scorsese's position was undoubtedly strengthened by his growing reputation as a film preservationist in the 1990s.

14 The Film Foundation's website links visitors to the World Cinema Project (WCP) and its pedagogical remit at http://www.film-foundation.org/world-cinema. The WCP "preserves and restores neglected films from around the world. To date, 40 films from Africa, Asia, Eastern Europe, Central America, South America, and the Middle East have been restored, preserved and exhibited for a global audience. The WCP also supports educational programs, including Restoration Film Schools; intensive, results-oriented workshops allowing students and professionals worldwide to learn the art and science of film restoration and preservation."

15 Once again, see Bickerton (2009, 21). In his "Preface" to *A Personal Journey*'s published script, Michael Henry Wilson "confesses" that Scorsese's "natural inclination was to favor the neglected figures—those forgotten artists or unsung craftsmen who somehow managed to communicate an original vision" (Scorsese and Wilson 1997, 8–9). See also Jim Hillier (1985, 1992) for collections of *Cahiers du Cinéma* criticism from the 1950s and 1960s. See James Naremore (1990) for a persuasive defense of *Cahiers du Cinéma*'s writings from this period and their ongoing pertinence, published at the very moment when such work had been dismissed by academic film studies. In the years since the first appearance of Naremore's essay, *Cahiers du Cinéma*'s 1950s criticism has been rehabilitated by the renewed theoretical-critical interest in cinephilia. See Christian Keathley (2006, 82–111), for instance. Dudley Andrew (2011, 2013) provides an excellent overview of André Bazin's—and by extension, 1950s *Cahiers du Cinéma*'s—changing value to scholars in the twenty-first century.

16 In an opinion piece for *The New York Times* (November 4, 2019), Scorsese writes: 1960s cinema "was about revelation—aesthetic, emotional and spiritual revelation." "It was about confronting the unexpected on the screen." The religiosity that still clings to Scorsese's popular image is usually dedicated to a discussion of Catholic themes in his fiction films, but this emphasis on the screen's capacity for "revelation" is probably better evidence of lingering patterns of religious thinking in the director's work.

17 See Truffaut's (1985) typically extravagant review of Ray's *Johnny Guitar* for *Cahiers du Cinéma*. See also Marc Raymond on *A Personal Journey*'s intersection with other strands of scholarly film criticism (2013, 141–2).

18 This pivotal sequence from Kazan's *America America* is also used briefly in Scorsese's *Lady by the Sea: The Statue of Liberty* (co-directed with Kent Jones, 2004).

19 Stanley Cavell's *The World Viewed*, essentially ignored by film studies scholars when it was first published in 1971, has been instrumental to this revivified philosophical thinking about photography, ontology, and film theory. See D.N. Rodowick (2007,

2014, 2015), for example. Early film theorists had made analogous assertions about the experience of looking at photographs and/or films, although unlike Rodowick, Rosen, and other present-day scholars, they did not use semiotic terminology such as "index" to do so. Walter Benjamin's and Siegfried Kracauer's film-related writings in the 1930s, reclaimed by film studies throughout the 1980s and 1990s, have provided a foundation for a great deal of this ongoing thinking about images and modernity, while the more recent rehabilitation of André Bazin's film criticism and theory also undergirds much contemporary discussion of these matters. See Miriam Bratu Hansen (2012) on Kracauer and Benjamin. See Dudley Andrew (2010, 2011) for an ongoing effort to demonstrate the pertinence of Bazin's thinking to present-day film and media studies. The 1990s "death of cinema" rhetoric paradoxically authorized the revivification of these once-hastily rejected positions, and the result has been a wide-ranging reassessment of so-called "classical" film theory for its insights about emergent media.

20 Scorsese often insists that he is not an "intellectual" (Christie and Thompson 2003, 231), and he certainly has no practical need for "film theory." But as a onetime instructor at New York University, he has significant experience in reading film criticism (André Bazin, Andrew Sarris, among other 1950s and 1960s fixtures). Moreover, the concluding section of *Street Scenes 1970* (Martin Scorsese, 1970) indicates an exposure to contemporaneous critical thinking about "ideology and representation," although the film's contentious afterlife is undoubtedly related to Scorsese's desire to distance himself from such political speculations (see Raymond 2013, 31–45). Nevertheless, if Scorsese's connection to present-day film theory is tenuous, his collaborators on these cinephile documentaries, Michael Henry Wilson and Kent Jones, are clearly knowledgeable about certain currents in film studies. In their promotional conversation about *A Letter to Elia* for PBS, for instance, Jones refers very briefly to "Heidegger's writings," and his film criticism indicates a significant—if understandably wary—interest in academic film studies. In short, the intersection between *Il mio viaggio in Italia* and contemporaneous trends in film studies scholarship isn't surprising or insignificant.

21 Daniel Morgan provides an excellent account of Godard's various statements about "projection" and his unequivocal judgment on television as a kind of "cancer" or "poison" (2013, 203–52). Dudley Andrew situates an analogous idea about "projection" at the center of his provocative defense of cinema in the digital age (2010, 66–74).

22 The personal, retrospective account of one's trips to movie auditoria in the 1960s became especially common after cinephilia was rehabilitated in the late-1990s. See Thomas Elsaesser for only one of many such descriptions: "Cinephilia meant being sensitive to one's surroundings when watching a movie, carefully picking the place

where to sit, fully alert to the quasi-sacral feeling of nervous anticipation that could descend upon a public space, however squalid, smelly or slipshod, as the velvet curtain rose and the studio logo with its fanfares filled the space" (2005b, 28–9).

23 See Peter Brown on the relocation of religious relics in late antiquity. "If relics could travel," he writes, "then the distance between the believer and the place where the holy could be found ceased to be a fixed, physical distance" (1981, 89). See also Noa Steimatsky's excellent *Italian Locations: Reinhabiting the Past in Postwar Cinema* for an examination of these matters as they relate to film theory (2008, 120–36).

24 This is not to say that Scorsese is incapable of these expressions of despair, nor do I mean to imply that such despair is necessarily unwarranted. The director's rejection of Marvel movies, for instance, a subject of intense backlash on social media throughout November 2019, was only partly an aesthetic judgment on the Marvel film franchises. In his explanatory opinion piece for *The New York Times* (November 4, 2019), Scorsese laments the current disappearance of what he describes as a Sixties-style cinephile spectatorship and filmmaking, and in this respect, he sounds a familiar "decay of cinema" note. Yet he also rightly refers to significant changes in the present-day distribution and exhibition of cinema around the world, corrosive effects of neoliberal corporate and governmental policies. In this sense, a vision of cinema—the classic cinephile's perception of film culture—has undoubtedly decayed gradually over the last two decades.

25 Other entries in the BFI's "Century of Cinema" series in 1995 were approximately one hour in length.

26 See Andrew Sarris (1996, 158). See also Susan Sontag for a common—and patronizing—rejection of Kazan's work during this period (1966, 9). This aesthetic assessment lingers in the present-day rehabilitation of cinephilia. See, for example, Christian Keathley's approving summary of the Sarris-Sontag dismissal of Kazan's films (2007, 73).

27 See Kazan's exceptional autobiography, *Elia Kazan: A Life* (1988), for descriptions of the immigrant's disposition, what he calls the "Anatolian smile," and his insights into his family's experience in America. See, for example, his incisive portrait of his father's perpetual wariness and anger (1988, 11–12). Admittedly, this can appear self-serving in the aftermath of his HUAC testimony and his lifelong quest to justify the events of April 1, 1952, but *A Life* returns continually to these observations about Kazan's "Anatolian cunning" and finally constitutes an indispensable depiction of the immigrant's life in America.

28 See, for instance, Aaron Baker (2015a, 124–9).

29 Following the release of *Il mio viaggio in Italia*, Scorsese had proposed the production of documentaries about "British and Russian cinema" (Christie and Thompson 2003, 271), but these films have not yet appeared.

30 For the prototypical utopian description of the internet and its promise of user "participation," see Henry Jenkins (2006). See Vincent Mosco (2004), Nick Dyer-Witheford (2015), and Ursula Huws (2014) for more sober—and very welcome—reassessments of the internet's "democratic" or "participatory" dimensions.

Conclusion

1 See Sharf (2018) on the forthcoming *An Afternoon with SCTV*. See Donnelly (2019) on Scorsese's planned documentary about New York City's 1970s music scene. See Strauss (2020) on the director's forthcoming SHOWTIME documentary about New York Dolls frontman David Johansen.

2 When asked if he was ever tempted by the "sort of collective cinema" practiced by the Drew Associates in the 1960s, for example, Scorsese simply says, "No. That was their temperament, and not my own. And it was a particular moment in history. Really, can there actually be such a thing as a group consensus as to what a film should say, or what it should be" (Donato 2007, 204)? Nonetheless, Scorsese's recent documentary work is clearly collaborative, even if he ultimately oversees these productions and their direction. In interviews, he refers repeatedly to his aging, his "limited time" and an attendant sense of urgency in making his planned films, and the presentation of others' work is approached in this same spirit: "I'm 77 and I've got things to do. Time is of the most value, right? I put my name on the line and say: 'Yes, I think you should see this picture'" (Pulver 2019). His collaborative documentary production appears to utilize his symbolic capital in a very similar way.

3 Scorsese is also credited as executive producer for the "eco" documentary, *Before the Flood* (Fisher Stevens, 2016), and its environmental activism should also be seen as a legacy of the 1960s.

4 On the creation of Imagine Entertainment's Documentary Unit, see Donnelly (2019).

5 Ken Burns's documentaries, for instance, are often said to epitomize PBS's general stolidity. Bill Nichols describes Burns as "a fundamentally conservative historian and filmmaker, albeit a very talented one" (2010, 171), and in his "list of distributors," Burns is the only filmmaker directly associated with the short PBS entry (2010, 314).

6 Scorsese is planning a documentary for Imagine Docs, for instance, and the new company's *modus operandi* appears to be both an opportunity and a substantial limitation. Imagine Docs proposes to make several documentaries in the coming years, but too much of its announced material is in the "celebrity profile" mold (Donnelly 2019). Nevertheless, Scorsese's projected study of New York City's 1970s

music scene at least promises to redress the perceived failure (both critical and commercial) of his HBO venture, *Vinyl* (2016).

7   Alex Gibney's *Sinatra: All or Nothing at All* (2015) also borrows heavily from *No Direction Home*'s approach. Like Dylan's 1966 tour with the Hawks, Sinatra's "retirement" concert in 1971 provides an anchor for *All or Nothing at All*'s editing structure. Admittedly, Elvis Presley, Johnny Cash, Frank Sinatra, and Bob Dylan all occupy comparable positions in the broader history of twentieth-century popular music, but Scorsese's *No Direction Home* has provided a durable template for these and other retrospective documentary examinations of legacy musicians.

8   More than anything, Scorsese's *Rolling Thunder Revue* rescues Dylan's *Renaldo and Clara* (1978) from obscurity. *Rolling Thunder Revue*'s concert segments look and sound much better than anything in Dylan's film, and if it doesn't completely connect with what Michael Denning calls *Renaldo and Clara*'s "symbolic itinerary," its way of mapping a form of "history-telling," Scorsese's documentary nonetheless indicates how Dylan's mid-1970s work "may yet come to figure America's Great Recession" (2009, 34; 41).

9   In his review of the thirtieth anniversary *Born to Run* CD box set (2005), rock critic Robert Christgau astutely outlines the overriding dilemma for "public Springsteen," particularly in his twenty-first-century legacy incarnation: how to "establish a seriousness that avoids the pomposity the music risks" (Christgau 2006). *Springsteen on Broadway* is in many ways the culmination to this lifelong "public" work, but its self-awareness cannot fully evade the persistent danger of self-seriousness. This continues to be the central aspiration in Thom Zimny's extensive work as Springsteen's primary archivist. In addition to *Springsteen on Broadway*, Zimny is co-director of *Western Stars* (2019) with Springsteen, but he has also created feature-length commemorative documentaries for the *Born to Run*, *Darkness on the Edge of Town* (2010), and *The River* (2015) CD box sets. This abundance of audiovisual material is, like any CD box set, ultimately aimed at burnishing the artist's legend.

10   Dylan has always adhered to this individualist ideal of self-invention, but his 2006 inventory of the last great "individualists" had spoiled badly by 2016: "the stuff that trained me to do what I do, that was all *individually* based. […] I'm talking about artists with the willpower not to conform to anybody's reality but their own. Patsy Cline and Billy Lee Riley. Plato and Socrates, Whitman and Emerson. Slim Harpo and Donald Trump. It's a lost art form" (Lethem 2006, 481). Dylan is often deliberately provocative and contrarian, and although he appears to be very serious here, the inclusion of Donald Trump on this short list of artists and thinkers could just as easily be a joke. Nevertheless, the "willpower not to conform to anybody's reality but [one's] own" is hardly a "lost art form," and it unfortunately describes

both Trump and the prevailing solipsism in contemporary American culture. Owen Gleiberman (2019) connects *Rolling Thunder Revue*'s mockumentary elements to a present-day "cult of put-on reality," although he rightly wonders about its meaning in Scorsese's film.

11 Even a cursory scan through the many readers' comments on Scorsese's *New York Times* editorial (November 4, 2019) reveals a general unwillingness to consider the political economy of the present-day media industries.

12 See Pulver (2019) for the director's description of an online streaming "revolution." But Scorsese has nonetheless urged viewers to not watch *The Irishman* on iPhones: "please, please don't look at it on a phone, please. An iPad, a big iPad, maybe" (Shoard 2019). Scorsese's commitment to the theatrical exhibition of his Hollywood movies continues to guide his approach. See Chris Lindahl (2020) on Apple's projected involvement in the director's next feature length production, *Killers of the Flower Moon*.

References

Adelt, Ulrich. 2010. *Blues Music in the Sixties: A Story in Back and White*. New Brunswick: Rutgers University Press.

Allen, Ray. 2010. *Gone to the Country: The New Lost City Ramblers and the Folk Music Revival*. Chicago: University of Illinois Press.

Allen, Robert C. and Douglas Gomery. 1985. *Film History: Theory and Practice*. New York: Alfred A. Knopf.

Allred, Jeff. 2002. "The Needle and the Damage Done: John Avery Lomax and the Guises of Collecting." *Arizona Quarterly: A Journal of American Literature, Culture, and Theory* 58.3 (Autumn): 83–107.

Álvarez López, Cristina and Adrian Martin. 2014. "Introduction to the Audiovisual Essay: A Child of Two Mothers." *NESCUS: European Journal of Media Studies* (December 3).

Ames, Eric. 2012. *Ferocious Reality: Documentary According to Werner Herzog*. Minneapolis: University of Minnesota Press.

Andrew, Dudley. 1998. "Film and History." In *The Oxford Guide to Film Studies*, edited by John Hill and Pamela Church Gibson, 176–89. New York: Oxford University Press.

Andrew, Dudley. 2010. *What Cinema Is!* Oxford: Wiley Blackwell.

Andrew, Dudley. 2013. *André Bazin, Revised Edition*. New York: Oxford University Press. (Orig. Pub. 1978.)

Andrew, Dudley with Hervé Joubert-Laurencin. 2011. *Opening Bazin: Postwar Film Theory and Its Afterlife*. New York: Oxford University Press.

Arthur, Paul. 1993. "Jargons of Authenticity (Three American Moments)." In *Theorizing the Documentary*, edited by Michael Renov, 108–34. New York: Routledge.

Arthur, Paul. 2003. "No Longer Absolute: Portraiture in American Avant-Garde and Documentary Films of the Sixties." In *Rites of Realism: Essays on Corporeal Cinema*, edited by Ivone Margulies, 93–118. Durham: Duke University Press.

Arthur, Paul. 2008. "Please Allow Me to Reproduce Myself." *Film Comment* (March–April): 46–51.

Baker, Aaron. 2015a. "*Alice Doesn't Live Here Anymore* and *Italianamerican*: Gender, Ethnicity, and Imagination." In *A Companion to Martin Scorsese*, edited by Aaron Baker, 117–32. Oxford: Wiley Blackwell.

Baker, Michael Brendan. 2015b. "Martin Scorsese and the Music Documentary." In *A Companion to Martin Scorsese*, edited by Aaron Baker, 239–58. Oxford: Wiley Blackwell.

Baron, Jaimie. 2014. *The Archive Effect: Found Footage and the Audiovisual Experience of History*. New York: Routledge.

Barthes, Roland. 1981. *Camera Lucida: Reflections on Photography*, translated by Richard Howard. New York: Hill and Wang.

Beattie, Keith. 2004. *Documentary Screens: Non-fiction Film and Video*. New York: Palgrave Macmillan.

Beattie, Keith. 2005. "It's Not Only Rock and Roll: 'Rockumentary,' Direct Cinema, and Performative Display." *Australasian Journal of American Studies* 24.2 (December): 21–41.

Beattie, Keith. 2011. *D.A. Pennebaker*. Chicago: University of Illinois Press.

Berman, Marshall. 1982. *All That Is Solid Melts into Air: The Experience of Modernity*. New York: Penguin Books.

Bickerton, Emilie. 2009. *A Short History of Cahiers du Cinéma*. London: Verso.

Birchall, Danny. 2008. "Online Documentary." In *Rethinking Documentary: New Perspectives, New Practices*, edited by Thomas Austin and Wilm de Jong, 278–83. Berkshire: McGraw-Hill.

Biskind, Peter. 1998. *Easy Riders, Raging Bulls*. New York: Touchstone.

Blake, Richard A. 2005. *Street Smart: The New York of Lumet, Allen, Scorsese, and Lee*. Lexington: The University Press of Kentucky.

Blistein, Jon. 2019. "Bob Dylan, Martin Scorsese 'Rolling Thunder Revue' Doc Hits Netflix." *Rolling Stone*, January 10.

Bowman, Rob. 2005. Liner Notes for *The Band: A Musical History*, Capitol Records CCAP77409-6, 5 CDs.

Brown, Lee B. 2002. "Jazz: America's Classical Music?" *Philosophy and Literature* 26.1 (April): 157–72.

Brown, Peter. 1981. *The Cult of the Saints: Its Rise and Function in Latin Christianity*. Chicago: University of Chicago Press.

Brunette, Peter. 1999. *Martin Scorsese: Interviews*. Jackson: University of Mississippi Press.

Bruzzi, Stella. 2006. *New Documentary, Second Edition*. New York: Routledge.

Buchsbaum, Jonathan and Elina Gorfinkel. 2009 "Introduction." *Framework* 50, 1.2: 176–80.

Cantwell, Robert. 1996. *When We Were Good: The Folk Revival*. Cambridge: Harvard University Press.

Cantwell, Robert. 2008. *If Beale Street Could Talk: Music, Community, Culture*. Chicago: University of Illinois Press.

Carruthers, Lee. 2016. *Doing Time: Temporality, Hermeneutics, and Contemporary Cinema*. Albany: SUNY Press.

Casetti, Francesco. 2015. *The Lumière Galaxy: Seven Key Words for the Cinema to Come*. New York: Columbia University Press.

Casillo, Robert. 2006. *Gangster Priest: The Italian American Cinema of Martin Scorsese*. Toronto: University of Toronto Press.

Caughie, John, ed. 1981. *Theories of Authorship*. London: Routledge.

Cavallero, Jonathan J. 2011. *Hollywood's Italian American Filmmakers: Capra, Scorsese, Savoca, Coppola, and Tarantino*. Chicago: University of Illinois Press.

Cavallero, Jonathan J. 2015. "Issues of Race, Ethnicity, and Television Authorship in *Martin Scorsese Presents the Blues* and *Boardwalk Empire*." In *A Companion to Martin Scorsese*, edited by Aaron Baker, 214–36. Oxford: Wiley Blackwell.

Cavaluzzi, Anthony D. 2015. "Music as Cultural Signifier of Italian/American Life in *Who's That Knocking at My Door* and *Mean Streets*." In *A Companion to Martin Scorsese*, edited by Aaron Baker, 277–91. Oxford: Wiley Blackwell.

Cavell, Stanley. 1979. *The World Viewed: Reflections on the Ontology of Film*, Enlarged Edition. Cambridge: Harvard University Press.

Cherchi Usai, Paolo. 2001. *The Death of Cinema: History, Cultural Memory and the Digital Dark Age*. London: BFI Publishing.

Christgau, Robert. 2006. "Re-Run: *Born to Run (30th Anniversary Edition)*." *Blender*, January–February.

Christie, Ian and David Thompson, eds. 2003. *Scorsese on Scorsese*. London: Farber & Farber.

Clapton, Eric. 2007. *Clapton: The Autobiography*. New York: Broadway Books.

Cohen, Ronald D., ed. 2003. *Alan Lomax: Selected Writings 1934–1997*. New York: Routledge.

Cohen, Ronald D., ed. 2011. *Alan Lomax, Assistant in Charge: The Library of Congress Letters, 1935–1945*. Jackson: University Press of Mississippi.

Cook, Pam. 2005. *Screening the Past: Memory and Nostalgia in Cinema*. New York: Routledge.

Corrigan, Timothy. 2010. "The Film Essay as a Cinema of Ideas." In *Global Art Cinema: New Theories and Histories*, edited by Rosalind Galt and Karl Schoonover, 218–37. New York: Oxford University Press.

Corrigan, Timothy. 2011. *The Essay Film: From Montaigne, After Marker*. New York: Oxford University Press.

Cran, Rona. 2014. *Collage in Twentieth-Century Art, Literature, and Culture: Joseph Cornell, William Burroughs, Frank O'Hara, and Bob Dylan*. Burlington: Ashgate.

Curtin, Michael. 1995. *Redeeming the Wasteland: Television Documentary and Cold War Politics*. New Brunswick: Rutgers University Press.

De Baecque, Antoine. 2008. *Camera Historica: The Century in Cinema*, translated by Ninon Vinsonneau and Jonathan Magidoff. New York: Columbia University Press.

de Peuter, Greig. 2014. "Beyond the Model Worker: Surveying the Precariat." *Culture Unbound* 6: 263–84.

de Valck, Marijke. 2010. "Reflections on the Recent Cinephilia Debates." *Cinema Journal* 49.2: 132–8.

Denning, Michael. 2009. "Bob Dylan and Rolling Thunder." In *The Cambridge Companion to Bob Dylan*, edited by Kevin J.H. Dettmar, 28–41. Cambridge: Cambridge University Press.

DeVeaux, Scott. 2001. "Struggling with Jazz." *Current Musicology* (Spring): 353–74.

Doane, Mary Ann. 2002. *The Emergence of Cinematic Time: Modernity, Contingency, the Archive*. Cambridge: Harvard University Press.

Donato, Raffaele. 2007. "Docufictions: An Interview with Martin Scorsese on Documentary Film." *Film History* 19 (2): 199–207.
Donnelly, Matt. 2019. "Imagine Docs Powers Up Slate, Including Scorsese's Return to Unscripted (Exclusive)." *Variety*, November 26.
Doyle, Peter. 2007. "Citizen Dylan." *Studies in Documentary Film* 1.1: 67–75.
Dry, Jude. 2017. "How the 'Pulp Fiction' Adrenaline Shot Scene Was Inspired by Scorsese's 'Lost Film.'" *IndieWire*, January 26.
Dyer-Witheford, Nick. 2015. *Cyber-Proletariat: Digital Labour in the Digital Vortex*. London: Pluto Press.
Dylan, Bob. 2004. *Chronicles: Volume One*. New York: Simon & Schuster.
Ebert, Roger. 2011. "Scorsese Meets the Sorcerer of Cinema," November 21. https://www.rogerebert.com/reviews/hugo-2011
Eisenberg, Evan. 2005. *The Recording Angel: Music, Records and Culture from Aristotle to Zappa*. New Haven: Yale University Press.
Elsaesser, Thomas. 2005a. *European Cinema: Face to Face with Hollywood*. Amsterdam: Amsterdam University Press.
Elsaesser, Thomas. 2005b. "Cinephilia or the Uses of Disenchantment." In *Cinephilia: Movies, Love and Memory*, edited by Marijke de Valck and Malte Hagener, 27–43. Amsterdam: Amsterdam University Press.
Filene, Benjamin. 2000. *Romancing the Folk: Popular Memory & American Roots Music*. Chapel Hill: The University of North Carolina Press.
Fried, Michael. 2005. "Barthes's *Punctum*." *Critical Inquiry* 31: 539–74.
Friedman, Lawrence S. 1997. *The Cinema of Martin Scorsese*. New York: Continuum.
Frith, Simon. 2007. *Taking Popular Music Seriously*. London: Routledge.
Garofalo, Reebee. 1999. "From Music Publishing to MP3: Music and Industry in the Twentieth Century." *American Music* 17.3 (Autumn): 318–54.
Giles, Paul. 1992. *American Catholic Arts and Fictions: Culture, Ideology, Aesthetics*. Cambridge: Cambridge University Press.
Gilmore, Mikal. 2006. "Interview with Mikal Gilmore, *Rolling Stone*, December 22, 2001." In *Bob Dylan: The Essential Interviews*, edited by Jonathan Cott, 437–546. New York: Simon & Schuster.
Gleiberman, Owen. 2019. "Why Did Martin Scorsese Prank His Audience in 'Rolling Thunder Revue'? Even He May Not Know." *Variety*, June 15.
Gracyk, Theodore. 2002. "Jazz after *Jazz*: Ken Burns and the Construction of Jazz History." *Philosophy and Literature* 26.1 (April): 173–87.
Gramsci, Antonio. 1971. *Selections from the Prison Notebooks*, edited and translated by Quintin Hoare and Geoffrey Nowell Smith. New York: International Publishers.
Grant, Catherine. 2014. "How Long Is a Piece of String? On the Practice, Scope and Value of Videographic Film Studies and Criticism." *The Audiovisual Essay: Practice and Theory in Videographic Film and Moving Image Studies*, September.

Grist, Leighton. 2000. *The Films of Martin Scorsese, 1963–77: Authorship and Context.* New York: St. Martin's Press.

Grist, Leighton. 2013. *The Films of Martin Scorsese, 1978–99: Authorship and Context II.* New York: Palgrave Macmillan.

Gunning, Tom. 2004. "What's the Point of an Index? Or, Faking Photographs." *Nordicom Review* 25.1–2 (September): 39–49.

Gunning Tom. 2007. "Moving Away from the Index: Cinema and the Impression of Reality." *Differences: A Journal of Feminist Cultural Studies* 18.1 (Spring): 29–52.

Guralnick, Peter. 1986. *Sweet Soul Music: Rhythm and Blues and the Southern Dream of Freedom.* New York: Little, Brown and Company.

Guralnick, Peter. 1995. *Last Train to Memphis: The Rise of Elvis Presley.* New York: Little, Brown and Company.

Guralnick, Peter. 2005. *Dream Boogie: The Triumph of Sam Cooke.* New York: Little, Brown and Company.

Guralnick, Peter. 2012. *Feel Like Going Home: Portraits in Blues and Rock 'n' Roll.* New York: Little, Brown and Company. (Orig. Pub. 1972.)

Hall, Jeanne. 1991. "Realism as a Style in Cinema Verite: A Critical Analysis of 'Primary.'" *Cinema Journal* 30.4: 24–50.

Hall, Jeanne. 2014. "Don't You Ever Just Watch?" In *Documenting the Documentary: Close Readings of Documentary Film and Video*, edited by Barry Keith Grant and Jeannette Sloniowski, 237–52. Detroit: Wayne State University Press.

Hall, Stuart. 2001. "Constituting an Archive." *Third Text* 15.54: 89–92.

Hansen, Miriam Bratu. 2012. *Cinema and Experience: Siegfried Kracauer, Walter Benjamin, and Theodor W. Adorno.* Los Angeles: University of California Press.

Harvey, David. 2005. *A Brief History of Neoliberalism.* New York: Oxford University Press.

Hell, Richard. 2013. *I Dreamed I Was a Very Clean Tramp: An Autobiography.* New York: HarperCollins Publishers.

Helm, Levon with Stephen Davis. 2013. *This Wheel's on Fire: Levon Helm and the Story of The Band, Updated Edition.* Chicago: Chicago Review Press. (Orig. Pub. 1993)

Hesmondhalgh, David. 2013. *Why Music Matters.* Oxford: Wiley Blackwell.

Heylin, Clinton. 2010. *Revolution in the Air: The Songs of Bob Dylan Vol. 1: 1957–73.* London: Constable.

Hillier, Jim, ed. 1985. *Cahiers du Cinéma, the 1950s: Neo-Realism, Hollywood, New Wave.* Cambridge: Harvard University Press.

Hillier, Jim, ed. 1992. *Cahiers du Cinéma, the 1960s: New Wave, New Cinema, Reevaulating Hollywood.* Cambridge: Harvard University Press.

Hobsbawm, Eric. 1997. *On History.* London: Weidenfeld & Nicolson.

Honneth, Axel. 2004. "Organized Self-Realization: Some Paradoxes of Individualization." *European Journal of Social Theory* 7.4: 463–78.

Hornby, Nick. 1995. *High Fidelity.* New York: Penguin Books.

Hoskyns, Barney. 2006. *Across the Great Divide: The Band and America, Revised Edition*. Milwaukee: Hal Leonard.

Huws, Ursula. 2014. *Labor in the Global Digital Economy: The Cybertariat Comes of Age*. New York: Monthly Review Press.

Jacobson, Matthew Frye. 2006. *Roots Too: White Ethnic Revival in Post-Civil Rights America*. Cambridge Harvard University Press.

James, David E. 2016. *Rock 'n' Film: Cinema's Dance with Popular Music*. New York: Oxford University Press.

Jameson, Fredric. 1990. *Signatures of the Visible*. New York: Routledge.

Jarmusch, Jim. 2017. "2006 Charles Guggenheim Symposium Honoring Martin Scorsese." In *Martin Scorsese: Interviews, Revised and Updated*, edited by Robert Ribera, 186–98. Jackson: University Press of Mississippi.

Jenkins, Henry. 2006. *Convergence Culture: Where Old and New Media Collide*. New York: New York University Press.

Jones, Kent. 2015. "NYFF: Martin Scorsese on Film Preservation." *Film Comment* (October 27).

Kahana, Jonathan. 1999. "The Reception of Politics: Publicity and Its Parasites." *Social Text* 58, 17.1: 92–109.

Kahana, Jonathan. 2006. "The 1970s and American Documentary." In *Contemporary American Cinema*, edited by Linda Ruth Williams and Michael Hammond, 199–209. New York: McGraw-Hill.

Kahana, Jonathan. 2008. *Intelligence Work: The Politics of American Documentary*. New York: Columbia University Press.

Kazan, Elia. 1988. *Elia Kazan: A Life*. New York: Alfred A. Knopf.

Keathley, Christian. 2006. *The Wind in the Trees: Or, Cinephilia and History*. Bloomington: Indiana University Press.

Keathley, Christian. 2007. "Sontag and Cinephilia." *Post Script* 26.2 (Winter–Spring): 72–80.

Keathley, Christian. 2011. "*La caméra-stylo*: Notes on Video Criticism and Cinephilia." In *The Language and Style of Film Criticism*, edited by Alex Clayton and Andrew Klevan, 176–91. London: Routledge.

Keathley, Christian. 2012. "Teaching the Scholarly Video." *Frames Cinema Journal* 1, July 2.

Keathley, Christian. 2014. "Teaching Videographic Film Studies." *The Cine-Files* 7 (Fall).

Kelly, Mary Pat. 1980. *Martin Scorsese: The First Decade*. Pleasantville: Redgrave Publishing Company.

Kelly, Mary Pat. 1991. *Martin Scorsese: A Journey*. New York: Thunder's Mouth Press.

Keyser, Les. 1992. *Martin Scorsese*. New York: Twayne Publishers.

Knopper, Steve. 2009. *Appetite for Self-Destruction: The Spectacular Crash of the Record Industry in the Digital Age*. New York: Free Press.

Kolker, Robert Phillip. 1988. *A Cinema of Loneliness, Second Edition*. New York: Oxford University Press. (Orig. Pub. 1980.)

Kolker, Robert. 2011. *A Cinema of Loneliness, Fourth Edition*. New York: Oxford University Press.

Kolker, Robert P. 2015. "The Imaginary Museum: Martin Scorsese's Film History Documentaries." In *A Companion to Martin Scorsese*, edited by Aaron Baker, 71–90. Oxford: Wiley Blackwell.

Kouvaros, George. 2018. *The Old Greeks: Photography, Cinema, Migration*. Crawley: The University of Western Australia Press.

Kozinn, Allan. 2013. "Sony Issues Dylan CDs to Extend Copyright." *The New York Times*, January 7.

Kubik, Gerhard. 1999. *Africa and the Blues*. Jackson: University Press of Mississippi.

Landau, Jon. 1971. "Ram." *Rolling Stone*, July 8.

Leacock, Richard. 2016. "For an Uncontrolled Cinema." In *The Documentary Film Reader*, edited by Jonathan Kahana, 490–1. New York: Oxford University Press.

Lethem, Jonathan. 2006. "The Genius and Modern Times of Bob Dylan, *Rolling Stone*, September 7, 2006." In *Bob Dylan: The Essential Interviews*, edited by Jonathan Cott, 469–81. New York: Simon & Schuster.

Letort, Delphine. 2015. *The Spike Lee Brand: A Study of Documentary Filmmaking*. Albany: SUNY Press.

Leyda, Jay. 1964. *Films Beget Films: A Study of the Compilation Film*. New York: Hill and Wang.

Lindahl, Chris. 2020. "Apple Steps in to Save Scorsese-DiCaprio-De Niro Reunion 'Flower Moon' as Budget Soars." *IndieWire*, May 27.

Lipsitz, George. 2006. *The Possessive Investment in Whiteness: How White People Profit from Identity Politics, Revised and Expanded Edition*. Philadelphia: Temple University Press.

Lomax, Alan. 1993. *The Land Where the Blues Began*. New York: Alfred A. Knopf Inc.

Lomax, John A. 1947. *Adventures of a Ballad Hunter*. New York: Macmillan.

Lopes, Paul. 2017. "The Power of Hyphen-Nationalism: Martin Scorsese's Sojourn from Italian American to White-Ethnic American." *Social Identities* 23.5: 562–78.

Lopes, Paul. 2019. *Art Rebels: Race, Class, and Gender in the Art of Miles Davis and Martin Scorsese*. Princeton: Princeton University Press.

MacCabe, Colin. 2003. *Godard: A Portrait of the Artist at 70*. London: Bloomsbury.

MacDougall, David. 2016. "Beyond Observational Cinema (1975)." In *The Documentary Film Reader: History, Theory, Criticism*, edited by Jonathan Kahana, 565–70. New York: Oxford University Press.

Mamber, Stephen. 1974. *Cinema Verite in America: Studies in Uncontrolled Documentary*. Cambridge: MIT Press.

Marcus, Greil. 2007. "The World Premiere of *No Direction Home*." *Studies in Documentary Film* 1.1: 49–52.

Marcus, Greil. 2010. *Bob Dylan: Writings 1968–2010*. New York: PublicAffairs.

Marcus, Greil. 2011. *The Old, Weird America: The World of Bob Dylan's Basement Tapes, Updated Edition*. New York: Picador. (Orig. Pub. 1997.)

Marcus, Greil. 2015. *Mystery Train: Images of America in Rock 'n' Roll Music, Sixth Revised Edition*. New York: Plume. (Orig. Pub. 1975.)

Marsh, Dave. 1985. *Fortunate Son: Criticism and Journalism by America's Best-Known Rock Writer*. New York: Random House.

Marsh, Dave. 1989. *The Heart of Rock and Soul: The 1001 Greatest Singles Ever Made*. New York: Plume.

Martin, Adrian. 2007. "Another Kind of River." *Studies in Documentary Film* 1.1: 53–8.

Martin, Adrian. 2014. "The Documentary Temptation: Fiction Filmmakers and Non-Fiction Forms." *NECSUS* 3.2: 5–20.

McDonough, Jimmy. 2002. *Shakey: Neil Young's Biography*. Toronto: Random House.

McElhaney, Joe. 2009. *Albert Maysles*. Chicago: University of Illinois Press.

McGee, Patrick. 2012. *Bad History and the Logics of Blockbuster Cinema: Titanic, Gangs of New York, Australia, Inglorious Basterds*. New York: Palgrave Macmillan.

Meneghetti, Michael. 2015. "Anamnesis in Acts: Documentary Performance as Intercession in *Italianamerican* and *American Boy*." *Studies in Documentary Film* 9.3 (Fall): 201–19.

Meneghetti, Mike. 2017. "Fearsome Acts of Interpretation: Audiovisual Historiography, Film Theory and *Gangs of New York*." *Film-Philosophy* 21.2 (June): 223–44.

Miller, Karl Hagstrom. 2010. *Segregating Sound: Inventing Folk and Pop Music in the Age of Jim Crow*. Durham: Duke University Press.

Moist, Kevin M. 2007. "Collecting, Collage, and Alchemy: The Harry Smith *Anthology of American Folk Music* as Art and Cultural Intervention." *American Studies* 48.4 (Winter): 111–27.

Monaco, James. 1979. *American Film Now*. New York: Oxford University Press.

Morgan, Daniel. 2006. "Rethinking Bazin: Ontology and Realist Aesthetics." *Critical Inquiry* 32.3 (Spring): 443–81.

Morgan, Daniel. 2013. *Late Godard and the Possibilities of Cinema*. Los Angeles: University of California Press.

Morin, Edgar. 2016. "Chronicle of a Film (1962)." In *The Documentary Film Reader: History, Theory, Criticism*, edited by Jonathan Kahana, 461–72. New York: Oxford University Press.

Mosco, Vincent. 2004. *The Digital Sublime: Myth, Power, and Cyberspace*. Cambridge: MIT Press.

Mulvey, Laura. 2006. *Death 24x a Second: Stillness and the Moving Image*. London: Reaktion Books.

Muscio, Giuliana. 2015. "Martin Scorsese Rocks." In *A Companion to Martin Scorsese*, edited by Aaron Baker, 259–76. Oxford: Wiley Blackwell.

Naremore, James. 1990. "Authorship and the Cultural Politics of Film Criticism." *Film Quarterly* 44.1 (Autumn): 14–23.

Nichols, Bill. 1991. *Representing Reality: Issues and Concepts in Documentary*. Bloomington: Indiana University Press.

Nichols, Bill. 1994. *Blurred Boundaries: Questions of Meaning in Contemporary Culture*. Bloomington: Indiana University Press.

Nichols, Bill. 2001. "Documentary Film and the Modernist Avant-Garde." *Critical Inquiry* 27: 580–610.

Nichols, Bill. 2010. *Introduction to Documentary, Second Edition*. Bloomington: Indiana University Press.

Nichols, Bill. 2014. "Remaking History: Jay Leyda and the Compilation Film." *Film History* 26.4: 146–56.

O'Farrell, Tim. 2006. "*No Direction Home*: Looking Forward from *Don't Look Back*." *Senses of Cinema* 38 (February).

Palmer, Robert. 1981. *Deep Blues*. New York: Penguin Books.

Parks, Justin. 2017. "Harry Smith, the *Anthology*, and the Artist as Collector." In *Harry Smith's* Anthology of American Folk Music: *American Changed through Music*, edited by Ross Hair and Thomas Ruys Smith, 65–81. New York: Routledge.

Perks, Robert and Alistair Thomson, eds. 1998. *The Oral History Reader*. New York: Routledge.

Pezzotta, Alberto. 2003. "A Journey Through Italian Cinema." *Senses of Cinema* 26 (May).

Pond, Steven F. 2003. "Jamming the Reception: Ken Burns, Jazz, and the Problem of 'America's Music.'" *Notes* 60.1 (September): 11–45.

Portelli, Alessandro. 1998. "What Makes Oral History Different?" In *The Oral History Reader*, edited by Robert Perks and Alistair Thomson, 63–74. New York: Routledge.

Pulver, Andrew. 2019. "Martin Scorsese: 'Maybe *The Irishman* Is the Last Picture I'll Make.'" *The Guardian*, December 20.

Pye, Michael and Linda Myles. 1979. *The Movie Brats: How the Movie Generation Took Over Hollywood*. New York: Holt, Reinhart and Winston.

Rabinowitz, Paula. 1994. *They Must be Represented: The Politics of Documentary*. New York: Verso.

Rancière, Jacques. 2014. *The Intervals of Cinema*, translated by John Howe. London: Verso.

Rascaroli, Laura. 2008. "The Essay Film: Problems, Definitions, Textual Commitments." *Framework* 49.2 (Fall): 24–47.

Raymond, Marc. 2013. *Hollywood's New Yorker: The Making of Martin Scorsese*. Albany: SUNY Press.

Renov, Michael. 2008. "First-Person Films: Some Theses on Self-Inscription." In *Rethinking Documentary: New Perspectives, New Practices*, edited by Thomas Austin and Wilm de Jong, 39–50. Berkshire: McGraw-Hill.

Ricoeur, Paul. 1988. *Time and Narrative, Vol. 3*, translated by Kathleen Blamey and David Pellauer. Chicago: The University of Chicago Press.

Robertson, Robbie. 2016. *Testimony*. New York: Penguin Random House.

Rodowick, D.N. 2007. *The Virtual Life of Film*. Cambridge: Harvard University Press.

Rodowick, D.N. 2014. *Elegy for Theory*. Cambridge: Harvard University Press.
Rodowick, D.N. 2015. *Philosophy's Artful Conversation*. Cambridge: Harvard University Press.
Rosen, Philip. 2001. *Change Mummified: Cinema, Historicity, Theory*. Minneapolis: University of Minnesota Press.
Rosenbaum, Johnathan. 2010. *Goodbye Cinema, Hello Cinephilia: Film Culture in Transition*. Chicago: The University of Chicago Press.
Ross, Andrew. 2009. *Nice Work If You Can Get It: Life and Labor in Precarious Times*. New York: New York University Press.
Rothman, William. 1997. *Documentary Film Classics*. Cambridge: Cambridge University Press.
Rothman, William. 2000. "Looking Back and Turning Inward: American Documentary Films of the Seventies." In *Lost Illusions: American Cinema in the Shadow of Watergate and Vietnam, 1970–1979*, edited by David A. Cook, 417–51. New York: Charles Scribner's Sons.
Rouch, Jean. 2003. *Ciné-Ethnography*, edited and translated by Steven Feld. Minneapolis: University of Minnesota Press.
Ruberto, Laura E. 2015. "Italian Films, New York City Television, and the Work of Martin Scorsese." In *A Companion to Martin Scorsese*, edited by Aaron Baker, 53–70. Oxford: Wiley Blackwell.
Said, Edward. 1975. *Beginnings: Intention and Method*. New York: Basic Books Inc., Publishers.
Sakamoto, John. 2014. "The copyright-extension album becomes a December tradition." *The Toronto Star*, December 12.
Sanjek, David with Benjamin Halligan. 2013. "'You Can't Always Get What You Want': Riding on the *Medicine Ball Caravan*." In *The Music Documentary*, edited by Robert Edgar, Kirsty Fairclough-Isaacs and Benjamin Halligan, 100–12. London: Routledge.
Sarris, Andrew. 1996. *The American Cinema: Directors and Directions, 1929–1968*. New York: Da Capo Press. (Orig. Pub. 1968.)
Schickel, Richard. 2011. *Conversations with Scorsese*. New York: Alfred A. Knopf.
Scorsese, Martin. 2003a. "Preface." In *Martin Scorsese Presents: The Blues*, edited by Peter Guralnick, Robert Santelli, Holly George-Warren and Christopher John Farley, 6–7. New York: Amistad.
Scorsese, Martin. 2003b. "Feel Like Going Home." In *Martin Scorsese Presents: The Blues*, edited by Peter Guralnick, Robert Santelli, Holly George-Warren and Christopher John Farley, 62–6. New York: Amistad.
Scorsese, Martin. 2015. "Film Preservation: A Dire Need." *Encyclopedia Britannica*, May 25.
Scorsese, Martin. 2019. "I Said Marvel Movies Aren't Cinema. Let Me Explain." *The New York Times*, November 4.

Scorsese, Martin and Michael Henry Wilson. 1997. *A Personal Journey with Martin Scorsese Through American Movies*. New York: Hyperion.

Severn, Stephen E. 2002. "Robbie Robertson's Big Break: A Reevaluation of Martin Scorsese's *The Last Waltz*." *Film Quarterly* 56.2 (Winter): 25–31.

Sharf, Zach. 2018. "Martin Scorsese Directing 'SCTV' Reunion Show for Netflix." *IndieWire*, April 12.

Shoard, Catherine. 2019. "Martin Scorsese on *The Irishman*: 'Please, please don't look at it on a phone.'" *The Guardian*, December 2.

Skinner, Katherine. 2006. "'Must Be Born Again': Resurrecting the *Anthology of American Folk Music*." *Popular Music* 25.1: 57–75.

Smail, Belinda. 2010. *The Documentary: Politics, Emotion, Culture*. New York: Palgrave Macmillan.

Sontag, Susan. 1966. *Against Interpretation, and Other Essays*. New York: Farrar, Straus & Giroux.

Sontag, Susan. 1996. "The Decay of Cinema." *The New York Times Magazine* (February 25): 60.

Sontag, Susan. 2001. *Where the Stress Falls: Essays*. New York: Picador.

Springsteen, Bruce. 2016. *Born to Run*. New York: Simon & Schuster.

Stahl, Matt. 2013. *Unfree Masters: Recording Artists and the Politics of Work*. Durham: Duke University Press.

Steimatsky, Noa. 2008. *Italian Locations: Reinhabiting the Past in Postwar Cinema*. Minneapolis: University of Minnesota Press.

Sterritt, David, ed. 1998. *Jean-Luc Godard: Interviews*. Jackson: University Press of Mississippi.

Strauss, Matthew. 2020. "Martin Scorsese to Direct New Documentary on New York Dolls' David Johansen." *Pitchfork*, July 7.

Svec, Henry Adam. 2012. "'Who Don't Care if the Money's No Good?': Authenticity and The Band." *Popular Music and Society* 35.3 (July 2012): 427–45.

Tarada, Rei. 2001. *Feeling in Theory: Emotion after the "Death of the Subject."* Cambridge: Harvard University Press.

Taubin, Amy. 2005. "From There to Here." *Film Comment* (November–December): 30–3.

Taylor, Deems. 1943. *A Pictorial History of the Movies*. New York: Simon and Schuster.

Telotte, J.P. 1979. "Scorsese's 'The Last Waltz' and the Concert Genre." *Film Criticism* 4.2: 9–20.

Testa, Bart and Jim Shedden. 2002. "In the Great Midwestern Hardware Store: The Seventies Triumph in Canadian Rock Music." In *Slippery Pastimes: Reading the Popular In Canadian Culture*, edited by Joan Nicks and Jeannette Sloniowski, 177–216. Waterloo: Wilfred Laurier Press.

Travers, Peter. 2010. "Shutter Island." *Rolling Stone*, February 19.

Travers, Peter. 2011. "Hugo." *Rolling Stone*, November 21.

Travers, Peter. 2019. "'Rolling Thunder Revue' Review: Scorsese's Dylan Doc Is Simply Brilliant." *Rolling Stone*, June 11.

Truffaut, François. 1985. "A Wonderful Certainty." In *Cahiers du Cinéma, the 1950s: Neo-Realism, Hollywood, New Wave*, edited by Jim Hillier, 107–10. Cambridge: Harvard University Press. (Orig. Pub. 1955.)

Verano, Frank. 2015. "Embodying 'Truthful Possibilities': An Interview with D.A. Pennebaker." *Studies in Documentary Film* 9.3: 250–9.

Verdicchio, Pasquale. 1999. "Unholy Manifestations: Cultural Transformation as Hereticism in the Films of De Michiel, Ferrara, Savoca, and Scorsese." In *Adjusting Sites: New Essays in Italian American Studies*, edited by William Boelhower and Rocco Pallone, 201–218. New York: *Forum Italicum*.

Waksman, Steve. 1999. *Instruments of Desire: The Electric Guitar and the Shaping of Musical Experience*. Cambridge: Harvard University Press.

Wald, Elijah. 2009. *How The Beatles Destroyed Rock 'N' Roll: An Alternative History of American Popular Music*. New York: Oxford University Press.

Ward, Brian. 1998. *Just My Soul Responding: Rhythm and Blues, Black Consciousness and Race Relations*. Berkeley: University of California Press.

Waugh, Thomas. 1985. "Beyond Vérité: Emile de Antonio and the New Documentary of the Seventies." In *Movies and Methods, Vol. II*, edited by Bill Nichols, 233–58. Los Angeles: University of California Press.

Wees, William C. 1993. *Recycled Images: The Art and Politics of Found Footage Films*. New York: Anthology Film Archives.

Wilentz, Sean. 2010. *Bob Dylan in America*. New York: Random House.

Wilentz, Sean. 2012. "Woody Guthrie and Bob Dylan Hit Manhattan." *American Music Review* 42.1: 1–5.

Willemen, Paul. 1994. *Looks and Frictions: Essays in Cultural Studies and Film Theory*. Bloomington: Indiana University Press.

Willman, Chris. 2019. "Bob Dylan, Martin Scorsese Reunite for 'Rolling Thunder' Film, Coming to Netflix in 2019." *Variety*, January 10.

Wilson, Michael Henry. 2011. *Scorsese on Scorsese*. Paris: *Cahiers du Cinéma*.

Witt, Michael. 1999. "The Death(s) of Cinema According to Godard." *Screen* 40.3: 331–46.

Witt, Michael. 2013. *Jean-Luc Godard: Cinema Historian*. Bloomington: Indiana University Press.

Witt, Michael. 2017. "Taking Stock: Two Decades of Teaching the History, Theory, and Practice of Audiovisual Criticism." *NECSUS: European Journal of Media Studies* (May 28).

Wollen, Peter. 2002. *Paris Hollywood: Writings on Film*. London: Verso.

Young, Neil. 2012. *Waging Heavy Peace: A Hippie Dream*. New York: Plume.

Zanes, Warren. 2015. *Petty: The Biography*. New York: Henry Holt and Company.

Index

Afternoon with SCTV, An (Scorsese) 197
Allred, Jeff 232 n.24, 234 n.36
All Things Must Pass (Harrison) 198
America America (Kazan) 165–6, 184, 187, 189–90, 239 n.18
American Bicentennial 6, 17–18, 203, 213 n.2, 216 n.29, 220 n.12
American Boy: A Profile of Steven Prince (Scorsese)
  and direct cinema 5, 8, 12, 45
  and ethnic revival 12, 44, 53, 56, 64, 107, 113
  and immigration 21, 44, 53, 113, 184, 216 n.25
  irony in 9, 45, 47, 49–50, 64
  and *The Last Waltz* 12–13, 57, 64, 94, 216 n.29
  and music industry 45, 64, 108, 226 n.47
  oral history in 5–6, 12–13, 44, 53–4, 56, 64, 107–8, 113, 155, 216 n.23
  Scorsese in 48–9
  and show business 45, 226 n.47
  storytelling in 7, 21–2, 45–6, 49, 51–4, 64
American Epic: The First Time America Heard Itself (MacMahon) 235 n.38
American Film Now (Monaco) 1
American Masters (PBS) 109, 143, 182, 184, 200
Ames, Eric 211 n.8
analogical imagination 179
Andrew, Dudley 168, 239 n.15, 239 n.19
Anthology of American Folk Music (Smith) 136–9, 235 n.38–40
anti-utopian 101
Antonioni, Michelangelo 158, 181
Apple 199, 210 n.6, 244 n.12
Armani, Giorgio 210 n.6
art cinema 107, 181, 229 n.8
Arthur, Paul 82–4, 132–3, 146–7
auteurism 151, 209 n.2, 229 n.8

"auteur theory" (Sarris) 107, 229 n.8
autobiography 105, 166, 181, 188, 227 n.1. *See also* memoir
avant-garde 114, 146–8, 225 n.46, 230 n.17
Aviator, The (Scorsese) 200

baby boomers 107, 129–30, 157, 188, 198, 217 n.33
Band, The
  Bob Dylan and 65, 77, 80
  breakup of 60–1, 94, 110, 219 n.6
  Canadian members of 88, 220 n.15
  and counterculture 72–3, 79–80, 221 n.16
  and documentary 62, 65–6
  in *Festival Express* 65–6, 221 n.19
  as The Hawks 65, 67, 77, 90, 111, 128, 130, 138, 140–1, 144, 222 n.28
  as Levon and The Hawks 65
  and Ronnie Hawkins 65, 77
  and the Sixties 57, 59, 66, 73, 108–9, 221 n.17
  and vernacular music 72, 76
  at Woodstock Music and Art Fair 65, 72
Band, The (The Band) 65, 72–3, 110, 148, 224 n.41
Band, The, works by. *See titles of specific works*
Baron, Jaimie 233 n.26
Barthes, Roland 33–4, 215 n.17
Bazin, André 172, 183, 239 n.15, 239 n.19
Baez, Joan 129
Beacon Theater 13, 63, 96, 98, 100–1, 103
Beatles, The 104, 108, 148, 198
Benjamin, Walter 239 n.19
Bergman, Ingrid 168
Berman, Marshall 234 n.35
Berry, Chuck 92, 229 n.7
BFI. *See* British Film Institute
Bickerton, Emilie 160, 183–4
bildungsroman 104

Biograph (Dylan) 228 n.3
biography 14, 28, 114, 116
Blonde on Blonde (Dylan) 130, 138, 140, 143
blues, the 13–14, 64, 76–7, 91, 104, 109, 113–28, 138, 150, 230 n.15, 230 n.17
Bodde, Margaret 197
Bootleg Series, The 106, 228 n.3
Brakhage, Stan 158
Brando, Marlon 188
Breathless (Godard) 189
Bringing It All Back Home (Dylan) 130, 138, 234 n.35
British Film Institute (BFI) 3, 157, 160, 165–6, 182, 199
Broonzy, Big Bill 113
Brown, Peter 217 n.30, 241 n.23
Buffalo Springfield 86
Buñuel, Luis 158
Burns, Ken 113–14, 116, 200, 230 n.17, 242 n.5
Butterfield, Paul 77–9
Butterfield Blues Band, The 79
Byrds, The 86
Byron, Joseph 35

Camera Lucida: Reflections on Photography (Barthes) 33–4
Cahiers du Cinéma 154, 157, 160, 163–4, 178, 183–4, 192, 239 n.15
Cahoots (The Band) 73, 110–11
Canned Heat 86, 98
Cantwell, Robert 108, 122, 124–5, 136, 150, 224 n.39
Capra, Frank 144–5
Carruthers, Lee 121–2
Casetti, Francesco 180–1, 193–4
Cash, Johnny 91, 202, 243 n.7
Casillo, Robert 209 n.2, 212 n.1, 213 n.3
Casino (Scorsese) 3, 161, 213 n.6
Cavallero, Jonathan J. 127, 216 n.20
Cavell, Stanley 31, 42, 173, 239 n.19
CDs. *See* compact discs
"Century of Cinema" (BFI) 160, 241 n.25
Channel 4 160
Charles, Ray 235 n.37
Christgau, Robert 217 n.35, 226 n.48, 243 n.9

Chronicles: Volume One (Dylan) 105–6, 130, 213 n.7, 227 n.1, 228 n.2
Chronique d'un été (Rouch and Morin) 232 n.22
cine-clubs 158, 159
Cinema of Loneliness, A (Kolker) 2, 209 n.2
cinematheques 159
cinephilia
    and cinema studies 157, 163, 237 n.2, 237 n.8
    and cinematic patrimony 154, 183, 192
    and collection 163–4
    and "death of cinema" 157, 239 n.19
    and digital media 157, 207, 237 n.2, 237 n.8
    in France 154, 158, 237 n.4
    in the Sixties 107, 154, 157, 160–1, 178, 183, 207, 240 n.22
    and spectatorship 153–4, 163–4, 178
Citizen Kane (Welles) 162
Clancy, Liam 143
Clapton, Eric 113, 115–16, 148, 223 n.31, 227 n.1, 231 n.17, 231 n.19
Cohen, John 129, 139
collectors 136, 163, 194, 235 n.37
Color of Money, The (Scorsese) 110
compact discs (CDs) 228 n.3, 230 n.17, 243 n.9
compilation film, the 233 n.26
computer-generated images (CGI) 172
concert film, the 8, 12–13, 57, 61–2, 64, 66, 73–5, 81–2, 95–6, 102
Concert for Bangladesh, The (Swimmer) 80
Cook, Pam 53
Cooke, Sam 86, 150
Coppola, Francis Ford 37, 189
Corrigan, Timothy 214 n.9
country rock 72, 222 n.28
Crisis: Behind a Presidential Commitment (Drew) 82

Danko, Rick 62, 64, 73, 75, 88–90, 94
Day for Night (Truffaut) 162
Dean, James 130, 188
De Baecque, Antoine 238 n.10
debts/indebtedness (historical)
    the historian as "collector of debts" 194

the historian as "insolvent debtor" 194–5
in *A Letter to Elia* 11, 15, 183–4, 194
Paul Ricoeur on 194–5
and Scorsese's auteurism 11, 154
Decade (Young) 228 n.3
Deep Blues (Palmer) 117, 126
Deep Blues: A Musical Pilgrimage to the Crossroads (Mugge) 116–17
Denning, Michael 204–5, 243 n.8
Delta blues 6, 13, 108–9, 114–17, 121–6, 128, 137–8, 150
Departed, The (Scorsese) 3, 200
De Sica, Vittorio 178–9
Diddley, Bo 77, 91–2, 233 n.28
Dig! (Timoner) 97
digital image-making 157, 237 n.8
direct cinema
 in the 1960s 8, 12–13, 25–8, 34, 57, 62–3, 67, 69, 82–5, 145–8, 223 n.33
 in the 1970s 25–8
 and candid photography 34
 and the concert film 8, 12–13, 57, 62–3, 65–71, 81–2, 95–6, 102, 223 n.33
 and individualism 8, 82–6, 95–6, 145, 148, 225 n.46
 and musician labor 13, 62–3, 81–2, 95–6
 portraiture 144–7
 and the public sphere 83, 145
 and rock music 67, 82
 and spectators 82–3, 145
directors
 Andrew Sarris on 154–5, 160, 166, 229 n.8
 as auteurs, *see* auteur theory *and* auteurism
 Cahiers du Cinéma and 154, 160, 184
 in *Il mio viaggio in Italia* 154–5, 166
 and New Hollywood 153
 in *A Personal Journey with Martin Scorsese Through American Movies* 154–5, 160, 166
Doane, Mary Ann 172, 237 n.8
documentary
 history of 25–7, 144–8
 performance in 31, 33–5, 41
 and photography 33–8

portraiture 64, 144–8, 199
profiles 15, 149, 197–208, 216 n.23
Doing Time: Temporality, Hermeneutics, and Contemporary Cinema (Carruthers) 121
Donato, Raffaele 23
Dont Look Back (Pennebaker) 8, 26, 34, 57, 67–8, 85–7, 89, 133, 144, 146, 224 n.38
Doyle, Peter 151, 167
Drew, Robert 26, 82–4
Drew Associates, The 83, 242 n.2
Duel in the Sun (Vidor) 163
DVD 194
Dwan, Allan 161
Dylan, Bob
 and *Dont Look Back* 34, 57, 67, 85, 144, 146, 224 n.38
 and *Eat the Document* 57
 and folk revival 67, 108, 128–9, 144, 201
 with The Hawks 65, 67, 77, 128, 141, 144
 and rock music 13, 57, 67, 109, 144, 224 n.39
 and the Sixties 14, 57, 104, 106–10, 128–30, 132, 137–8, 143, 217 n.33
Dylan, Bob, works by. *See titles of specific works*

East of Eden (Kazan) 187–9, 191
Eat the Document (Dylan and Alk) 57
Ebert, Roger 153
editing
 and archival materials 10, 109, 121, 125, 126, 133
 and compilation 109, 121, 129, 133, 145
 digital editing 159, 237 n.8
 in *Feel Like Going Home* 6, 10, 109, 120–6, 128–9
 in *No Direction Home* 6, 10, 14, 109, 128–9, 132–3, 235, 140, 146
 and time 120–5, 132, 140
Elia Kazan: A Life (Kazan) 183, 241 n.27
Ellis Island 18–19, 35, 189
Elsaesser, Thomas 229 n.8, 240 n.22
Elvis on Tour (Abel and Adidge) 1, 6, 222 n.25

Elvis Presley: The Searcher (Zimny) 202, 225 n.43
emotions, the
 in documentary 26
 and interpretation 24, 53, 122
 in *Italianamerican* 21–2, 24, 27–8, 39, 53, 214 n.8
 and oral history 28, 53
 Scorsese on 21–2, 24–8, 122, 214 n.8
 and subjectivity 24, 26–8, 214 n.8
 and theory 82, 214 n.8
Eric Clapton: Nothing but the Blues (PBS) 113, 115–17, 148, 197, 230 n.14
Ethnic Revival
 and *American Boy* 11–12, 44–5, 53–4, 56, 64, 107, 113
 and genealogy 6
 and heritage 17, 18, 35, 54
 and *Italianamerican* 7–8, 12, 17–22, 25, 28, 35–7, 53–4, 56, 107, 113, 127, 190
 Matthew Frye Jacobson on 17–18, 20, 35–6
 Scorsese and 6–7, 12, 17–21, 53–4, 189–90
 visual iconography 35–7, 189–90
ethnographic filmmaking 232 n.22

Feel Like Going Home (Scorsese) 6, 10, 13, 105, 107, 109–10, 113–30, 137–8, 150–1, 203
"Feel Like Going Home" (Waters) 231 n.18
Fellini, Federico 181
Festival Express (Smeaton and Cvitanovich) 221 n.19
50 Year Argument, The (Scorsese and Tedeschi) 3, 55, 197
Filene, Benjamin 231 n.18, 232 n.24, 236 n.41
film criticism 107, 237 n.5, 239 n.17
Film Foundation, The 9, 112–14, 159, 229 n.11, 239 n.14
Film History: Theory and Practice (Allen and Gomery) 83
film noir 1, 161
film preservation 4, 9, 107, 111–12, 154, 159, 229 n.11
folklore 13, 92, 109, 115, 121, 123, 126, 129, 198

folk music 67, 128, 130, 134, 138–40, 228 n.2, 232 n.24
folk processes 106, 128, 228 n.2
folk revival 67, 104, 108, 128–9, 139, 144, 201, 224 n.39, 235 n.40
Force of Evil (Polonsky) 161
Frampton, Hollis 158
French New Wave 158
Fried, Michael 34

Gangs of New York (Scorsese) 200
George Harrison: Living in the Material World (Scorsese) 109, 129, 148–9, 167, 197–8
Gibney, Alex 243 n.7
Gift, The: The Journey of Johnny Cash (Zimny) 202
Giles, Paul 42, 179
Gimme Shelter (Maysles) 26, 63, 67, 99, 101, 103
Ginsberg, Allen 129
Godard, Jean-Luc 158–9, 177–8, 226 n.50
Godfather Part II, The (Coppola) 37, 189
Godfather and Sons (Levin) 230 n.16
Good As I Been to You (Dylan) 106
Goodfellas (Scorsese) 3, 161
Gramsci, Antonio 21
Grateful Dead 65, 86, 222 n.28
Griffith, D.W. 158
Grist, Leighton 210 n.4, 215 n.15, 217 n.31, 218 n.1
Grossman, Albert 65,
Gunning, Tom 237 n.8
Guralnick, Peter 150, 231 n.18, 236 n.48
Guy, Buddy 116

Hall, Jeanne 84, 224 n.38
Hall, Stuart 229 n.6
Happy Mother's Day (Leacock and Chopra) 82
harmonious deportment 13, 63, 92, 101
Harris, Corey 114, 122, 128, 137, 150, 233 n.27
Harrison, George 14, 80, 104, 108–9, 148–51
Harvey, David 225 n.45
HAVANA MOON – The Rolling Stones Live in Cuba (Dugdale) 103
Hawkins, Ronnie 65, 77

Hawks, The 65, 67, 77, 90, 111, 128, 130, 138, 140–1, 144, 222 n.28
Hell, Richard 227 n.1
Helm, Levon 60–1, 91–2, 219 n.6
Hendrix, Jimi 65, 86–7, 93
heritage
  cultural 6, 9, 17, 35, 54, 111, 159
  and ethnic revival 17–18, 35, 54
  and film preservation 9, 11, 159
  and photography 35
  and Scorsese 6, 9, 17–18, 54, 111, 159, 198, 202, 213 n.3, 238 n.9
Herzog, Werner 211 n.8
Hesmondhalgh, David 233 n.25
Heylin, Clinton 236 n.41–2
Hibbing, Minnesota 130–1, 134–5
Highway 61 Revisited (Dylan) 130, 138
Hine, Lewis 35
Histoire(s) du cinéma (Godard) 159
historiography 20, 56, 158–9, 169, 172, 194–5
Hitchcock/Truffaut (Jones) 198
Hobsbawm, Eric 45
Holly, Buddy 93
Hollywood Renaissance 1–2, 11
Hooker, John Lee 120–1, 124–6
House, Son 126
House Un-American Activities Committee (HUAC) 185–7, 192, 196, 241 n.27
Hudson, Garth 62, 64, 77, 88, 94, 140, 218 n.4
Hugo (Scorsese) 153, 200

icons 179
Il mio viaggio in Italia (Scorsese) 14–15, 54–5, 151–7, 164–84, 191–6, 211 n.10
immigration 7–8, 12, 14, 19–21, 23, 31–2, 35–6, 40–4, 53, 113, 127, 129, 151, 165, 169, 176, 184, 188–92, 196, 199, 216 n.25
I'm Not There (Haynes) 141
index 172–3, 237 n.8
individualist 25, 83–4, 96, 245, 148, 151, 184, 199, 207, 225 n.46, 243 n.10
individualization 225 n.45
intercession 39–41, 63–4, 217 n.30
internet 159, 193–4, 237 n.2, 242 n.30

Irishman, The (Scorsese) 3, 200–1, 207, 244 n.12
Islands (The Band) 111
Italian Cinema 155–6, 166–8, 172–4, 179
Italian Immigration 7, 12, 21, 42, 169, 176
Italian Neorealism 156, 177, 181
Italianamerican (Scorsese)
  and 1970s documentary 27–8, 215 n.12
  and direct cinema 5, 8–9, 12, 25–8, 33, 45
  and ethnic revival 7, 8, 12, 17–20, 25, 28, 35–7, 56, 107, 113, 127, 190, 212 n.1
  and immigration 7–8, 12, 14, 19–23, 31–2, 35–6, 40–3, 127, 129, 151, 169, 184, 190–2, 216 n.25
  and oral history 5–6, 12, 20, 28, 37, 56, 107, 113, 129, 182, 199
  performance in 31, 33, 41
  and photography 33–7
  Scorsese in 29, 40–1, 90
  storytelling in 7, 11–12, 18–24, 27–33, 35, 39–43, 53–5, 129, 169, 190, 213 n.7

Jacobson, Matthew Frye 17–18, 20, 35–6, 213 n.3
Jagger, Mick 13, 63, 96, 98–103, 226 n.51
James, David E. 66, 68, 103, 224 n.40, 226 n.50
Jameson, Fredric 38
Jazz (Burns) 113–14, 116, 200, 230 n.17
Jean-Luc Godard: Cinema Historian (Witt) 158
Jefferson Airplane 65, 73, 222 n.28
Johansen, David 242 n.1
Johnny Guitar (Ray) 64
Johnson, Robert 116, 150, 231 n.19
Jones, Kent 182, 198, 229 n.11, 240 n.20
Joplin, Janis 65, 86

Kahana, Jonathan 28, 83–4
Kazan, Elia 11, 14, 152, 154–6, 165, 181–7, 196, 198, 241 n.27
Keathley, Christian 163–4, 238 n.11, 241 n.26
Keita, Salif 127
Kelly, Mary Pat 209 n.2, 213 n.4
Key to Reserva, The (Scorsese) 210 n.6

Keyser, Les 19, 212 n.1, 213 n.2
King, B.B. 116
King, Willie 127
King of Comedy, The (Scorsese) 110
Koité, Habib 127
Kolker, Robert 2, 164, 210 n.4, 237 n.5
Kouvaros, George 181, 190–1, 237 n.6
Kracauer, Siegfried 172, 239 n.19
Kuleshov, Lev 158
Kuras, Ellen 197, 226 n.49

labor
  in *American Boy: A Profile of Steven Prince* 45, 64, 108, 226 n.47
  autonomous 63, 82, 95
  in direct cinema 13, 61–2, 81–2, 95–6
  in *Dont Look Back* 87
  expressive 63, 81
  in *Italianamerican* 226 n.47
  in *The Last Waltz* 13, 61–3, 81–2, 94–6, 219 n.6, 226 n.47
  and musicians 13, 61–2, 81–2, 96, 226 n.50
  and rockumentaries 97
  self-actualizing 62, 65
  self-realizing 87, 96
Ladri di bicilette (De Sica) 178
Ladies and Gentlemen: The Rolling Stones (Binzer) 103, 227 n.53
Lady by the Sea: The Statue of Liberty (Scorsese and Jones) 210 n.6, 239 n.18
Landau, Jon 220 n.14
Last, Bob 160
Last Waltz, The (soundtrack) 80, 111, 219 n.4
Last Waltz, The (Scorsese) 1–2, 4, 8–10, 12–13, 57, 59–64, 66, 69, 71–82, 87–104, 107–12, 123, 148, 149, 150, 203, 205, 218 n.1, 220 n.12
Last Year at Marienbad (Resnais) 189
La terra trema (Visconti) 178
Leacock, Richard 26, 82–4, 145, 223 n.37
Lead Belly (Huddie Ledbetter) 137, 232 n.24
Lebowitz, Fran 55, 198–9
Lee, Spike 211 n.8
Lethem, Jonathan 217 n.33, 234 n.32
Letort, Delphine 211 n.8

Let's Spend the Night Together (Ashby) 101–2
Letter to Elia, A (Scorsese and Jones) 11, 14–15, 54–5, 151–5, 161, 164, 166, 181–96, 198, 200, 211 n.10
Levon and The Hawks 65
Leyda, Jay 233 n.26
liberalism 25, 83–4
Life Itself (James) 197
"Like a Rolling Stone" (Dylan) 131, 138, 141, 147, 234 n.34
Linklater, Richard 44, 216 n.22
Little Italy 14, 19, 38, 45, 48, 153, 156, 165–6, 169–72, 174–5, 178–9, 181, 182, 188–9, 192
Living in the Material World (Harrison) 198
Lomax, Alan 122, 125, 128, 134, 137, 231 n.18
Lomax, John 119, 134, 232 n.24, 234 n.36
Long Strange Trip (Bar-Lev) 197–8
Lopes, Paul 209 n.2, 213 n.3
L'oro di Napoli (De Sica) 179
"Love and Theft" (Dylan) 106, 213 n.7

MacCabe, Colin 160
Made in Milan (Scorsese) 210 n.6
Mahal, Taj (musician) 115, 122–3, 128, 233 n.27
Mali, West Africa 114, 126
Mamber, Stephen 26, 223 n.33
Mann, Anthony 161
Manuel, Richard 62, 78, 111, 224 n.41
Marcus, Greil 65, 73, 89, 106, 132, 139, 219 n.6, 220 n.15, 221 n.18, 222 n.25, 228 n.2
Martin, Adrian 210 n.5, 213 n.6, 234 n.35
Martin Scorsese Presents: The Blues (various directors) 3, 13, 107, 113–14, 197, 230 n.14–17
Marvel Comics (movie franchise) 207, 241 n.24
Masked and Anonymous (Charles) 213 n.7
mass culture 137, 138
mass media 26
Maysles, Albert 226 n.49
McCartney, Paul 220 n.14
Mean Streets (Scorsese) 3, 43, 59, 188
mediators (cultural) 117, 137, 138

Medicine Ball Caravan (Reichenbach) 1, 222 n.25,
Mekas, Jonas 148
memoir 61, 94, 227 n.1. *See also* autobiography
memory 124, 136, 163-4, 171-2, 174, 176-7, 181. *See also* recollection
Midnight Ramble 91-2
migration 5, 14, 21, 107, 123, 125, 164-5, 169, 175, 181, 189, 192
"Mirror, Mirror" (Scorsese) 210 n.6
Mississippi Delta 13, 108-9, 114-15, 117, 121-2, 124-5
mobile relics 14, 156, 181, 194. *See also* religious artifact
Modern Times (Dylan) 106, 213 n.7
modernist aesthetics 2, 114, 168, 210 n.3, 217 n.31, 218 n.1
Monaco, James 1-2, 209 n.1
montage 121, 167
Monterey Pop (Pennebaker) 12, 67-74, 79, 81-2, 86, 99, 222 n.23, 224 n.40
Moondog Matinee (The Band) 111
Morgan, Daniel 237 n.8, 240 n.21
Morin, Edgar 232 n.22
Morrison, Van 91
Mulvey, Laura 168, 237 n.8
Music from Big Pink (The Band) 65, 72, 80, 110, 148
musician labor 13, 62-3, 82, 96. *See also* labor

Naremore, James 239 n.15
National Endowment for the Humanities (NEH) 6, 8-9, 11, 17-19, 22, 24, 54
"Neighborhood, The" (Scorsese) 210 n.6
neoliberalism 207, 225 n.46
Netflix 3, 15, 197, 199-203, 205, 207
"Never Get Out of These Blues Alive" (Hooker) 124-5
New Hollywood 8, 64, 149, 153, 165
New York City 14, 50, 55, 96, 105, 130, 133, 139, 143, 156, 169, 171, 177, 179, 181-2, 197
New York Film Festival 17, 199
New York Public Library 105, 161, 176, 228 n.2
New York Review of Books, The 55
Newport Jazz Festival 123

Nichols, Bill 25-6, 48, 225 n.46, 242 n.5
Night and Fog (Resnais) 233 n.26
No Direction Home: Bob Dylan (Scorsese) and *Anthology of American Folk Music* 136-9
  editing in 6, 10, 14, 109, 128-9, 132-5, 140, 146
  folk music in 128-30, 134-40
  and folk revival 104, 128-9, 139, 144, 201
  and PBS 143, 200, 234 n.31
  and record collecting 133-137
  and rock music 13, 57, 109, 139
  and vernacular culture 147, 150
  and vernacular music 106, 109, 128-9, 133-40, 143-4, 199
Northern Lights – Southern Cross (The Band) 73, 111
nostalgia 9, 38, 55, 108, 110, 114, 129, 154, 181, 195, 218 n.1, 222 n.28

observational documentary 27, 84, 144
Once Were Brothers: Robbie Robertson and The Band (Roher) 198, 218 n.4
On the Waterfront (Kazan) 187-9, 191
oral history 28

Paisà (Rossellini) 169, 178, 184
Palmer, Robert 117, 126, 232 n.20
participatory interviews 27-8, 55, 232 n.22
Patton, Charley 127
PBS. *See* Public Broadcasting Service
Pennebaker, D.A. 8, 12, 26, 34, 67-9, 84, 86, 133, 140, 144, 146-7
Perkins, Carl 91
Personal Journey with Martin Scorsese Through American Movies, A (Scorsese) 3, 10, 14, 54, 113, 151, 157, 159-66, 182-3, 189, 193-4
Pezzotta, Alberto 155
Phillips, John 68
photography 33-5, 172-3, 239 n.19
Piano Blues (Eastwood) 230 n.16
Pictorial History of Movies, A (Taylor) 161, 163, 176
politiques des auteurs 161, 183
Polonsky, Abraham 161

"Portal to America" (photo exhibit, 1966) 35
Portelli, Alessandro 20, 28
Presley, Elvis 91–3, 150, 202
Primary (Drew) 26, 82–4
Prince, Steven 43–54, 64, 226 n.47
Public Broadcasting Service (PBS) 6, 17, 107, 109, 113, 143, 182, 197, 199, 200, 235 n.38
Public Speaking (Scorsese) 3, 10, 55–6, 198–9
Pulp Fiction (Tarantino) 216 n.22

Rabinowitz, Paula 26, 33
Raging Bull (Scorsese) 3, 22, 55, 110–11, 159, 161, 188
Rancière, Jacques 196
Rascaroli, Laura 214 n.9
Ray, Nicholas 148, 165
Raymond, Marc 210 n.3, 237 n.5, 238 n.13
recollection 39, 162–3. *See also* memory
record collection 133–7
Red, White & Blues (Figgis) 230 n.16, 231 n.19
Redding, Otis 69, 70, 74, 86, 93
relics 180–1, 241 n.23. *See also* mobile relics
Renaldo and Clara (Dylan) 201, 203–4, 220 n.12, 243 n.8
Renov, Michael 214 n.9, 225 n.46
Resnais, Alain 189, 233 n.26
Richards, Keith 96, 98, 100–2
Richardson, Robert 197, 226 n.49
Ricoeur, Paul 194–5
Riis, Jacob 35
ritual of origins 108–9, 128
rituals
    and cinephilia 154
    in the concert film 62, 64–71, 86
    in *Feel Like Going Home* 109, 128
    and film spectatorship 154
    in *Il mio viaggio in Italia* 174
    in *The Last Waltz* 74
    in *No Direction Home* 135
    in rock music 62, 64–71
    in *Shine a Light* 96

Road to Memphis, The (Pearce and Kenner) 230 n.16
Roaring Twenties, The (Walsh) 161
Robertson, Robbie 9, 13, 60–3, 73, 81, 87–96, 98, 100, 102–3, 110–11, 218 n.1, 218 n.4, 224 n.41
rock music 5, 8–9, 12–13, 57, 59–60, 62–72, 76, 97–8, 103–4, 108–9, 139, 148, 197, 224 n.39,
rock 'n' roll music 13, 64–7, 91–3, 128, 138, 143, 229 n.7
Rock of Ages (The Band) 110–11
rockumentary 62–71, 200–203, 205–7, 212 n.11
Rodowick, David 237 n.8, 239 n.19
Rogers, Jimmy 116
"Rollin' Stone" (Waters) 123, 127, 233 n.27
Rolling Stone (magazine) 153, 237 n.1
Rolling Stones, The 63, 65, 96–104, 146
Rolling Stones, The: Live at the Max (Temple) 103
Rolling Thunder Revue: A Bob Dylan Story by Martin Scorsese (Scorsese) 3, 10–11, 148, 150, 197, 200–7
roots music 109, 138–9. *See also* vernacular music
Roots Too: White Ethnic Revival in Post-Civil Rights America (Jacobson) 18
Rosen, Jeff 106, 129, 143–4, 167, 217 n.32
Rosen, Philip 172–3, 237 n.8
Rosenbaum, Jonathan 229 n.8
Rossellini, Roberto 168–9, 179
Rothman, William 26, 213 n.2, 223 n.33
Rotolo, Suze 143
Rouch, Jean 232 n.22

Said, Edward 21
Salesman (Maysles) 8, 26, 84, 85
Sanders, George 168
Santana 70, 87
Santana, Carlos 70
Sarris, Andrew 107, 154–5, 160, 164, 166, 183–4, 229 n.8, 237 n.5
Scorsese, Catherine 29–31, 38–43, 45, 50–3, 55, 191
Scorsese, Charles 29–31, 38, 43, 45, 47, 52, 55, 169, 191

Scorsese, Martin
    and auteurism 107, 151, 154–5, 160–1, 166, 183–4
    and cinephilia 14–15, 153–65, 178–85, 192, 194, 196, 207, 241 n.24
    as documentarian 1–2, 6, 8, 12, 20
    as editor 1, 6, 69, 222 n.24
    as executive producer 15, 113, 197–8, 242 n.3
    and The Film Foundation 9, 112–14
    and film preservation 9–10, 111–13
    illustrated lecture-presentations by 9, 111–12, 229 n.11
    and Netflix 15, 197, 199, 200–5, 207
    and New Hollywood 8, 64, 149, 153, 165
    and rock music 57, 107–8
    and rock 'n' roll music 229 n.7
    and *Woodstock* 1, 6, 69–70, 222 n.24
Scorsese, Martin, works by. *See titles of specific works*
Scorsese Shorts (The Criterion Collection) 211 n.7
Seeger, Pete 129
Severn, Stephen E. 61, 89, 93
Shine a Light (Scorsese) 13, 63, 96–104, 132–3, 148, 150, 205, 226 n.49
Shines, Johnny 150
Shutter Island (Scorsese) 153, 200
similitude 179–80
Sinatra, Frank 243 n.7
Sixties, The 14, 57, 66–75, 104, 106–10, 128–32, 137–8, 143, 148–9, 151, 157, 181, 198, 206, 217 n.33
Sly and the Family Stone 70–1, 74
Smith, Harry 136–9
Sontag, Susan 157, 241 n.26
Soul of a Man, The (Wenders) 230 n.16
spiritual biography 110, 144, 149, 167
Springsteen, Bruce 205–6
Springsteen on Broadway (Zimny) 202–3, 205–7, 243 n.9
Stage Fright (The Band) 110–11
Stahl, Matt 63, 85, 95, 97, 215 n.13, 223 n.35
Stewart, Dave 117, 232 n.21
Street Scenes 1970 (Scorsese) 1, 6, 218 n.3, 240 n.20

Tarantino, Quentin 44, 216 n.22
Taxi Driver (Scorsese) 3, 22, 43–4, 198
Taubin, Amy 132
Taylor, Deems 161, 176
Tedeschi, David 3, 55, 133, 197–8
television (TV) 152, 129, 175–8, 194
Telotte, J.P. 80–1
Telluride Film Festival 199
Theme Time Radio Hour with Your Host Bob Dylan 106
This Wheel's on Fire: Levon Helm and the Story of The Band (Helm with Davis) 60
Time (magazine) 72
Time and Narrative (Ricoeur) 194
Toronto International Film Festival 199
Toure, Ali Farka 127–8
Travers, Peter 153, 237 n.1
Truffaut, François 162, 164, 183
Turner, Otha 125–6
TV. *See* television

universalism 39, 52, 127
utopianism (counterculture) 66–8, 72, 81–2, 86, 97–8

Val Lewton: The Man in the Shadows (Jones) 198
Van Ronk, Dave 143
Verdicchio, Pasquale 216 n.25
vernacular music 13–14, 72, 76, 90–1, 106, 117, 128–9, 134–44, 150, 228 n.2. *See also* roots music *and* folk music
Viaggio in Italia (Rossellini) 168
video-sharing platforms 194
Vidor, King 163
vimeo 159
Vinyl (HBO) 227 n.54, 242 n.6
vinyl records 235 n.37
Visconti, Luchino 178

Wadleigh, Michael 1, 6, 65, 100
Waking Life (Linklater) 216 n.22
Walsh, Raoul 161
Warhol, Andy 147
Warming by the Devil's Fire (Burnett) 230 n.16

Waters, Muddy 78–9, 86, 91, 113–14, 122–4, 128, 137, 150
Watts, Charlie 98, 101
Waugh, Thomas 26
Welles, Orson 162
When We Were Good: The Folk Revival (Cantwell) 136
White, Bukka 113
Who, The 65, 86–7
Wilentz, Sean 105, 130, 139, 220 n.12, 236 n.43
Willemen, Paul 163
Williams, Hank 93, 134
Winterland Ballroom 60, 62, 73, 75–7, 81–2
Witt, Michael 158, 177, 238 n.11
Wolf, Howlin' 113, 127

Wollen, Peter 196
Wood, Ronnie 98
Woodstock (Wadleigh) 1, 6, 12, 65, 67–8, 70–4, 79, 81–2, 86–7, 98–100
Woodstock Music and Art Fair 65
World Cinema Project 112, 159, 239 n.14
World Gone Wrong (Dylan) 106

Yarrow, Peter 129, 140
You Know Something Is Happening (Pennebaker) 133, 140, 144, 146
YouTube 159, 194, 202–3
Young, Neil 44, 227 n.1, 228 n.3

Zanes, Warren 202, 220
Zimny, Thom 202, 206, 243 n.9

www.ingramcontent.com/pod-product-compliance
Lightning Source LLC
Chambersburg PA
CBHW072130290426
44111CB00012B/1852